BEWITCHED: THE RISE OF NEO-GALATIANISM

David R. Anderson, Ph.D.

GRACE THEOLOGY PRESS

Bewitched: The Rise of Neo-Galatianism

Published by Grace Theology Press

The website addresses recommended throughout this book are offered as a resource to you. These websites are not intended in any way to be or imply an endorsement on the part of the author or publisher, nor do we vouch for their content.

Unless otherwise noted, all Scripture quotations are taken from the New King James Version®. Copyright © 1982 by Thomas Nelson, Inc. Used by permission. All rights reserved. Scripture quotations marked ESV are taken from The Holy Bible, English Standard Version® (ESV®), copyright © 2001 by Crossway, a publishing ministry of Good News Publishers. Used by permission. All rights reserved; KJV are taken from the King James Version of the Bible. (Public Domain); NASB are taken from the New American Standard Bible®, Copyright © 1960, 1995 by The Lockman Foundation. Used by permission. (www.Lockman. org); NIV are taken from the Holy Bible, New International Version®, NIV®. Copyright © 1973, 1984 by Biblica, Inc.™ Used by permission of Zondervan. All rights reserved worldwide. www.zondervan.com; and NRSV are taken from the New Revised Standard Version Bible, copyright 1989, Division of Christian Education of the National Council of the Churches of Christ in the United States of America. Used by permission. All rights reserved. The author has added italic and bold treatment to words in Scripture quotations for emphasis.

ISBN 10: 099165885X
ISBN 13: 978-0-9916588-5-5

© 2015 David Anderson

Printed in the United States of America

First Edition 2015

1 2 3 4 5 6 7 8 9 10

DEDICATION

I would like to dedicate this work to Bob Tebow and
his fifty Filipino evangelists who encouraged me
to write this book.

CONTENTS

ACKNOWLEDGEMENTS

Most births in America are accompanied by a medical team: an obstetrician, an anesthetist, and a nurse or two. Books are no different. It is usually a team effort. This book is no exception. I am deeply grateful to three men who helped edit this work: Tim Dunn, Ken Wilson, and Jack Campbell. I am especially grateful to Tim Dunn for not only his editing work, but also for his authorial contributions. Ken Wilson, who is not only an accomplished hand surgeon but also a theologian of the first order with a DPhil from Oxford, scoured this work with his theological scalpel to make sure it was theologically coherent and as consistent as possible. And Jack Campbell's eye for detail is a gift I appreciate and will never possess. Thanks to my team.

PREFACE

Some years ago a pastor friend from Mississippi encouraged me to buy an ultra-light airplane. He belonged to a club of fifty guys who flew them and thought I would enjoy the experience. So he took me to a catfish farm near his home in Starkville, Mississippi, to take a ride in a double-seater. After the ride, as we were driving away, he said, "Did you notice the girl standing in the door to the hanger?" I replied, "Well, I remember her standing there, but that's about it. What about her?" "Did you notice her dress?" "No." "The owners of the farm are Mennonites who don't allow their women to wear buttons on their dresses. The dresses are held together by safety pins. They think buttons are worldly right along with wearing lipstick and other forms of make-up. They are very legalistic."

Spirituality from the outside in. Yes, that was my understanding of legalism—a set of rules to measure our spirituality from the outside. Jesus accused the Pharisees of this approach to spirituality. They had all kinds of rules about what you could and could not do on the Sabbath. Somehow what you did on the outside was going to make you holy on the inside. Jesus said it doesn't work. He accused the Pharisees of being whitewashed tombs—white on the outside, but rotting on the inside. With his "Sermon on the Mount" he tried to show them that true spirituality is from the inside out. You have heard it said that it is wrong to commit murder (external), but I say unto you, it is wrong to be angry against your brother without a cause (internal). You have heard it said that it is wrong to commit adultery (external), but I say unto you it is wrong to lust after a woman in your heart (internal).

Jesus certainly made it clear that trying to legislate morality from the outside in is a form of legalism. But does it stop there? After decades of serving as a pastor I have come to believe that legalism can also come from the inside out. I am referring to our basic drives and motives. My desire to please people (internal) may cause certain types of behavior (external) in order to reach my goal. That might mean living according to a set of rules established by my particular religious group or church. Even my desire to please God (internal) can lead to a certain type of behavior (external) in order to reach that goal. Of course, the desire to please God is good (2 Cor. 5:9), and that desire can lead to a certain type of behavior on the outside that is good as well. But in Galatians Paul shows us that even the desire to please God can be corrupted (Gal. 3:3). How? Perhaps legalism actually begins on the inside.

The thought that legalism could begin on the inside led me to believe that each of us wrestles with legalism every day. And you don't have to be a Christian to be legalistic. Just be human. Legalism is a consequence of the fall. I come into this world feeling so insecure and insignificant (a result of the fall of Adam) that I try to expunge these feelings through my performance. If I perform well, I feel more worthy of being loved and accepted (sources of security) and more worthy of being admired and approved (sources of significance). Thus the default setting of my flesh is on performance.

In this book I try to show that every religion and every branch of any religion leans toward legalism, an innate desire (internal) to please God or the gods through our performance (external). As you read this, you will be tempted to say, "He is throwing every Christian group under the bus." That would be correct. But remember, I am also throwing myself under the bus. I wrestle with legalism every day. I was trained to be a legalist from the womb, you might say. I cut my teeth on performance. Performing well, be it in the classroom or the athletic field, was my drug of choice to take away the pain of feeling insecure and insignificant. Winning made me feel better about myself.

I do believe some forms of religion and even some branches of Christianity make it easier for the legalist to reach his goal (the desire to feel secure and significant) than others. Nevertheless, all three main branches of Christianity (Catholicism, Arminianism, and Calvinism) leave an open door for the legalist to operate. And if it is true that the compulsion to perform stems from my flesh (my sinful nature passed down through Adam), then I can find plenty of opportunity to feed my flesh no matter what my religious stripe might be. I cannot blame my legalism on the system. It goes to the very root of my being.

What about you? Do you wrestle with legalism? Read on and find out.

1

THE TRUE GOSPEL
Galatians 1:1-10

Have you ever known someone who seems addicted to bad news? They just stay glued to news channels that focus on all the mayhem and tragedies in the world. It reminds me of the redhead and blond gals who were best friends. They regularly met after work down at the local pub to watch the evening news. This particular evening they got there for the six o'clock news only to witness a man standing on the edge of a tall building and threatening to jump. Captivated, the blond said, "I've got fifty bucks that says he won't jump." Redhead: "I'll take that bet." Well, sure enough, he jumped. Hands shaking, the blond reached in her purse for fifty dollars and gave it to her friend. The redhead said, "Oh, I can't take this. You see, I watched the five o'clock news and I already knew he was going to jump." The blond replied, "No, you keep it. I watched the five o'clock news too, but I was willing to bet he wouldn't do it again."

We like good news. You have to be a little weird to like to hear bad news all the time. I'm sure you've met someone who doesn't even read the front page or listen to the news channel just because they get worn down by all the bad news out there. Well, we are no different from the people who lived in central Turkey two thousand years ago, an area known as Galatia. There was a southern part and a northern part, and Paul bisected that region in his missionary journeys. He camped on the southern part in his first journey, and he passed through the upper part in his next two journeys. These people were also tired of bad news, so when the good news of Jesus Christ came to their region, it was like manna from heaven. They ate it up faster than I can eat a half gallon of, you know what, Homemade Vanilla Blue Bell Ice Cream. The Galatians loved good news, and there was plenty of it.

But not everyone welcomes good news, especially if it involves change. While visiting my family back in Kentucky recently, I drove by so many of those horse farms where they raise the thoroughbreds that race in the Kentucky Derby that I decided to read the story of Seabiscuit by Laura Hillenbrand. In an early chapter she described the early resistance here in America to the automobile during the era of horse and carriage:

> So sleekly efficient on paper in practice it was a civic menace, belching out exhaust, kicking up storms of dust, becoming hopelessly mired in the most innocuous-looking puddles, tying up horse traffic, and raising an earsplitting noise that sent buggy horses fleeing. Incensed local lawmakers responded with monuments to legislative creativity. The laws of at least one town required automobile drivers to stop, get out, and fire off Roman candles every time horse-drawn vehicles came into view. Massachusetts tried and, fortunately, failed to mandate that cars be equipped with bells that would ring with each revolution of the wheels. In some towns police were authorized to disable passing cars with ropes, chains, wires, and even bullets, so long as they took reasonable care to avoid gunning down the drivers.[1]

---

1   Laura Hillenbrand, *Seabiscuit: An American Legend* (New York: Random, 2001), 17.

Paul's gospel announced change—serious change. In fact, very few questions in the spiritual life are as important as this one: What is the true gospel? After all, our eternal destinies hang on our understanding of the gospel. Get it wrong, and the Bible says we spend eternity in the lake of fire. Paul's MO was to begin his work in each town at the synagogue. Everything he had to say could be found in the Jewish Bible, so he started with the Jews in his evangelism. Many received his good news eagerly, but others became his bitter enemies. They resisted change.

No sooner had Paul left the region than people who opposed his message followed his trail and tried to undermine his converts. So he wrote this letter to try to clear up the confusion. Many believe this was his first apostolic letter (written about AD 49). His gospel was such radical truth, the Galatians could hardly believe it, and Paul's detractors certainly didn't believe it. Paul had been commissioned by God to go to the Gentiles. The future of the Gentiles and their ability to participate in the early church hung on his message. So he wrote this letter to defend his gospel.

Ironically, that gospel still needs defending today. We face today what I will call Neo-Galatianism. It is the same thing Paul faced but in a different time and in different cultures. But the Scriptures we believe offer us "timeless truths," truths that transcend time and space and cultures, truths that are just as valid for twenty-first-century people in New York as they were for first-century people in Galatia. In fact, we probably have less agreement on the true gospel today than they did in Paul's day. He faced three factions; we probably have hundreds. To name just a few, here are various requirements suggested by different groups to get the gates of heaven open: repentance, water baptism, trying our best, faith that produces works, doing more good than bad, a commitment to stop sinning and to do good, tithing, church membership, taking communion, total surrender to the Lordship of Christ, and on it goes.

So in this study we want to focus on the true gospel. And we shall see that understanding that gospel affects not only our future in the next life but also our present situation in this life. The issues at stake affect not only our justification salvation but also our sanctification salvation.[2] So let's see what the Holy Spirit says about the gospel in Galatians 1:1-10. But first, let's propose an outline for the letter:

GALATIANS
"The Gospel of Grace"

SALUTATION/INTRODUCTION	
A. Paul Announces the True Gospel	1:1-5
B. Paul Denounces the False Gospel	1:6-10
BODY	1:11-6:10
I. A HISTORICAL DEFENSE OF HIS GOSPEL	1:11-2:21
A. Justification by Faith	1:12-2:10
B. Sanctification by Faith	2:11-21
II. A THEOLOGICAL DEFENSE OF HIS GOSPEL	3:1-6:10
Introduction	3:1-5
A. Justification by Faith	3:6-4:20
B. Sanctification by Faith	4:21-6:10
CONCLUSION/FAREWELL	6:11-18
A. Paul Denounces the Proponents of the False Gospel	6:11-13
B. Paul Announces the Exponents of the True Gospel	6:14-18

---

2   Many Bible teachers like to talk about salvation in three tenses: (1) salvation from the penalty of sin in the past (justification); (2) salvation from the power of sin in the present (sanctification); and (3) salvation from the presence of sin in the future (glorification). The book of Romans includes all three (see *Portraits of Righteousness* by David R. Anderson and James S. Reitman [Lynchburg, VA: Liberty University Press, 2013]).

As you can see, there is a historical section in which Paul picks three historical events as witnesses for the defense of his gospel. Then he dives into a theological defense. But in both sections he starts with a defense of the correct view of how we are justified and then explains how we are sanctified. Included in both our justification and our sanctification are the requirement (faith) and the means (grace), two words we find side by side in Ephesians 2:8: "For by **grace** you have been saved through **faith**." But right now we are in his salutation/introduction (1:1-10).

I. PAUL ANNOUNCES THE TRUE GOSPEL   1:1-5

> Paul, an apostle (not from men nor through man, but through Jesus Christ and God the Father who raised Him from the dead), and all the brethren who are with me, to the churches of Galatia: Grace to you and peace from God the Father and our Lord Jesus Christ, who gave Himself for our sins, that He might deliver us from this present evil age, according to the will of our God and Father, to whom be glory forever and ever. Amen.

Paul identifies himself as an "apostle." He certainly wasn't one of the twelve. Nor was he in the running to replace Judas Iscariot. And Jesus said the twelve would be sitting some day on thrones ruling over the twelve tribes of Israel. So Paul's apostleship had to be different. He did not travel with Jesus before the crucifixion. His introduction to Jesus, as far as we know, was on the road to Damascus—a direct, postresurrection appearance of Jesus. In time, as we shall see, he was given a unique apostleship, an apostleship to the Gentiles.

It might be significant to note that there were three types of apostles in the NT. The first had the office. An office carries with it both authority and sphere. An apostle or an elder or a deacon has certain authority, but only in a well-defined sphere. You cannot be an elder in Bent Tree Bible Church in Dallas and an elder in Spring Baptist Church in Spring, Texas, at the same time. And so Paul had authority in a certain sphere. Peter had authority in another.

There is also the gift of being an apostle. Barnabas had that gift, as did Apollos. It is estimated that there were around fifty apostles who had the gift but not the office. The gift was given to help plant churches. It is very much like some of our missionaries today. In fact, the words *apostle* and *missionary* mean the same thing—"sent one." But the gift carries no authority and is not confined to any particular sphere. If I have the gift of evangelism, I can use it in Houston or Vietnam. But I do not have the authority to command people to receive Christ as their Savior. I can only persuade or invite.

Thirdly, there is the function of a messenger. Epaphroditus was called an apostle to the Philippians. As their messenger, he carried money to Paul and a letter from Paul back to the Philippians. So: the office, the gift, and the messenger. The latter two uses are around today, but the first one died out with the twelve and Paul. No one today can meet the qualifications of the office of apostle (see Acts 1:21-22). So if you hear someone telling you he is the apostle to the Western Hemisphere (as I have heard), you know something is amiss. They will try to use their title to gain authority over you. But remember, the office ended in the first century, and we have no evidence that it was passed along to succeeding generations (apostolic succession). Only the office had authority.

Now, since this is just a salutation, we don't expect to get all the details of Paul's gospel in these five verses, but it is interesting to see how many there are:

1. "Jesus Christ"—the gospel is about a Savior from our sins, and his name is Jesus Christ. What will you do with the person of Jesus Christ?

2. "Raised"—this is the promise of life after death.

3. "Grace"—here is the MO for salvation. "For by grace you have been saved."

4. "Peace"—that peace that passes understanding can only come from God and always follows grace, not law.

5. "Gave"—God's provision was the giving of Jesus. Here it

emphasizes that he gave himself. It is a gift. Giving is what gifts are all about.

6. "Our sins"—here is humanity's problem. Without a spiritual problem, we don't need a spiritual Savior.

7. "Deliver"—that's what Saviors do; they deliver or rescue or save you from something, in this case the evil age in which we live.

8. "Will of our God"—this salvation desire is God's, not man's. If we could save or rescue ourselves, we certainly wouldn't need a Savior. No other major religion in the world offers a Savior from our present sinful state.

Though faith is conspicuous by its absence, Paul is not trying to cover all the bases here in his salutation. Faith is picked up in Galatians 3, where it is mentioned thirteen times.

Yes, the true gospel is really good news. There is no bad news mentioned in these first five verses—just one piece of good news after another. But so many people associate Christianity (and all religion for that matter) with bad news. For most people religion is a set of rules that they can never consistently keep. For the Jews it is the Law of Moses and the oral tradition of the Pharisees or the rabbis.

For the Buddhists it is the Eightfold Path. The goal of their Eightfold Path? To cease to exist. To exist is to have pain. So you can stop hurting if you just cease to exist. Now there is good news!

For the Hindus it is the law of karma and living a life good enough to merit ascending the ladder to the next higher caste. I remember a little fellow I saw in Delhi. He was about sixty years old, about ninety pounds, and naked. He had a little broom in his hands and was sweeping the walkway with each step he took. I asked someone what was going on, and the person explained that the man believed in the law of ahisma (life principle) such that if he stepped on an insect, it might be one of his ancestors who had slid down the ladder of karma. The man was gaining karma by protecting tiny insects. Only the male Brahmans can enter nirvana. That is the highest caste, and only a tiny percentage of people in India belong to that caste. For everyone else—bad news.

And then there is Islam. Oh, they have good news, all right. Just blow yourself up for Allah and you win a get-out-of-jail-free card that takes you straight to paradise. (Of course the rulers aren't asking their children to blow themselves up.) Otherwise, you have to keep the Five Pillars. One of their pillars is almsgiving, but if you follow the Koran, you don't give 10 percent or 20 percent. No. You are supposed to give 40 percent. Isn't that good news?

Paul doesn't mention works-based obligations and rules because he has good news. As Young Life claims, Christianity is not about a set of rules; it is about a personal relationship with Jesus Christ, who offers his love without any strings. Do you have a personal relationship with him?

II. PAUL DENOUNCES THE FALSE GOSPEL   1:6-10

> I marvel that you are turning away so soon from Him who called you in the grace of Christ, to a different gospel, which is not another; but there are some who trouble you and want to pervert the gospel of Christ. But even if we, or an angel from heaven, preach any other gospel to you than what we have preached to you, let him be accursed. As we have said before, so now I say again, if anyone preaches any other gospel to you than what you have received, let him be accursed. For do I now persuade men, or God? Or do I seek to please men? For if I still pleased men, I would not be a bondservant of Christ.

Paul is simply amazed that his converts have turned away so quickly to a different gospel. "Turning away" is the word *metastithesthe*, which is used in secular Greek of a turncoat who switches from one philosophical school to another. And so "soon" as they turned—if written in AD 49 it has been only a year or two since Paul evangelized this area. But Acts 14 demonstrates how quickly opposition to Paul's gospel arose. Everywhere he went, those who promoted keeping the Law of Moses followed after him.

Those who were troubling the Galatians were charged with

perverting the "gospel of Christ," most likely meaning the "good news about Christ." Paul has just mentioned the "grace of Christ." Gospel and grace are parallel here and practically interchangeable. Wherever the gospel of grace goes, opposition is soon to follow. Suffering is the caboose that follows the engine of grace down the tracks of this evil age (Acts 14:22). The word translated "pervert" here is *metastrephō*, which quite often means to turn from better to worse or from light to darkness (see Acts 2:20 where the sun *turns* from light to darkness and James 4:9 where laughter *turns* to mourning). This word definitely includes the idea of "changing or altering."

But how will these troublemakers alter the gospel? Well, if grace is the core of the gospel, which the parallelism above would indicate, then to subvert the gospel is to subvert grace. And if saving grace is an undeserved favor, then to change the message or subvert it is to add something to saving grace, some sort of human merit—in front of, behind, or in the middle of the grace message. That's the danger we should watch for intently. Hebrews 13:7 says to test any church or Christian organization by grace. If grace is not at the core of that church or organization, get out.

I watched a DVD the other night that appealed to people to oppose abortion on the grounds that not doing so is like the Germans who did nothing to resist the Holocaust. An interviewer was stopping people on the street and bombarding them with questions about Hitler and what they would have done to stop him. He transferred the discussion to the abortion issue and convinced many to change their approach to abortion. Then he tried to lead them to Christ. Everything was beautiful up to this point. Then he said you have to do two things to have your sins forgiven: (1) repent and turn from your sins (which he apparently viewed as one thing, making the two synonymous); and (2) receive Jesus as your Savior. Notice how he asked people to "turn from their sins." We would suggest he was asking an unbeliever to do something the unbeliever was powerless to do. Jesus wants to save us from the penalty of our sins (hell) and the power of our sin nature (hell on earth). The first Paul calls justification; the second he calls sanctification. But asking for an unbeliever to get sanctified before he

9

is justified is a classic case of putting the cart before the horse. We like to say that Jesus catches his fish before he cleans them.

The word "different" (*heteros*) might imply that there are many valid gospels, many ways to salvation. But Paul clears that up with the word "another" (*allo*), which means "another of the same kind." *Not. Allo* means "different," *unlike* the true gospel! Paul is saying there is no other good news like the gospel he has preached; it is unique. Anyone, even an apostle or an angel from heaven, who says otherwise is under an apostolic curse (*anathema*). Strong language. But how about it? Suppose you show up at church one Sunday morning only to be surprised by a guest speaker, and that speaker is none other than the angel Gabriel. His brilliance is such that the ushers pass out sunglasses as you enter the auditorium. He tells you God has given him a word of knowledge to share with you. He says there is still lots of room in heaven, and God wants all humans to be saved, so he is prepared to make a new offer for gaining entrance to heaven: faith + works = salvation. Finally, all those who think you don't get something for nothing have a chance earn their entrance. Would you say, "Amen"? Would you clap? Would you sing a praise song? If the apostle Paul were there, he would curse. Oh, I don't mean he would cuss. He would say the angel is accursed. *Anathema* was used on numerous occasions by Paul (Rom. 9:3; 1 Cor. 12:3; 16:22) to refer to being delivered over to divine wrath for destruction.[3]

According to Joseph Smith, an angel appeared to him at the beginning of Mormonism. According to Muhammad, an angel appeared to him and gave him the sayings of the Koran. But their gospels are not the same gospel that Paul preached. And some would say those angels were demons, fallen angels. But this text says "an angel from heaven." That's not a demon. Paul extends the curse even to angels from heaven, that is, if one were to preach a different gospel.

Strong language, yes. But just in case we didn't get the message,

---

3   Richard N. Longenecker, *Word Biblical Commentary*, vol. 41 (Dallas: Word Books), Logos on Gal. 1:9.

Paul essentially repeats himself for emphasis in verse 9. The interesting thing here is that he includes himself in the potential for being cursed. He is saying that in ten years if he is preaching a different gospel from the one they had heard from him in the beginning, he himself should be accursed. Most authors give themselves a little wiggle room, a little room for future enlightenment or progressive illumination. Not on this issue. Do you think Paul was strong on grace? Do you think he thought it was something to fight for?

Paul senses that some will react to his strong language. So he immediately says he realizes his words will not be popular. But he isn't writing to please men; his only concern is to please God, and he cannot please both. Like Jesus who says we cannot serve two masters (God and mammon), Paul says he cannot serve to please both men and God. This would seem to contradict Christ's teaching on serving men, but this is more along the lines of Luke 14 where Christ says there are times when we will have to reject the will (desires) of men to follow the will (desires) of God. This passage would suggest that when we water down the message to tickle the ears of men (men pleasers), we are no longer serving God.

Of course, preachers can hide behind this passage as their defense for being obnoxious with truth. This passage is no excuse for what I call "In Your Face Grace." People who believe in grace should be gracious. We will see this principle in more detail when we get to the fruit of the Spirit in Galatians 5. But alas, Paul's stern warning apparently did not stick for more than a generation at best. We don't know much about what happened in Christianity from AD 70 until AD 100 (unless the works of John were written in the 90s). But from AD 100 forward, grace appears to have fallen through the cracks, at least as it relates to salvation.

The earliest Christian literature we have, other than the Bible, is *The Shepherd of Hermas*, written around AD 100-120. Never does it mention salvation by faith or by grace. It does mention salvation by doing good and by water baptism. The writer claims to have been a contemporary of Clement, the presbyter-bishop of Rome (AD 92-101). Hermas is instructed by the "angel of repentance," who is dressed up like a shepherd. The call is for a lackadaisical church to repent. The writing is thoroughly legalistic. He speaks of the meritorious system of good works and the atonement of sin through martyrdom. There is no mention of justification by faith, but water baptism is indispensable for salvation.[4] Water baptism is the seal of repentance that "makes Christians into Christians.... Asceticism [denial of the flesh] and penal suffering are the school of conversion."[5] Faith is the fruit of repentance and the baptism that seals it.[6]

Justin Martyr (d. AD 165) followed on the heels of Hermas and also saw water baptism as the work of regeneration. He said, "Those who are convinced of the truth of our doctrine...are exhorted to prayer, fasting, and repentance for past sins.... Then they are led by us to a place where there is water, and in this way they are regenerated, as we also have been regenerated.... For Christ says: Except you are born again, you cannot enter into the kingdom of heaven."[7] The importance of water baptism for Justin Martyr was underscored when he said, "The laver of repentance...is baptism, the only thing which is able to cleanse those who have repented."[8]

But Paul never mentions water baptism as a requirement for salvation. He mentions only one thing: faith in the Lord Jesus's death and resurrection. Just simple trust; this is how justification takes place. Jesus called it a new birth, and Paul says we are a new creation in Christ. A new birth is not something that happens gradually. We don't go to the hospital to wait for a new birth and expect to be there for a period of months or years. It happens at a moment in time. One moment the baby is in the womb; the next moment the baby is out of

---

4   Philip Schaff, *History of the Christian Church*, 5th ed., vol. 2, *Ante-Nicene Christianity* (Grand Rapids, MI: Eerdmans, 1967), 684-87.

5   Behm, "μετανοέω," *TDNT*, 4:1008.

6   Ibid., 4:1007.

7   Justin Martyr, *Apology* I.

8   Justin Martyr, *Dialogue*, 14.1.

the womb and crying. And we never wonder whether or not we were born, because birth is not something that repeatedly happens, then "unhappens."

It is no accident Jesus and Paul use physical birth to explain justification, because justification is spiritual birth. Just like physical birth, it takes place all at once. And just like physical birth, the baby, the new creation in the womb, receives life as a gift. Babies have nothing whatsoever to contribute to their births (although my physician friends tell me they send a hormone that initiates the process). They are just born. In like fashion, new creations in Christ simply receive the free gift of the grace of God in making us a new creation. This is the beginning. And the new birth is by faith.

Just as Paul states in Romans, the Christian life is also *lived* by faith. So both justification and sanctification are by faith. But the Galatians have another gospel being presented that involves following the law. As we will see, that has no place in bringing righteousness in either justification or sanctification. Rules do not change the heart. Justification gives us a new nature. Sanctification is letting that new heart beat strongly, walking in our new nature, which requires daily faith. The lack of beating strongly in no way affects the reality that we were born any more than not living up to our full physical potential would ever mean we were not physically born.

Neo-Galatianism is requiring adherence to a particular set of rules or standards to "prove" we have been born again, that we are justified. It says if we are *really* justified then we will *inevitably* be sanctified. As we will see, Paul is clear in this letter that justification has *nothing* to do with our life choices after our birth; justification is only our spiritual birth. In contrast, our sanctification is exercising our hearts and is dependent on our daily walking in faith. Our lack of doing so creates loss in our lives but has nothing whatsoever to do with whether or not we were born again.

2

A HAND FROM HEAVEN
Galatians 1:11-24

One of the strangest expressions of pride is the "desire to deserve." We want to earn what we get. A prideful person has some difficulty accepting something for nothing. This is one of the reasons some people have difficulty receiving God's grace.

For the Greeks, who prided themselves in their philosophical speculations, the grace of the cross was just plain foolishness. It made no sense to them. That's too bad on the one hand, but on the other hand it tells us they understood the message. Why? Because on the surface the message of grace does not make sense. One preacher defined saving grace as God's "unreasonable kindness." He said that grace offends our sense of reason, and until one stands back and shakes his head at the absurdity of grace, he probably doesn't understand what it means.

Well, grace may have many shades of meaning, but it certainly means man cannot earn God's favors. That really offended the Jews. They had set up a system of external righteousness that they believed would open the gates of heaven. Grace made them mad. So they went out to destroy the messenger and the message. Galatians is Paul's defense. There were three types of "law lovers" attacking Paul. Scholars call these law lovers the Judaizers. Here are the three categories or types of Judaizers:

1. **Judaizers who maintain Gentiles must become Jews and keep the Law of Moses to go to heaven.** These were the Pharisees, Sadducees, and their followers. These are the people who put Jesus on the cross and opposed Peter and John in the early chapters of Acts. They believed you had to keep the Law of Moses in order to be accepted by God into heaven after death. This controversy was between unbelieving Jews outside the church and believing Jews inside the church. It was assumed that only Jews by birth or conversion could go to heaven. They opposed Paul in Turkey and were the ones who stoned him and left him for dead (Acts 14).

2. **Judaizers who said Gentiles can be saved without becoming Jews but must keep the Law of Moses in addition to believing in Jesus.** This controversy was inside the church. The early church was almost 100 percent Jewish. They did not think Gentiles could go to heaven unless they became proselytes to Judaism by keeping the Law of Moses and being circumcised. The conversion of Cornelius and his family in Acts 10-11 changed the mind of the early church. In Acts 15, Paul received letters from the Jerusalem Council to deliver to the Gentile churches in Turkey. Those letters said the Gentiles did not have to keep the Law of Moses and be circumcised to go to heaven. But this group did not agree with these letters.

3. **Judaizers who said both Jews and Gentiles are justified by faith alone but must keep the Law of Moses in order to be sanctified.** After the Jerusalem Council in Acts 15, the law lovers could not claim either the Jews or the Gentiles

15

had to keep the Law of Moses and be circumcised to go
to heaven. So the issue changed from how to be justified
to how to be sanctified. In other words, they claimed a
believer could not become a mature Christian without
keeping the Law of Moses. We see an example of this type
of law lover in Acts 21:19ff. Many Jews believed in Jesus
but were still zealous for the Law of Moses. When they
heard that Paul was saying they no longer had to keep the
law, they became angry and tried to kill him.

Paul answers all three types of law lovers here in Galatians. His
argument is both historical and theological. In the first two chapters
he gives three historical vignettes, each undermining a different
type of Judaizer. Then he argues theologically against each type of
Judaizer in the rest of the body of this letter. In chapter 1, he uses
his own conversion story to refute the first type; in 2:1-10 he refutes
the second type by calling Titus to the witness stand, since he was
a Gentile; in 2:11-21 he uses his confrontation of Peter to refute
the third type of law lover. But just the fact that Paul is so strongly
attacked for this gospel of grace tells us how deeply ingrained within
us is the "law principle," that is, the sense that we should get only
what we deserve. So to go to heaven or enjoy heaven on earth we
instinctively think we have to deserve it by earning it. Galatians says,
"No!"

LAW—DO AND YOU WILL BE BLESSED

Here is the essence of legalism. We think we can rack up points
with God because we do good works. As such, *we think we can put
him in our debt.* He **owes** us blessings. There is no question rewards
(blessings) are promised to those who are faithful and live righteous
lives—on earth and in heaven. The problem lies in thinking God **owes**
us these rewards or blessings. It's the difference between a **have-to
life** and a **thank-you life**. Grace leads to a thank-you life. Because of
our many blessings in heavenly places in Christ Jesus (Eph. 1:3ff.),

we **want to** live a life pleasing to God. And the beauty of this kind of life is that God promises to reward us for living this thank-you life. **The subtlety of legalism is to turn the promised reward into an obligatory debt. This may appeal to humans because it puts us in control of God, but Paul will have none of it!**

GRACE—YOU ARE BLESSED; THEREFORE, DO

The grace-oriented Christian has two motivating factors behind what he does. The first, as mentioned, is gratitude. As Larry Moyer likes to say, it is a **thank-you life.** Here is where we look back at the cross and the innumerable blessings that accrue to us because of what Christ did for us so many years ago. But sometimes gratitude is not enough. So God promises something more. He promises us a richer life now and hereafter if we live a life pleasing to him. Call these rewards or blessings, it doesn't matter. What matters is our attitude toward them. We can easily become legalists as we live for these rewards. How? Simply by thinking we will get what we are owed. Again, that is the flesh creeping in. It is always on the lookout for "what I am entitled to." That is the law principle with me as the judge.

Jesus told a parable in order to try to discourage that kind of thinking. You know which one, don't you? The parable of the vineyard in Matthew 20. Those who had worked through the heat of the day got what they earned and got what they were promised. But they were unhappy. Why? Because they thought they deserved more than those who had not worked as long as they had worked. The Lord responded by asking them if he had shortchanged them in any way. Hadn't he given what he had promised? Yes, of course. But to the legalist it was not fair for others who had not worked as long or endured the heat of the day to get as much as they received. The Lord was upset with these legalists. That is why he told his steward to begin by paying those who went to work in the vineyard last. Why? Because he knew these latecomers would be overjoyed by getting more than they thought they deserved.

To whom do you really enjoy giving? Those who think you owe them, or those who have appreciation for getting an undeserved favor? The latter, obviously, because they are just so happy to get anything. The owner of the vineyard did not bargain with those who worked only a small part of the day. He just said, "Go work. I'm a just man. I will take care of you. Don't worry about it." The other guys wanted to hammer out all the contractual details. They wanted to know exactly what was coming to them. Well, they got it. But they weren't happy. Jesus is trying to teach us that even these rewards are not a debt God is obliged to pay us. Everything from his hand is born out of grace. It's only his grace that allows us to go to work in the vineyard at all.

So, legalism can creep in on the macro level or the micro level, the justification level or the sanctification level, the level of this life or the level of the next life. Paul wants to undercut legalism at every level. That is the purpose of Galatians. He begins the body of his letter with a historical defense of his gospel. He does this by telling three stories: one about himself, one about Titus, and one about Peter. The first story is just his testimony (1:11-24). In this testimony Paul will make it clear that he did not become a believer by keeping the law. Not only that, but Peter himself wound up putting his stamp of approval on the legitimacy of Paul's conversion. His testimony unfolds in three visits: a visit from Christ, a visit to Arabia, and a visit to Jerusalem.

By the way, as we go through this study, we will be looking at modern-day examples of Neo-Galatianism, or legalism. It may appear that we are throwing all Christian groups under the bus except ourselves. In other words, everyone else missed it—we are the only ones who have it right. Not so. The truth is, we **are** throwing everyone under the bus, **including ourselves**. Legalism is something we all wrestle with. The default setting of our flesh is performance. That is inbred in every person who has a sin nature. So the examples we choose come from all walks and all brands of Christianity. Legalism is a drift we must all resist. Part of the victory comes from recognizing how it creeps into our lives. In Galatians, Paul offers us freedom from the ridiculous burden of "being owed," which leads to trying to control God and judge others.

I. A DAZZLING VISIT—FROM CHRIST   1:11-16a

> But I make known to you, brethren, that the gospel which was preached by me is not according to man. For I neither received it from man, nor was I taught it, but it came through the revelation of Jesus Christ. For you have heard of my former conduct in Judaism, how I persecuted the church of God beyond measure and tried to destroy it. And I advanced in Judaism beyond many of my contemporaries in my own nation, being more exceedingly zealous for the traditions of my fathers. But when it pleased God, who separated me from my mother's womb and called me through His grace, to reveal His Son in me, that I might preach Him among the Gentiles...

Paul's main point here is that he was converted by a direct, postresurrection appearance of Jesus Christ. His gospel did not come from men; it came directly by revelation from Jesus. He was not taught this gospel by man, nor did he cook it up himself. Obviously something dramatic had taken place. Here was a man more zealous for Judaism than anyone in the country, to the point that he was trying to destroy the early church by killing off its members. Something awfully dramatic must have taken place to cause him to do a complete about-face. That something was a vision from God. And to prove how independent this entire event was, he did not go immediately to Jerusalem to tell everyone. Instead, he went to Arabia.

II. A DIRECT VISIT—TO ARABIA   1:16b-17

> I did not immediately confer with flesh and blood, nor did I go up to Jerusalem to those who were apostles before me; but I went to Arabia, and returned again to Damascus.

Through the years it has amazed me how many people think Paul spent three years in Arabia and that is where God taught him his wonderful insights. But a quick look at the text makes it obvious we don't really know how long he was in Arabia because sometime thereafter he returns to Damascus. Then verse 18 tells us after three years in Damascus he went to Jerusalem.

What happened in Arabia? We are pretty sure he went to Petra and preached to Aretas IV, the king of the Nabateans who lived in Petra. His territory extended all the way up to at least Damascus, which would be in modern-day Syria. Damascus had a governor under King Aretas, according to 2 Corinthians 11:32. Aretas controlled the trade routes along which spices came from the Persian Gulf area. That is how the Nabateans became wealthy. Paul was upsetting things with his preaching in Damascus, so after three years of it, Aretas tried to have Paul killed. He escaped by being lowered in a basket from a window.

Paul's rejection, or rather the rejection of his message, by King Aretas was cemented by the king's decision to help the Roman army in their siege against the Jews in Jerusalem in AD 66. That was the beginning of the end for the Nabateans. One generation later their fortified city of Petra, seemingly impregnable, was conquered by the Romans and essentially lost for over seventeen hundred years. This judgment for rejecting the gospel was similar to the one Jesus put on the Jews of his generation (Matt. 23:36). It was one generation (forty years) after his ministry began (AD 30) that Titus came in to sack Jerusalem (AD 70). God had given them one generation to repent. When they did not, his temporal wrath was poured out on that generation. According to Josephus Flavius, about 1,100,000 Jews were killed and 97,000 were deported as captives.[9]

Finally, after escaping from Damascus, Paul goes to Jerusalem to meet some of the apostles.

---

9   Josephus Flavius, *The Works of Josephus: The Wars of the Jews*, VI 9.3 (Peabody, MA: Hendrickson, 1993), 749.

III. A DELAYED VISIT—TO PETER   1:18-24

> Then after three years I went up to Jerusalem to see Peter, and remained with him fifteen days. But I saw none of the other apostles except James, the Lord's brother. (Now concerning the things which I write to you, indeed, before God, I do not lie.) Afterward I went into the regions of Syria and Cilicia. And I was unknown by face to the churches of Judea which were in Christ. But they were hearing only, "He who formerly persecuted us now preaches the faith which he once tried to destroy." And they glorified God in me.

Everywhere he went, Paul spread the good news of Christ, and the good news of his own conversion was cause for great rejoicing. It is interesting that James is listed as an apostle. James the son of Zebedee was killed by Herod in Acts 12:2. Perhaps James, the brother of Christ and the writer of the epistle of James, replaced James the son of Zebedee just as Matthias replaced Judas Iscariot. But this is not likely in that James the son of Zebedee will still sit on one of the thrones ruling over one of the tribes of Israel. There would not be enough thrones for a thirteenth apostle to the Jews. So James probably fits into the category of men with the gift of an apostle (see Rom. 16:7) like Andronicus and Junia.

After leaving Jerusalem, you would expect Paul to start preaching in Judea. Instead he headed back into Syria and Cilicia. He didn't go back to Damascus for obvious reasons, but Antioch was in Syria, so he probably preached in and around Antioch. Then, as we might expect, he went home. Tarsus was on the coast of southeastern Turkey, but it was also in the region of Cilicia. So Paul went back to his own roots to share his testimony and preach grace.

Paul probably avoided Judea for the simple fact that he had killed a lot of the Christians in that region. It wouldn't be unreasonable for him to think that he wouldn't get very far in Judea before some families might take revenge on him. So for fourteen years (2:1) he preached the gospel outside of Judea. But they heard of his conversion and his preaching. Since it lasted so long, it was not a flash in the pan. He finally established enough credibility to return to Jerusalem. But we are getting ahead of ourselves. Let's back up and make an observation about his testimony.

Paul's conversion had nothing to do with the Law of Moses. It didn't have anything to do with any kind of law. There was no list of requirements. I read a popular book by a popular Christian writer. It was very inspiring until he got to his chapter on how we get to heaven. Here is his list of requirements, which he introduces with this statement:

> Saving faith is no simple thing. It has many dimensions. "Believe on the Lord Jesus" is a massive command. It contains a hundred other things. Unless we see this, the array of conditions for salvation in the New Testament will be utterly perplexing. Consider the following partial list.
>
> 1. Believe on the Lord Jesus and you will be saved (Acts 16:31).
> 2. Receive Christ (John 1:12).
> 3. Repent and turn from your sins (Acts 3:19).
> 4. Obedience (Heb. 5:9; John 3:36).
> 5. Childlikeness (Matt. 18:3).
> 6. Self-denial (Mark 8:34-35).
> 7. Love Jesus more than anything else (Matt. 10:37; 1 Cor. 16:22).
> 8. Free from love of possessions (Luke 14:33).

He concludes his discussion by saying:

> These are just some of the conditions that the New Testament says we must meet in order to inherit final salvation. We must believe on Jesus and receive him and turn from our sin and obey him and humble ourselves like little children and love him more than we love our family, our possessions, or our

own life. This is what it means to be converted to Christ. This alone is the way of life everlasting.[10]

The list he offers, according to him, is just a **partial** list. It could include **"a hundred other things."** This is such a blatant works approach to justification salvation that he cannot escape the hole he has dug, so he tries to find a way out. He asks, "And what keeps them [these conditions] from becoming a way of earning salvation by works?" He goes to the parable of hidden treasure and concludes: "I conclude from this parable that we must be deeply converted in order to enter the kingdom of heaven, and we are converted when Christ becomes for us a Treasure Chest of holy joy." Which being interpreted means, when Christ becomes the joy of our lives, we will produce the fruit of turning from our sins, obedience, humility, self-denial, and so on, which "alone is the way of life everlasting."[11]

My friends, this is Neo-Galatianism pure and simple, because sanctification, according to John Piper, is required for justification. As we shall see in Galatians 3, Paul has a "list" of one, only one, single condition for life everlasting: faith. Undoubtedly our list maker would agree. But this confused author goes on to say, "Saving faith is no simple thing."[12] On the contrary, justifying faith is as simple as trusting. And it is given completely freely. Living daily by faith is sometimes "no simple thing"; life has genuine difficulties. But that is sanctification, and while greatly to our benefit, sanctification has no bearing on whether we go to heaven.

When Piper begins to list salvation's many dimensions, most of which look like works to any unbiased reader, he is saying these are *requirements* to be justified, to go to heaven. Faith mixed with works to go to heaven—yep, that's the heart of Neo-Galatianism. How can

---

10   John Piper, *Desiring God* (Colorado Springs: Multnomah, 2003), 65-66.

11   Ibid., 70.

12   Ibid.

you tell if you have slipped into Neo-Galatianism? Here are a few of the symptoms:

1. **Little Peace.** *Neo-Galatianism is characterized by fruit inspecting.* Whenever fruit inspecting begins, peace takes a hike. One of the many problems with fruit inspecting is whose list to use. Most people wind up making their own list, which is usually a combination of Scriptures they have heard and rules from their own local culture. Whatever the list, there is never any certainty that the person has been good enough long enough. Consequently, there is no inner peace or rest. There is always a striving to be good enough, which leaves the performer restless and unsatisfied. In addition, we can self-justify our own imperfections by judging the faults of others (based on our list), which often leads to conflict and division.

2. **Little Joy.** Fruit inspecting robs us of joy. The fruit inspectors encourage their followers to examine themselves to see if they are "in the faith." I remember when James Montgomery Boice was on his deathbed. R. C. Sproul was speaking at a conference where he asked for prayer that James would die in the faith. The implications were that if he did not, he would not find himself in heaven after he died. Of course, this is consistent with their teaching that the believer must remain faithful until he dies before he can know his eternal destiny. So, they live a "have-to" life. They "have to" be good and faithful until the end of their lives, according to their interpretation of Matthew 24:13. Thus, they cannot know until death if they are "elect." If you find yourself in constant fear of failing God, you might be a victim of Neo-Galatianism.

3. **More Sin.** Paul teaches that the law incites sin: "For when we were in the flesh, the sinful passions which were aroused by the law were at work in our members to bear

24

fruit to death" (Rom. 7:5). The law acts like the bumblebee on which Ferdinand the Bull sat: sting! Tell the sin nature you "have to," and watch what happens. Oh, you might get the victory more or less, but every time the sin nature hears "have to," it says, "Just watch me." The more it hears "have to," the more it rebels. End result? More sin. If you find yourself sinning more, but expending great energy to hide it from certain people, you might be a victim of Neo-Galatianism.

4. **More Guilt.** Known sin and guilt are connected, right? If I know I am sinning, then unless my conscience is seared, I will sense more guilt. That kind of living is not living at all. Paul calls it "death" (1 Tim. 5:6; Rom. 7:7-10, 24; 8:6). The death he speaks of has nothing to do with eternity. It is the defeated Christian life and all its attendant misery, defeat, and depression—the living death.

5. **Anger at God.** The four symptoms above are often accompanied by anger at God. In fact, anger at God tells me I have been a legalist. Anger comes when I am disappointed with the way things have turned out in my life. If I have been a faithful follower of God and believe he is in control, then I expect better from him. After all, I deserve better, don't I? I have served in the church. I have been a faithful spouse and parent. What more can God expect? Ah, that is the voice of Neo-Galatianism. Are you angry at God?

6. **Disillusionment.** I have performed well. God has not come through with his blessings. Over and over I have resisted temptation. And I have put my life on the Christian altar to be used however God wishes. But now look at my daughter. She's grown up in a loving home, the daughter of a preacher, gone off to one of the best Christian universities in America, but she's sleeping around. It was just with her boyfriend. But when he dumped her, she

has now become completely promiscuous. I don't trust God anymore. I did my part, but he hasn't delivered. He hasn't been faithful to me; why should I be faithful to him? If this is the way God treats his faithful children, then I just won't be faithful. If you can phrase any of your disappointment with God as "God owes me because…," you are probably practicing Neo-Galatianism.

So goes the death spiral of the defeated Christian, a spiral experienced more often than not by those caught in the spider web of legalism. We have probably all been there; I know I have. Of course, as Paul argued in Romans 7, it's not that there is anything wrong with the Law of Moses. And many of our self-imposed laws—ones not even found in the Law of Moses—are good. The problem is the attempt to use the law to reform our sin nature. The sin nature can't be reformed; it can only be crucified, and to attempt to reform really just pours fuel on the fire. It can produce a firestorm of sin.

On the other hand, God's grace is the most transforming power in the world. Whereas the law is limited and rigid, grace is unlimited and pliable. It is also why Scripture says, "Mercy triumphs over judgment" (James 2:13). No one has captured this truth in novel form better than Victor Hugo in his famous work *Les Misérables*. Jean Valjean was not a bad man, at first. Times were tough in France around 1765. Hunger gnawed at his insides. But more than that, there was no one to feed his sister and his mother. A little bread in the store window. A little theft. But Jean Valjean was caught and sent to prison. He fought the law and the law won. Prison didn't rehabilitate Jean Valjean. Every time he did something wrong they extended his sentence. Finally, after over twenty years in prison for what began as a stolen loaf of bread, he is released, broken and bitter. But is he better? Not a chance.

The first opportunity he gets, Jean Valjean steals some silver from a local priest who has shown him a little hospitality. Again he is caught, but when the priest is called to witness against him by the *gendarmes*, to his amazement, the priest defends Jean Valjean and even offers him some of the more valuable objects he had left behind. With his kindness the priest whispers in the ear of Jean Valjean, "Go and show this kindness to others." **An unreasonable kindness—grace.** Jean Valjean is at first stupefied by what he considers the stupidity of the priest. But he can't escape the unreasonable kindness. It follows him like a dog tracking everywhere he goes. Finally, he finds himself wanting to help others as he had been helped. **This unreasonable kindness is transforming his life.** He finds business success and even becomes the mayor of a small French town where he provides honest jobs for hundreds of workers at his factory. He leaves his old identity and becomes another man.

But Jean has an archenemy—the law, which is personified by Javert, a police inspector. Like a bloodhound, Javert catches the scent of Jean Valjean. He hunts him down, but Valjean escapes. Javert is relentless. It takes years, but Javert finally catches up with Valjean. The law never changes; the law cannot be broken with impunity. But in a twist of events Javert feels the knife of Jean Valjean at his neck. Certain death is imminent for Javert, and thus finally, after all these years, Valjean will be free. Javert even assures Valjean that Valjean must kill him, because if Valjean refuses, he, Javert, will track Valjean down again and bring him to justice. After all, he is the law, and the law is perfect and unyielding.

But the grace of an unreasonable kindness and its opposite, vengeance, are contradictory. Jean Valjean does not thrust his knife home. He sets Javert free despite the inevitable consequence of reimprisonment. And, sure enough, the inevitable happens. Javert captures Jean Valjean. But when face-to-face with his prey, Javert becomes confused and even agitated about the conflict between justice and grace. How could this man, Jean Valjean, Hugo's personification of grace, not kill him when he had the chance? It was an **unreasonable kindness.** The law is unable to defeat the higher principle of grace. So instead of slaying Valjean (grace), Javert (law) kills himself by throwing himself into the Seine River to drown. Mercy triumphs over judgment (James 2:13). Grace fought the law, and grace won. Grace will also win in your life, if you will let it transform you into another man or woman.

3

THE JERUSALEM SUPER BOWL
Galatians 2:1-10

The Super Bowl—arguably the greatest annual athletic gala in America, maybe the world. A friend offered me a ticket to the Super Bowl at the Superdome in New Orleans—the Baltimore Ravens versus the San Francisco Forty-Niners, 2013. Seeing it as a bucket-list opportunity, I decided to go. I soon realized this wasn't just a game; it was an event. The initial goal was to find a parking place along the narrow New Orleans streets some distance from the Superdome. Then a sea of people flowing along on its way to the dome joined me. It was apparent from all the purple that the Ravens fans greatly outnumbered the Forty-Niners fans. All those fans must have helped; the Ravens won a close contest despite a forty-five minute blackout in the middle of the game.

Of course, there was not a Super Bowl in Israel during the first century, but the Jerusalem Council of Galatians 2:1-10 and Acts 15 was the closest thing to it, at least in the Christian world. But the contest was not over football; it was over the gospel. The Forty-Niners (Jewish Christians living in Israel) versus the Ravens (Gentile Christians from outside Israel), with each group contending their view of the gospel was the correct view. The outcome of this council would determine the future course of Christianity.

The battle was between law and liberty. If the Forty-Niners won, the Ravens would be subjected to the Law of Moses. If the Ravens won, the Gentiles were free from having to observe the Law of Moses. Who would win the first Christian Super Bowl? The Holy Spirit gives us the color commentary as found in Galatians 2:1-10.

GALATIANS
"The Gospel of Grace"

SALUTATION/INTRODUCTION

A. Paul Announces the True Gospel		1:1-5
B. Paul Denounces the False Gospel		1:6-10
BODY		1:11-6:10
I. A HISTORICAL DEFENSE OF HIS GOSPEL		1:11-2:21
A. Justification by Faith		1:12-2:10
1. For the Jew		1:11-24
2. For the Gentile		2:1-10
a. His Gospel Appraised Privately		2:1-7
b. His Gospel Approved Publicly		2:8-10

I. PAUL'S GOSPEL APPRAISED PRIVATELY   2:1-7

Then after fourteen years I went up again to Jerusalem with Barnabas, and also took Titus with me. And I went up by revelation, and communicated to them that gospel which I preach among the Gentiles, but privately to those who were of reputation, lest by any means I might run, or had run, in vain. Yet not even Titus who was with me, being a Greek, was compelled to be circumcised. And this occurred because of false brethren secretly brought in (who came in by stealth to spy out our liberty which we have in Christ Jesus, that they might bring us into bondage), to whom we did not yield submission even for an hour, that the truth of the gospel might continue with you. But from those who seemed to be something—whatever they were, it makes no difference to me; God shows personal favoritism to no man—for those who seemed to be something added nothing to me. But on the contrary, when they saw that the gospel for the uncircumcised had been committed to me, as the gospel for the circumcised was to Peter...

Apparently, Paul had not been to Jerusalem since his first trip, and that trip occurred after he had been a believer for three years. It is hard to say how old Paul was at this point, but somewhere between forty-five and fifty-five would make sense. Though it cannot be proven that Paul was ever a member of the Sanhedrin, we do know that they gave him authority to round up and persecute Christians (Acts 26:9-10). Presumably this kind of authority would not be given to someone in his early twenties. If we leave a year between the death of Christ and the death of Stephen, then Paul is probably at least thirty-five when he oversees the stoning of Stephen.

We belabor this point only to reflect on how long God prepared Paul for his greatest work, his missionary journeys. And how long does it take to become a mature Christian, one ready to persevere through the onslaught of satanic opposition every soldier of Christ will face? It would seem that Paul was called to his greatest work in his early fifties. Your greatest work for the Lord may come after age fifty. And how long does it take to become a mature Christian? Perhaps as long as it takes to become mature physically—about eighteen years. There are certainly exceptions, especially in the case of martyrs where it seems the Lord compresses the growth process for them (Stephen, the first Christian martyr, and missionaries like Jim Elliot). However, as someone once observed, the Lord can grow a squash overnight, but it takes decades to grow a red oak tree.

Too often we see Christians most active for Christ during their twenties, thirties, and forties. Why not in their fifties, sixties, and seventies? Unless bad health slows us down, we may have more to offer in the autumn of our lives than in the spring or summer. Just this morning an accomplished physician told me his dream during the spring and summer of his practice was to retire in his fifties and spend the last thirty years of his life traveling around with his wife in their motor home and playing golf five days a week. After all, he had earned it. But the Holy Spirit turned his life around in his midfifties. Now, after over ten years walking by the Spirit, he says his greatest joy is to help someone understand a passage of Scripture or the grace of God or the gospel itself. He attends or leads three Bible studies a week and participates in a weekly prayer meeting. Without doubt he would say that the autumn and winter of his life will have a greater impact on eternity than the spring and summer will.

A key to understanding the issue at this council is the mention of "Titus"—twice. Titus went with Paul to the council as an object lesson. It was apparent he was a new believer with the gift of the Holy Spirit, but he was not circumcised. He served as an object lesson of Gentile salvation—not a Jew, not a proselyte, not observant of the law, and not circumcised; but he believed in Jesus and had the Holy Spirit.

The Acts 15 council marks the transition from the second type of Judaizer to the third type. Remember, the first type says one must be a Jew or become a proselyte to Judaism and keep the law to go to heaven. The second type acknowledges that Gentiles can go to heaven without becoming proselytes to Judaism, but they would have to believe in Jesus as well as keep the law. The third type agrees that keeping the law has nothing to do with justification but is still a requirement for sanctification, whether one is a Jew or a Gentile.

The second type of Judaizer (Gentiles can be saved without becoming proselytes but must believe in Jesus, keep the law, and be circumcised) is represented by both believers and unbelievers, but all professing Jesus. This gets a bit complicated, but Acts 15:1 tells us that "certain men came down from Judea and taught the brethren, 'Unless you are circumcised according to the custom of Moses, you cannot be saved.'" These men must have been professing Christ or they would not have gotten an audience in the church at Antioch. But they were teaching that the Gentiles must keep the law to "be saved."

We cannot be certain whether these men are believers or unbelievers. Some at the Jerusalem Council in Acts 15 are called believers, and they thought the Gentiles must keep the law to be saved (Acts 15:5). The fact that these believing Pharisees thought the law must be kept for justification salvation is made clear by Peter's speech in which he concludes in Acts 15:11 that "we believe that through the grace of the Lord Jesus Christ we shall be **saved** in the same manner as they." So these Pharisees are identified by Luke as believers who thought the Gentiles must keep the law to "be saved."

But according to Galatians 2:4 there were also "false brethren" at the council who crept in secretly to spy out the freedom these new Gentile Christians were experiencing through Paul's gospel. It was their goal to bring these new believers "into bondage," that is, bondage to keep the law and be circumcised. And so it goes with Galatianism or legalism. It is hard to tell the believers from the unbelievers when both groups say the law must be kept to go to heaven. If we take the text at face value, then these Pharisees were believers, that is, Christians. But they were teaching false doctrine; at least that is what the council determined.[13]

Is it possible for a born-again person headed for heaven to teach a false gospel? Of course. That is exactly what these Pharisees were doing, unless you want to say these believing Pharisees were the false brethren Paul references in Galatians 2:4. But if that is true, it is the only example of Luke's use of the term "believer" or "disciple" of someone who was not headed for heaven. Best to say that both unbelievers and believers get confused when it comes to the requirements for going to heaven. And if they got confused when Christ and the apostles were around, what about today?

---

13   Ken Wilson, MD, DPhil, offers this insight: "Could 'false brothers' be 'lying brothers' = Christians who are lying about the gospel? The Greek *pseudo* most often means 'wrong' or 'liar' not fake— *pseudodidaskalos* = real teachers teaching falsely; *pseudomarturia* = lying witness, not that he is a fake witness; *pseudomai* = I lie, not that I am." From correspondence with this author.

Fortunately, the Jerusalem Council drew a definitive line in the sand. They sent letters to the churches in Antioch, Syria, and Cilicia making it completely clear the Gentiles did not have to keep the law and be circumcised. These letters should have silenced the second type of Judaizer forever. Not. The law principle (performance) can be like a deadly cancer in remission. For a period of time both the first type and second type of Judaizers (whose error was teaching one must keep the law and be circumcised to go to heaven) were "put in remission." So a third type of Judaizer arose who said both Jewish and Gentile Christians had to keep the law and be circumcised to be sanctified, to become mature Christians, as we shall see in the second half of Galatians 2.

The Jerusalem Council should have settled once and for all the justification issue, that is, no one (Jew or Gentile) has to keep the law and be circumcised to go to heaven when they die. All anyone must do is trust (believe) in the person and work of Jesus Christ. The council recognized the validity of Paul's gospel and his apostleship to the Gentiles, just as they recognized Peter's apostleship to the Jews. But right now we must note that Paul's gospel was not only appraised privately (2:1-7), it was also approved publicly (2:8-10).

II. PAUL'S GOSPEL APPROVED PUBLICLY   2:8-10

(For He who worked effectively in Peter for the apostleship to the circumcised also worked effectively in me toward the Gentiles), and when James, Cephas, and John, who seemed to be pillars, perceived the grace that had been given to me, they gave me and Barnabas the right hand of fellowship, that we should go to the Gentiles and they to the circumcised. They desired only that we should remember the poor, the very thing which I also was eager to do.

The council was one thing. Perhaps even more important to Paul was the affirmation of James, Peter, and John. Peter and John were, of course, part of the inner circle of Christ's disciples. James, the brother of John, was martyred in Acts 12:2. So this James is the half brother of

Jesus (see Gal. 1:19), who became increasingly influential in the early Jerusalem church (see 2:12). These three "pillars" gave their stamp of approval to Paul's gospel of "grace." Note that this one word, **"grace,"** is the word Paul chose to characterize his gospel. The requirement for our justification salvation is faith, but the means of this salvation is grace (all works excluded). This is what we mean by "faith alone in Christ alone."

So Paul's gospel has been appraised privately and approved publicly. But what does the Holy Spirit have for us today from these verses? Here are three simple applications:

1. The church soon (by AD 100) substituted baptism for circumcision.

Using an incorrect interpretation of Acts 2:38 and Titus 3:5 as a basis, water baptism became the rite of passage into heaven. *The Shepherd of Hermas* (c. AD 100), Justin Martyr (d. 165), Irenaeus (d.c. 200), Cyril of Jerusalem (d. 386), Augustine (d. 430), Thomas Aquinas (d. 1274), the Council of Trent (1545-63), Martin Luther (d. 1546), the Second Vatican Council (1963-65), Anglicans, Episcopalians, Methodists, Presbyterians, Reformed, the churches of Christ—many if not most, that water baptism is required in order to go to heaven.

But Titus 3:5 says, "Not by works of righteousness which we have done, but according to His mercy He saved us, through the washing of regeneration and renewing of the Holy Spirit." Nowhere do we find the word "water." The mention of "washing" is just a reference to the cleansing work of the Holy Spirit in the heart of the one regenerated. It is used in a similar way in Ephesians 5:25-26—"Husbands, love your wives, just as Christ also loved the church and gave Himself for her, that He might sanctify and cleanse her with the **washing of water by the word**." No one (I hope) would dare suggest that the washing here is talking about Jesus baptizing wives in water. And in this case water is even mentioned, but the water is a figure of speech for the Word of God. It is God's Word that does the washing (see John 17:17).

Acts 2:38 may be the most misunderstood and misapplied verse in the entire Bible. The verse says, "Then Peter said to them, 'Repent, and let every one of you be baptized in the name of Jesus Christ for the remission of sins; and you shall receive the gift of the Holy Spirit.'" At first blush, without any reference to the context of this verse, it appears to say the Holy Spirit will not be given and remission of sins not granted until one is water baptized. But several things have been overlooked in most explanations of the verse:

a. There are people listening to these words who are already headed for heaven. We call them OT saints. In Acts 2:5 it tells us many of the Jews from various nations who heard these words were "devout" men. Luke is the only NT author to use this word. The first use is in Luke 2:25 where it refers to Simeon, a just and devout man upon whom was the Holy Spirit. The only other use besides Acts 2:5 is in a description of the men who carried Stephen's body away after his stoning. Acts 8:2 says these men were "devout" men who buried Stephen and made "great lamentation" for him. Surely no one would venture to claim these men in Acts 8 and Simeon in Luke 2:25 were not believers. Even if we say that the men in Acts 8 were water baptized (which they most certainly were), the same word (devout) is used of the unbaptized men of Acts 2:5. These devout men in Acts 2:5 already had a personal relationship with God.

b. All the listeners were Jews or proselytes to Judaism (Acts 2:10). This is true in every case where there is a gap of time between receiving Christ by faith and the Holy Spirit; it is always Jews (Acts 2; 9; 19) or half-Jews (the Samaritans, Acts 8). The significance of this cannot be overlooked. When a Gentile believed (Cornelius, Acts 10), he received the Holy Spirit immediately, prior to water baptism. But before a Jew could receive the Holy Spirit, he needed to be water baptized. Why? Because there was a special curse of destruction imposed on the generation of Jews who crucified Jesus (see Matt. 23:36). Jesus gave them one generation (forty years) to repent of their sinful association with corrupt Judaism in order to avoid imminent destruction and death. Jesus began his ministry in AD 30. Titus came in AD 70. That's forty years. During that time period and that one only, the Jews had to be water baptized to disassociate themselves from the generation that would suffer the curse of destruction and death imposed by Jesus.

c. Invariably Acts 2:40 is overlooked: "And with many other words he testified and exhorted them, saying, 'Be saved from this perverse generation.'" Will you please notice that the salvation mentioned here is not from hell or the lake of fire or eternal damnation? They needed to be water baptized in order to be saved from that perverse *generation*. What generation? The generation that would spill an amount of blood equal to all the blood shed from righteous Abel until Zechariah the son of Berechiah (Matt. 23:35-36). The call for repentance was to the nation. To avoid the bloodletting of Matthew 23:36 the leaders of the nation had to repent. Throughout the Gospels there was a tension between the leaders and the general populace. In Matthew 12:23 the people were ready to proclaim Jesus the Messiah, the Son of David. But the leaders demurred, assigning his healing miracle to the devil. At that point Jesus changed his ministry from one of open miracles to the subtle teaching of parables. He realized the leaders of the nation were not going to receive him. But in his grace he continued to offer himself even after his ascension. Acts 2 was a reoffer of the kingdom. So was the sermon in Acts 3. At the end (Acts 3:19-20) Peter says, "Repent therefore and turn around, that your sins may be blotted out, so that times of refreshing may come from the presence of the Lord, and that He may send Jesus Christ" (translation mine). Even at that point had the leaders of the nation repented, Christ would have returned and set up his kingdom. A sign of that repentance would have been for the leaders of the nation to proclaim Christ to be their Messiah and to be water baptized.

By the way, have you ever noticed the similarities between circumcision and water baptism? Some interesting parallels can be made between water baptism and circumcision, not in their meaning but in their mode. Circumcision was definitely considered to be a work by the writers of Scripture. It was directly associated with the Law of Moses. As noted above, the Jerusalem Council of Acts 15 (15:1, 7, 9, 24) established faith alone as the only requirement for eternal life. The Law of Moses and circumcision (part of the law) were not required for eternal life, explicitly. Apparently, the early church leaders recognized circumcision as a work. I wonder why.

Perhaps a few observations about circumcision will help us understand the difference between circumcision and faith. Then if we find the same contrasts between water baptism and faith, we can conclude that the early church would lump water baptism into the works category. What can we say about circumcision versus faith?

1. Circumcision is a physical act; faith is not.
2. Circumcision is accomplished through physical means (a knife); faith is not.
3. Circumcision is accomplished by a human (the circumciser); faith is not.
4. Circumcision is physically observable by others; faith is not.

Now, what can we say about water baptism with regard to faith?

1. Water baptism is a physical act; faith is not.

2. Water baptism is accomplished through physical means (water); faith is not.

3. Water baptism is accomplished by a human (the baptizer); faith is not.

4. Water baptism is physically observable by others; faith is not.

From the foregoing contrast between circumcision and faith, we can see why the early church leaders put circumcision into the category of works and the law (Gal. 5:1-6). But wait a minute. If water baptism can be contrasted to faith in the same manner as circumcision, and if circumcision was thought to be a work, then so is water baptism. If A = B and C = B, then A = C.

Circumcision was a physical sign or symbol of something spiritual. So many Protestants believe the elements in the Lord's Supper (communion) are physical signs or symbols of something spiritual. Likewise, many believe water baptism is a sign or symbol of something spiritual. These signs or symbols do not validate the spiritual realities they represent. Nor does the absence of these signs or symbols invalidate the spiritual realities they represent. In today's world Paul would argue for the great significance of water baptism, but that significance falls under the category of our sanctification, not our justification. In other words, water baptism does not pry open the doors of heaven for us (justification—salvation from the eternal penalty of sin, that is, hell), but our open, public identification with Christ (water baptism) is a very important first step down the road of progressive sanctification (salvation from the power of sin, that is, a life of slavery to our sin natures).

2. God looks for godly radicals, not godly revolutionaries.

According to Webster, a radical makes "changes in existing views, habits, conditions or institutions," but a revolutionary tries to "overthrow the existing government." Paul was a church planter, not a church splitter. He operated under the authority of the apostles and elders in Jerusalem. He sought to change existing views, etc., but he did not seek to undermine the authority of the church leadership. Unity among Christians is one of the highest priorities in the NT.

But "radical" can also refer to that which is not routine, customary. It also has a slang usage meaning "wonderful or excellent." Dorothy Sayers says of the church:

> The dogma we find so dull, this terrifying drama of which God is the victim and the hero—if this is dull, then what in heaven's name is worthy of being called exciting? The people who hanged Christ never (to do Him justice) accused Him of being a bore. On the contrary, they considered Him too dynamic to be safe. It has been left for later generations to muffle up that shattering personality and surround him with an atmosphere of tedium. We have very efficiently pared the cause of the Lion of Judah, certified Him meek and mild, and recommended Him as a fitting household pet for pale curators and pious old ladies. Those who knew Him, however, objected to Him as a dangerous firebrand.[14]

3. God shows personal favoritism to no man or woman.

The gospel of grace reaches out to every man, woman, and child of every race without favoritism. The proof text is Titus, the Gentile. Respect for every life is woven into the fabric of the Scriptures and especially the gospel of grace. This is one of the many great truths lost in communism, where the individual exists for the good of the state. The individual is expendable. But Christianity teaches that if only one human being were to receive the wonderful offer of salvation through Christ, Jesus would have laid down his life for that one person. What is an individual life worth? Apparently the life of God's only begotten Son.

Professing Christians have not always lived out this truth. In

---

14   Dorothy Sayers, *Letters to a Diminished Church: Passionate Arguments for the Relevance of Christian Doctrine* (Nashville: W Publishing Group, 2004), 1.

Germany the atrocities committed at Auschwitz and other camps were done with clear consciences by many in charge because they did not believe the Jews were human. The commander at Auschwitz, Rudolf Höss, defended his actions in his memoirs, always believing the Jews were the enemy of the state and were subhuman.

The Nazis are always an easy target. What about closer to home? The science of eugenics was actually developed here in America with over twenty thousand forced sterilizations in California alone.[15] In 1934 Hitler gave an honorary doctorate to Harry H. Laughlin, the American scientist who led the field in the science of "racial cleansing." The Nazis used the American practice as justification for their own eugenic policies. No, the idea of a superior race did not begin with Hitler.

In his book *The Imperial Cruise*, James Bradley documents the nefarious philosophy and atrocities of the man who may well have been the most destructive white supremacist president America has ever known: Theodore Roosevelt. He learned his white supremacy while studying at Harvard and under Professor John Burgess at Columbia Law School. The white Christian male sat perched at the top of the evolutionary ladder, according to Professor Burgess. Only those with Teutonic blood were fit to rule the world. The "Manifest Destiny" of these Aryans was to go west from the Atlantic to the Pacific and from the Pacific coast to Asia, ultimately circumnavigating the globe and conquering the world with democracy. Of course, the ruling class would be all white Christian males.

Many races were too dark to be considered human. Of the American Indians Roosevelt wrote that "life was but a few degrees less meaningless, squalid and ferocious than that of the wild beasts [who] seemed to the White settlers devils and not men."[16] The Hawaiians and the Filipinos were Pacific Negroes. When a provisional government

---

15   "Eugenics in the United States," Wikipedia, accessed August 7, 2014, http://en.wikipedia.org/wiki/Eugenics_in_the_United_States.

16   James Bradley, *The Imperial Cruise* (New York: Little, Brown and Company, 2009), 58.

was established in the Hawaiian "colony," only white Christian males (less than 2 percent of the population) were allowed to vote. Bradley's entire book is an exposé on the history of white supremacy and how it led to WWII. The saddest and sickest part of all this is that the proponents of white supremacy in America were doing it in the name of Christ. Yet the greatest racial barrier the history of mankind has ever known was the barrier between the Jews and the Gentiles. If anyone could claim special favor from God, it had to be the Jews. But Acts 15:9 says the gospel broke that barrier and God made no distinction between the Gentiles and the Jews. Later in Galatians 3:28 we read, "There is neither Jew nor Greek, there is neither slave nor free, there is neither male nor female; for you are all one in Christ Jesus."

CONCLUSION

The law principle focuses on the **externals**; liberty focuses on the **internals**. What we are saying is that spirituality does not come from the outside; it comes from the inside. Whenever great attention is given to the externals, especially a list of things that defines "good" as the Pharisees concocted, it is usually a sign there is something wrong on the inside. In fact, I would go so far as to suggest that the greater the focus on external cleanliness, the greater the probability for internal ugliness.

My first lesson in this principle was when my wife and I tried to rent our starter home. A man and his wife showed up with cash in hand for the first and last months' rent and even a damage deposit. They said they loved the home but would only move in if we would allow them to repaint the entire inside of the house. Strange request. He said he used to be a commercial painter and would do the labor for free if we would buy the paint. So, for a hundred dollars we got a fresh paint job. It was perfect. And it was also amazing to watch this man and his wife scrub down the bathrooms. Everything had to be spotless. I think you could fry eggs on the bathroom floor.

Unfortunately, a couple of months later we got a call from the police around eight in the evening. "Did you rent your home to...?" No. "To...?" No. "To...?" No. "To...?" Yes. "Well, he has many aliases, but he is wanted by the law for extortion, bank robbery, car theft, kidnapping, and impersonating a military officer. We have set up a roadblock around your rental house." Needless to say, we were a little stunned. A few minutes later, we heard screeching tires. This guy and his wife escaped the roadblocks and were not apprehended for another month. My experience with rental houses has not been stellar.

You have to wonder what was going on in their minds. I mean, really, there was nothing wrong with the paint inside our house. But he did not only paint all the walls but also the ceilings and trim work. It took him two weeks. Why? The only thing I can conclude was he felt so guilty on the inside, he compensated by compulsive attention to cleanliness on the outside.

Jesus taught us that spirituality does not go outside in; it goes inside out. Stated inversely, it is not what goes into a man's mouth that defiles him, but what comes out. And David wrote in his great confession, "You do not desire sacrifice, or else I would give it; You do not delight in burnt offering. The sacrifices of God are a broken spirit, a broken and contrite heart—these, O God, You will not despise" (Ps. 51:16-17).

4

THE LAW OF SUBSTITUTION
PART 1
Galatians 2:11-16

What is the road to a victorious and fulfilling Christian life? According to Elisabeth Elliot in her book *The Liberty of Obedience*, most sects of Christianity try to measure spirituality based on a list of things they can observe. Here, for instance, is the reply a prospective student got when he asked what he must forsake before entering a Christian school:

> Colored clothes, for one thing. Get rid of everything in your wardrobe that is not white. Stop sleeping on a soft pillow. Sell your musical instruments and don't eat any more white bread. You cannot, if you are sincere about obeying Christ, take warm baths or shave your beard. To shave is to lie against him who created us, to attempt to improve on his work.[17]

---

17   Elisabeth Elliot, *The Liberty of Obedience* (Nashville: Abingdon, 1968), 45-46.

Granted these requirements pertained to a second-century Christian school, but it is just one more illustration of how early legalism spread its wings. Here is another example of legalism run amok. A youth worker showed a missionary film to the high school kids of a church with Scandinavian roots. Several elders showed up an hour later and asked, "Did you show the young people a film?" "Well, yeah, I did." "We don't like that," they replied. Without trying to be argumentative, the youth worker reasoned, "Well, I remember that at the last missionary conference, our church showed slides—" One of the church officers put his hand up signaling the youth worker to stop talking. Then, in these words, he emphatically explained the conflict: "If it's still, fine. If it moves, sin! You can show slides, but when they start moving, you're getting into sin."[18]

No, any kind of list making and the enforcement thereof does not create spirituality; rather, it impedes it since it stirs up our sin natures to rebellion. Is there any single key to a victorious Christian life? Perhaps not. Perhaps it is a combination of things like: obedience, discipline, study, prayer, worship, fellowship, evangelism, service, and giving. Unfortunately, this is just another list of things we can see and measure. But we all know that what's happening on the outside does not necessarily reveal what is happening on the inside. Ultimate freedom from slavery to our sin nature has to happen on the inside.

Fortunately, the Bible does not keep the key to victory a secret. In a word, the key to a victorious Christian life is: **substitution**. Let's see how Paul develops this key to victorious Christian living as he faces the third type of law lover, those who claim we must keep the Law of Moses and be circumcised in order to be sanctified.

---

18   Charles R. Swindoll, *The Grace Awakening* (Dallas: Word, 1990), 160-61.

GALATIANS
"The Gospel of Grace"

SALUTATION/INTRODUCTION

Note carefully the shift from the arena of justification to the arena of sanctification. The Jerusalem Super Bowl is over; the Ravens won. No Gentile has to keep the Law of Moses and be circumcised to be justified. As Peter stated, we are "saved by grace." So the primary argument left for the law lovers was that Christians had to keep the Law of Moses and be circumcised to be sanctified. Now "sanctified" is just a fancy word for "holy." And "holy" is just another way to say righteous, God-like, or Christ-like. In 1 Peter 1:16 God says through Peter, "Be holy, for I am holy." Sanctification, in other words, is how to grow into Christian maturity. And just as the flesh tries to mess up our understanding of justification, it will try to mess up the sanctification process. God justifies us by faith; the devil wants us to attempt to be justified by the flesh. God wants us to be sanctified by faith; the devil wants us to try to be sanctified by the flesh. And he, the devil, will deceive well-meaning, highly qualified Christian leaders into teaching sanctification by the flesh to their followers—even Christian leaders like Peter. Let's see how.

I. PAUL RECOGNIZES PETER'S HYPOCRISY   2:11-13

> Now when Peter had come to Antioch, I withstood him to his face, because he was to be blamed; for before certain men came from James, he would eat with the Gentiles; but when they came, he withdrew and separated himself, fearing those who were of the circumcision. And the rest of the Jews also played the hypocrite with him, so that even Barnabas was carried away with their hypocrisy.

Here we have the great apostle Peter once again saying one thing and doing another, just as he did with his denial of Christ. We can understand his fear of dying and thus his denial of Christ, but we also see his boldness in the face of death after his reception of the Holy Spirit at Pentecost. Thus, his second dissembling may be more shocking than the first if we realize it happened post–Holy Spirit.

At the same time, even this hypocrisy is understandable when we think a bit about Peter's personality. We know enough from the Gospels to know that he was always out front, speaking without thinking, wanting the approval of men, wanting to be liked and popular. It is hard to be popular if you go around speaking the blunt truth all the time. Therefore, the popular person adapts to his environment. "When in Rome, do as the Romans do." So when he was with the Gentiles, he acted accordingly. But when the Jews from Jerusalem showed up, Peter pulled away from the Gentiles and apparently practiced the dietary rules of the Jewish law.

Poor Peter. He's always getting a bad rap. We so easily forget he had enough faith to get out of the boat. For the rest of his life he could tell his grandkids about the day he walked on water—for a little while. But if Peter could slip into this kind of hypocrisy, what about us? Jesus warned his disciples, "Beware of the leaven of the Pharisees" (Luke 12:1), which is hypocrisy. Legalism is the shortest path to hypocrisy. Legalism turns us into junk jewelry—all pretty on the outside, but not much substance on the inside.

Leaven was a great illustration since it would often spread undetected through the entire lump of dough. Paul will say later in Galatians (5:9) that "a little leaven leavens the whole lump." Prior to that he wants to know who hindered the Galatians. They were running well. The "who" (*tis*) in 5:7 is singular. The Greek implies that one person began the legalistic teaching until it spread through the entire area. Same thing with Peter. He was a leader. It says the rest of the Jews followed him so that even Barnabas got carried away with their hypocrisy. Like a growing cancer, Neo-Galatianism can spread through the whole church or the whole denomination.

A friend of mine pastors in a "dying denomination" (his words). They never were big by some denominational standards, but they used to have four thousand churches. Now they are down to around twenty-six hundred churches. Their Bible college has fared even worse—from twenty-five hundred to about three hundred students. Fortunately, new leadership is turning the ship around. But what caused the implosion over the past couple of decades? According to my friend, rampant legalism caused one split after another. They are being destroyed from the inside out and outside in. Inside out since they are doing it to themselves, but outside in because they are measuring one another by externals. It was Charles Spurgeon who said:

> I have found, in my own spiritual life, that the more rules I lay down for myself, the more sins I commit. The habit of regular morning and evening prayer is one which is indispensable to a believer's life, but the prescribing of the length of prayer, and the constrained remembrance of so many persons and subjects, may gender unto bondage, and strangle prayer rather than assist it.[19]

Joseph Stowell observes that the list approach taught by the Pharisees (365 negative commands and 248 positive ones) had at least ten fatal flaws:

(1) New laws continually need to be invented for new situations. (2) Accountability to God is replaced by

---

19   Charles Spurgeon, in *Wycliffe Handbook of Preaching & Preachers*, W. W. Wiersbe, ed. (Chicago, IL: Moody Publishers), 235.

accountability to men. (3) It reduces a person's ability to personally discern. (4) It creates a judgmental spirit. (5) The Pharisees confused personal preferences with divine law. (6) It produces inconsistencies. (7) It created a false standard of righteousness. (8) It became a burden to the Jews. (9) It was strictly external. (10) It was rejected by Christ.[20]

Bad as this appears, it's not a lot different from the system set up by John Calvin in Geneva during the sixteenth century. According to Will Durant in his book on the Reformation:

> To regulate lay conduct a system of domiciliary visits was established: one or another of the elders visited, yearly, each house in the quarter assigned to him, and questioned the occupants on all phases of their lives. Consistory and Council joined in the prohibition of gambling, card-playing, profanity, drunkenness, the frequenting of taverns, dancing (which was then enhanced by kisses and embraces), indecent or irreligious songs, excess in entertainment, extravagance in living, immodesty in dress. The allowable color and quantity of clothing, and the number of dishes permissible at a meal, were specified by law. Jewelry and lace were frowned upon. A woman was jailed for arranging her hair to an immoral height. Theatrical performances were limited to religious plays, and then these too were forbidden. Children were to be named not after saints in the Catholic calendar but preferably after the Old Testament characters; an obstinate father served four days in prison for insisting on naming his son Claude instead of Abraham.... To speak disrespectfully of Calvin or the clergy was a crime. A first violation of these ordinances was punished with a reprimand, further violation with fines, persistent violation with imprisonment or banishment. Fornication was to be punished with exile or drowning; adultery, blasphemy,

20   Joseph M. Stowell, *Fan the Flame* (Chicago: Moody, 1986), 52.

or idolatry, with death. In one extraordinary instance a child was beheaded for striking its parents. In the years 1558-59 there were 414 prosecutions for moral offences; between 1542 and 1564 there were seventy-six banishments and fifty-eight executions; the total population of Geneva was then about 20,000. As everywhere in the sixteenth century, torture was often used to obtain confessions or evidence.[21]

Calvin's Geneva was Neo-Galatianism on steroids. Unrestrained legalism knows no limits. The Pharisees came up with 613 laws to help define and protect the first ten. Like our legal system, new laws have to be written to interpret the old laws. No, Neo-Galatianism does not promote godliness. Godliness self-destructs when the rules are all external. And as the laws multiply, the yoke gets heavier and heavier, reminding us of Peter's words to the Jerusalem Council: "Now therefore, why do you test God by putting a yoke on the neck of the disciples which neither our fathers nor we were able to bear?" (Acts 15:10). We do not know how long after this speech to the council the confrontation of Peter by Paul took place. But we do know that by the time of Galatians 2:11-13, Peter had slipped away from the very principle of grace and freedom he defended so boldly. So Paul confronted Peter's hypocrisy. Then he reproved his heresy.

II. PAUL REPROVES PETER'S HERESY   2:14-16

But when I saw that they were not straightforward about the truth of the gospel, I said to Peter before them all, "If you, being a Jew, live in the manner of Gentiles and not as the Jews, why do you compel Gentiles to live as Jews? We who are Jews by nature, and not sinners of the Gentiles, knowing that a man is not justified by the works of the law but by faith in Jesus Christ, even we have believed in Christ Jesus, that we might be justified by faith in Christ and not by the

---

21   Will Durant, *The Story of Civilization: Part VI, The Reformation* (New York: Simon & Schuster, 1957), 474.

works of the law; for by the works of the law no flesh shall be justified.

Part of the "truth of the gospel," part of the good news, is that we have been set free from the works of the Law of Moses. Such works are not required for justification; nor are they required for sanctification. *Justification* means "to be declared righteous." In this context it refers to justification before God; that is, in God's court of law he, the righteous judge, looks at the perfect righteousness of his own Son that was credited to our account when we believed in him and his work on the cross as our **substitute** in death, and God says, "Not guilty; perfectly righteous." This opens the gates of heaven.

This was the only kind of justification discussed by the early church fathers until Augustine (about AD 400), not knowing his Greek, understood the Greek word for "to justify" as "to **make** righteous"[22] instead of "to **declare** righteous." That simple difference became the single greatest point of contention between Catholics and Protestants about eleven hundred years after Augustine. "To make righteous" meant a continual infusion of the character of Christ until, hopefully, at the end of our lives we have been "made" righteous in our walk or *condition* on earth. "To declare righteous" was not a change in our character on earth but our standing in heaven; not a change in our *condition* or walk but a change in our *position* before God. Augustine and the Roman Catholic Church (RCC) that followed him believed in a lifelong process of justification—what Protestants would call progressive sanctification. But if justification means "to declare righteous," then this legal declaration of righteousness occurred in God's courtroom at a single moment in time.

What is highly significant about a correct understanding of justification is that without it, there can be no assurance of salvation in this life. In Augustine's system there was no forgiveness for future sins. All known sins must be confessed to the local priest for forgiveness. One's future was always in question. If a person died with unconfessed

---

22   In Latin, of course.

mortal sins, he went to hell. With this approach, as Augustine and the RCC taught, no one could have assurance of his salvation in this life. In fact, to make a claim in this life that one was sure he would go to heaven when he died was considered the height of hubris or spiritual pride.[23]

But 1 John 5:13a says we *can know* in this life that we have eternal life: "These things I have written to you who believe in the name of the Son of God, that you may **know** that you have eternal life." With Augustine's approach to justification, one could never know in this life since he could not know if he were "made righteous" to the extent necessary for entrance to heaven. Furthermore, there was no way to deal with sins I might commit in the future. My relationship with God was only as good as my last confession. But if a person is "declared righteous" in the courtroom of heaven based on the blood of Christ, then all his sins (past, present, and future) are buried at the bottom of the sea. Of course, future sins are covered by the blood. For anyone born after the cross, all his sins were "in the future" with respect to the time of the cross itself (AD 33). In other words, Jesus's sacrifice was sufficient to cover sins not yet committed—future sins. At a moment in time all one's sins (past, present, and future) are wiped away. They were already paid for by Christ's work. Although the price has been paid, one must still receive the gift. Like a gift fully paid for on layaway, until the one to whom it is offered claims his gift, it will never be his. This biblical truth of "knowing" opens the door to assurance.

Augustine pioneered a number of new doctrines—some good, some not so good. His linear view of justification (being made righteous in our character over a period of time) helped pave the way for the doctrine of purgatory.[24] It was the logical conclusion to his system of justification. At the end of one's life, if a person had not progressed in righteousness to the necessary point (only God knows what that would be), he is sent to purgatory to suffer for his sins

---

23 It still is among the Amish, who have a completely works-oriented system for going to heaven (http://en.wikipedia.org/wiki/Amish).

24 The actual noun *purgatory* was not in use until around AD 1200.

through which he is purged of the vestiges of sin that would keep him below the cutoff for entering heaven. Once purged, the person goes through the pearly gates.

This approach to justification not only robs a believer of any chance for assurance of his salvation in this life, but it is a gospel different from the one Paul preached. How do we know? Because it teaches that a person who winds up in purgatory can still get to heaven through his own personal suffering for his sins in addition to the suffering of Christ. Instead of Christ's work of suffering on the cross being sufficient, we now have: personal suffering + Christ's suffering = my works + Christ's work = justification. That is another gospel.

As we shall see in more detail in Galatians 3:13, we believe the Bible teaches a substitutionary atonement. That means Christ was our substitute on the cross. He took the punishment we deserved. He died in our place. And his work completely satisfied God (propitiation—1 John 2:2). To say we must suffer for our own sins either in this life or the next to enter heaven is to say Christ did not do enough. Biblical justification takes place in God's court, not in our character. It takes place because of the *law of substitution*: Christ died in our place.

Paul intends to show how the law of substitution extends beyond justification to sanctification. He wants to show us how Christ is not only our substitute in death, but he is also our substitute in life. That is where he is going (Gal. 2:20). But in order to get around to sanctification, he reminds Peter of a proper understanding of justification, which they both share: no man is justified by works of the law. The performance principle just won't work when it comes to justification. Nor will it work when it comes to sanctification, or the victorious Christian life, or progressively becoming more and more like Christ.

We also want to move on to the issue of sanctification in Galatians 2:17-21. But right here we want to pause to further explain how works became inextricably intertwined with faith for justification in most forms of Christianity. We looked at the issue of infant baptism in an earlier lesson. This time we want to look at the issue of perseverance. By perseverance we are not talking about eternal security, a popular way to redefine what the early theologians meant by perseverance.

No, we are talking about remaining faithful in your walk until the end of your life. For most branches of Christian theology (Roman Catholic, Orthodox, and Protestant) this doctrine of perseverance has become inseparable with faith in Christ.

It should come as no surprise that the doctrine of perseverance is a corollary to Augustine's view of justification—an ongoing process in one's life until he dies. If one must have his character progressively "made" righteous throughout his life, it only makes sense that he must also persevere in the faith until the end of his life. How else could the finishing touches on his righteousness be completed so he can enter heaven?

Although anyone who reads Augustine realizes he does not pretend to be an exegete, he does make reference to verses out of context to support his logical conclusions. He found one to support perseverance in Matthew 24:13—"But he who endures to the end shall be saved." Although I have done an engine search on only about a fourth of his writings, Augustine refers to this verse as a requirement for going to heaven far more than any other verse in the Bible (over 250 times in the writings I searched). (This occurs only after AD 412, whereas prior he believed deliverance from physical death was meant in Matthew 24:13.)

For Augustine, after his transition in AD 412, perseverance does not play second fiddle to faith; it plays first violin. He actually believed someone could be regenerated, receive the Holy Spirit, and have genuine faith in Christ but not be elect to go to heaven if he did not persevere in the faith until the end of his life.[25] On top of that, he believed God sovereignly chose those to whom he would give this gift of perseverance. It is what Calvinists later called "irresistible grace." The elect have no choice in whether they receive this gift or not—it is irresistible. Some baptized believers got it; some didn't. Why do some get it and others don't? It's a mystery, according to Augustine.[26] So it

---

25 Augustine, *Rebuke and Grace*, 5.18; and *The Gift of Perseverance*, 9.21; 11.25.

26 Ibid., *Gift of Perseverance*, 9.21; 11.25.

is that no one in the RCC has assurance of his or her salvation. And so it is that the Council of Trent (the RCC answer to the teachings of Calvin and Luther) anathematized anyone who challenged their doctrine that works are meritorious for salvation.

Do you see it? The RCC did. If you are going to say someone *must* persevere in good works until the end of his life in order to go to heaven, then of course good works are an essential part of the salvation equation. But the Protestants were no different. Let us understand that the Protestants were steeped in Augustinian doctrines. After all, where did the Protestants come from? The RCC. The Protestants split off into two directions: the Arminians and the Calvinists. The Arminians believe the Christian who does not persevere in his walk until the end of his life loses his salvation. The Calvinists don't think someone who is elect can lose his salvation. So they think Matthew 24:13 teaches the elect will persevere until the end of their lives. If they don't, then they were never elect to begin with.[27]

Do you see it? They did not. As this fruit-inspecting industry crossed the ocean from Europe to America, there is a familiar ring. Charles Hodge typifies the error of this group:

> Election, calling, justification, and salvation are indissolubly united; and, therefore, he who has clear evidence of his being called has the same evidence of his election and final salvation.... **The only evidence** of election is effectual calling, that is, the production of holiness. And **the only evidence** of the genuineness of this call and the certainty of our perseverance, is a patient continuance in well doing [emphasis mine].[28]

---

27   See appendix A in David R. Anderson, *Free Grace Soteriology* (Houston: Grace Theology Press, 2013) for a development of how Matthew 24:13 became a soteriological verse.

28   Charles Hodge, *St. Paul's Epistle to the Romans* (Grand Rapids, MI: William B. Eerdmans, 1950), 212.

Or, as John Murray put it, "The perseverance of the saints reminds us very forcefully that only those who persevere to the end are truly saints."[29] These men fall into the Calvinistic camp.

But how does this understanding of perseverance differ from "the churches of Christ," which think salvation can be lost? Robert Shank, one of their chief spokesmen, writes: "Obviously, it can be known only as one finally perseveres (or fails to persevere) in faith. There is **no valid assurance** of election and final salvation for any man, **apart from deliberate perseverance in faith**" (emphasis mine).[30] But Shank is a pure Arminian who left the Southern Baptist Convention over the issue of eternal security. It is strange how alike aspects of these two systems (Calvinism and Arminianism) become when one studies their doctrines of perseverance based on an Augustinian interpretation of Matthew 24:13.

Yet surely the modern advances of exegesis under the scrutiny of a careful study of Greek grammar and the historical setting (the grammatico-historical method) have cleared away the brush hiding the inconsistency of interpreting "the end" of Matthew 24:13 differently from "the end" of Matthew 24:3, 6, and 14. "The end" in Matthew 24:3, 6, and 14 obviously means the end "of the age." But right in the midst of these verses it is claimed that "the end" in Matthew 24:13 means "the end of one's physical life." That is an amazing inconsistency. Common sense would argue that a word found in the same context four times should mean the same thing all four times. Surely. But, as we shall see, Neo-Galatianism will not allow it to be so. Let us take a contemporary NT scholar who teaches at a respected, conservative seminary as a case in point: Scot McKnight.

In a 1992 article McKnight addressed the warning passages of

---

29   John Murray, *Redemption Accomplished and Applied* (Grand Rapids, MI: Wm. B. Eerdmans Publishing Company, 1955), 155.

30   Robert Shank, *Life in the Son: A Study of the Doctrine of Perseverance* (Springfield, MO: Westcott, 1961), 293.

Hebrews.[31] The first question he had to settle was whether the recipients of the epistle were believers or unbelievers. Like a prospector panning for gold, he sifted through the evidence very carefully. Page after page of research amassed the evidence and concluded the obvious: these are actual believers, not fake believers—professors, not possessors. He does not like the implications connected with Calvin's solution of "temporary faith," so he searches for another explanation as to how actual believers can wind up in hell (his conclusion).

McKnight is to be commended for not allowing his Calvinistic approach to perseverance to cause him to declare these recipients unbelievers. However, because he is convinced that only believers who persevere to the end of their lives are elect, he must make categories among those who have actually believed. So he distinguishes between "genuine, true, real, or saving" faith and what he calls "phenomenological" faith.[32] Those who are phenomenological believers are those who, from the human perspective, have been observed to have all the fruits of genuine faith but may have fallen short of the same.[33] Because these believers have genuinely experienced the Holy Spirit, the powers of the age to come, the taste of God's Word, and so on, they have enjoyed spiritual *phenomena* that are genuine spiritual experiences shared by the elect.[34] But, alas, they are not elect. How do we know? Because they do not persevere in the faith until the

---

31 Scot McKnight, "The Warning Passages of Hebrews: A Formal Analysis and Theological Conclusions," *Trinity Journal* 13 (Spring 1992): 22–59.

32 Ibid., 24, n. 12.

33 Ibid., n. 10.

34 McKnight recognizes these believers as regenerate, but for him regeneration does not necessitate perseverance and is, by his definition, a lifelong process. So, much like Augustine, these believers can be regenerated but fall away from the faith and be eternally damned.

end of their lives, and Matthew 24:13 tells us that people who do not persevere until the end cannot be saved (notice that Hebrews never uses such terminology).

McKnight's entire article is a classic study in circular reasoning. He assumes what he is trying to prove. He assumes incorrectly (from Matt. 24:13) that anyone who does not persevere in the faith until the end of his life cannot go to heaven. But the evidence he amasses from Hebrews demonstrates the readers to be believers. Now the only way to keep these believers out of heaven is to say they lose their salvation (an Arminian option), they go to purgatory for further cleansing (a Catholic option), or there must be different categories of believers (his final option). On this basis, he understands only Joshua and Caleb from the redeemed "Egyptian" generation of Israelites to be with the Lord today (see below). How Moses appeared with the Lord at the transfiguration he does not explain. Why Michael the archangel contended with the devil over the body of Moses (Jude 9) remains a mystery.

Yes, McKnight recognizes the recipients of Hebrews as believers, but they may be only phenomenological believers who wind up in hell because of apostasy. He uses the severe language in the warning of Hebrews 10:26ff. to determine that all the warning passages in Hebrews are alluding to the danger of hellfire if one does not persevere:[35]

> The following logic is at the heart of the author's exhortations: if willful disobedience and apostasy in the Mosaic era brought discipline and prohibited entrance into the Land (a type of the eternal rest), then surely willful disobedience and apostasy in the new era will bring eternal exclusion from the eternal rest.

---

35 The approach to interpretation is called "analogy by faith." It just means we should try to interpret an unclear passage in the same book by a clear passage. He thinks it is clear the warning in Hebrews 10:26ff. is hell for those who do not persevere. By analogy, then, the other warning passages, which are not quite as clear, refer to the same warning: hell.

In light of the final sense of several of these expressions (cf. especially the harsh realities of 10:30-31, 39) and the use of imagery in Hebrews that elsewhere is used predominantly of eternal damnation, it becomes quite clear that the author has in mind an eternal sense of destruction. The author of Hebrews makes it *unambiguously clear* [when we authors claim a doctrine is unambiguously clear, it is usually a red flag that it is not—italics mine] that those who do not persevere until the end will suffer eternal punishment at the expense of the wrath of God. There is no escape; like the children of Israel who disobeyed, those who shrink back will be destroyed. The consequences for those who apostasize [*sic*] are eternal damnation and judgment; therefore, the author has exhorted his readers to persevere until the end.[36]

Never mind the fact that the words "hell," "lake of fire," "eternal," "everlasting," "forever," "damnation," and the like never occur in any of these warning passages. He is convinced the language of 10:26-39 is so

---

36   Ibid., 35-36. His view of "fire" and "burning" is limited to hellfire. But note Deuteronomy 4:24 and the consuming fire, the jealous God, and the utter destruction (the LXX uses *apōleia/apoleisthe* to emphasize the **utter** destruction to come upon Israel if she is unfaithful, and this is the same term used in Heb. 10:39). Malachi 4:1 also points to the fire, and this fire will destroy the Jews in the land. They will not prolong their days in the land.

Interpreters who object to the warning in Hebrews 10 as being a temporal judgment instead of eternal speak of the much worse judgment to come upon believers in Christ who apostatize as opposed to the judgment that came upon the unfaithful Israelites at Kadesh-Barnea. However, they overlook the fact that a judgment that affects one's rest in the Millennium (one thousand years) is much worse than a judgment that affects one's rest in the land for forty years.

severe it must refer to eternal damnation. Does he conclude the same for Deuteronomy 4:24's *apōleia/apoleisthe* (utterly destroy) and *ektribē/ektribēisthe* (utterly destroy), expressions that are even more emphatic than the *apōleian* (destruction) of Hebrews 10:39?[37] Not likely. The curses in Deuteronomy are temporal curses. God's covenants with Abraham and David ensure an eternal relationship with Israel. The issue in Deuteronomy 4 and 30 is fellowship, not relationship. Then could the same not be said of the Hebrew Christians of Hebrews, especially when drawing on the warnings of temporal judgment given in Deuteronomy 32 (32:35 and 36 are quoted in Heb. 10:30), the language of which is even more graphic than that of Hebrews 10:26ff.?

McKnight concludes that those who do not persevere until the end cannot go to heaven, since that is the "single condition"[38] for final salvation (whatever happened to believing in Jesus?). With the circle complete, he warns his own readers that we should not be hasty in giving assurance of salvation to people who look like genuine believers. Why? Because they may only be phenomenological believers.

How can one know if he is a phenomenological believer instead of a genuine believer, since the observable fruit for each category is the same until the former falls away somewhere before the end of his life? Obviously, one cannot know which category he belongs to until the end of his life. Again, McKnight is to be credited for some consistency. That is, he warns us that no one can have assurance of his salvation in this life. McKnight, by his own admission, has said nothing new.[39] He merely traded Calvin's conclusion for Augustine's earlier error. His term "phenomenological believers" simply describes Augustine's regenerated believers who received the Holy Spirit but who never received God's additional required gift of perseverance for ultimate salvation.

---

37   When a verb in Hebrew or Greek is preceded by a noun with the same root as the verb, the action of the verb is being emphasized.

38   McKnight, *Warning Passages*, 59.

39   Ibid., 22.

Even Wayne Grudem (another Calvinist) admits that his fellow Calvinist Scot McKnight teaches a view that would preclude even the elect of having assurance in this life: "This position [McKnight's] would mean that no Christian could ever have *present* assurance of salvation, but would simply have to wait and persevere until the end of life in order to have confidence that he or she would be saved."[40] Exactly.

But is this not the very conclusion of Augustine and Calvin? Augustine specifically rejected assurance of salvation before death. Calvin, writing against the RCC, initially embraced assurance. Assurance was of the essence of faith in his early writings, but not after his interaction with the Council of Trent, which said assurance led to a license to sin. It would seem the apple does not fall very far from the tree.

Yes, an inaccurate interpretation of Matthew 24:13 as applying to the end of our lives rather than the end of the age has become over the centuries the single most relied upon verse in the Bible for defining gaining life after death with God, or *the* requirement for going to heaven, if you will. The RCC leans on it. The Calvinists claim it. And the Arminians use it as their final arbiter. Could this be Neo-Galatianism? Is it not a subtle way of adding something to the gospel either on the front end (Arminians) or the back end (Calvinists) or for the duration (RCC)? We can see that the basic struggle Paul fights in Galatians rages on in the twenty-first century with Neo-Galatianism.

---

40 Wayne Grudem, "Perseverance of the Saints," in *Still Sovereign*, ed. Thomas R. Schreiner and Bruce A. Ware (Grand Rapids, MI: Baker, 1995), 165.

5

THE LAW OF SUBSTITUTION PART 2

Galatians 2:17-21

INTRODUCTION

I have done a lot of stupid things in my life. I don't know where this ranks on the list, but it has to be up there near the stupidest. It was in the early '80s. The cold war with the Soviets was still underway. Two brilliant brothers, one a seminary professor and the other an ophthalmologist had made a wall-sized US map in their home in Dallas. This map identified the "hot spots" in America where the Soviets might hit first in a preemptive strike. They also had all of our missile silos identified. Then they found what they considered the safest place in America and bought a home there. The ophthalmologist never practiced medicine. He made plenty of money during medical school by tape recording the professors' notes, transcribing them, and selling them to other medical students so they didn't have to take their own notes. He moved to Whitefish, Montana.

Now I was good friends with one of their good friends who knew all about the plan. Houston was a hot spot because of its refineries.

We needed to be able to get out of Texas and up to Montana on one refill. At the time there was only one way to do it: diesel gas and lots of it. Well, it just so happened that GM had come out with their first diesel engine for a car. It was the old 350cc block made to use diesel. We figured if I bought a station wagon with a twenty-gallon gas tank and put a trucker's tank (fifty gallons) in the back with a gravity feed down to the twenty-gallon tank, that would give us seventy gallons to work with. Start full and refuel just once, and you're there—Houston to northern Montana with just one stop.

Now I have learned through my many mistakes through the years (most of which have involved believing other people when I shouldn't) that I must have some neon lights on my forehead that read: Sucker. Now my friends were dead serious about all this, and I was commuting at the time to work on a PhD in Dallas, so I thought, why not? Of course, it is illegal to ride with a tank of gas inside your car—unless it is diesel, which is not combustible. So I filled up and did a trial run to Dallas. Only one serious problem—the smell. Can you imagine going up and down the freeway smelling diesel fuel?

Well, it turns out this experiment by GM didn't work so well. These engines were breaking down all over the place. Ours broke down three times. I really thought I could drive so far with that car that I would ultimately drive it to heaven. Finally, when all looked lost and I was about to bury this car, GM stepped forward with a solution. To avoid a class action lawsuit, they were willing to convert these cars from diesel to regular gas. And they would pay for the conversion.

Voilà! My car could be saved. But there was only one way to do it. It had to be "born again" by replacing the old, defunct engine with a brand-new engine that really worked. That's right. My car was born again. They substituted the old engine with a new one that ran on regular gasoline. Of course, we gave up our master plan to escape to Montana, especially after the collapse of the Soviet Union. It's all quite laughable (or pitiable) right now, but at the time it seemed like a really good idea.

I realize this illustration is a stretch and breaks down at certain points, but I have only one main point to make—**substitution**. That was the only hope for that old car if it were ever going to get anywhere. The same is true in our Christian lives. Sooner or later we will discover that trying to putt around the highways and byways of Christianity will cause motor problems. Very likely, our engines will just conk out on us. If we are ever going to make it (sanctification), we need to substitute our old engines with new ones.[41] And that's what sanctification is all about. *Christ was our substitute in death to deliver us from the eternal penalty of sin (justification), and he must be our substitute in life to deliver us from the present power of sin (sanctification).*

Nothing can sap the joy out of the tree of Christian living faster than living under the yoke of legalism. In Acts 15:10, Peter argued against legalism by saying, "Why do you test God by putting a yoke on the neck of the disciples which neither our fathers nor we were able to bear?" But the desire to perform for the approval of either God or men or both is so strong that not long after making this speech at the Jerusalem Council we find Peter caught up in legalism in Antioch. Paul confronts him face-to-face. Peter is wearing the very yoke he preached against. Paul wants to take that heavy yoke off Peter and all his own followers through the law of substitution.

GALATIANS
"The Gospel of Grace"

---

41   We are not teaching exchanged life theology here.

If we view Galatians 2:1-10 as the Jerusalem Council, which I do, then we have to wonder why there is still discussion going on about justification. The council made it clear that no one had to be justified by works of the law. Letters were put in hand for Paul to nail to the church bulletin boards. Since this issue was settled, much of the discussion turned to what is required for sanctification instead of justification. But the specter of inevitable death looms so large in the human experience that the discussion keeps drifting back to justification because people really want to know, if possible, where they are going to go after they die. We will see this in 2:17. The Galatians were getting justification and sanctification all mixed up, just like the Neo-Galatianists are. Here Paul discusses the accusation of license (2:17) and the answer of liberty (2:18-21).

I. ACCUSATION OF LICENSE   2:17

> But if, while we seek to be justified by Christ, we ourselves also are found sinners, is Christ therefore a minister of sin? Certainly not!

Just as in Romans 6:1, when justification by faith alone in Christ alone is taught, there are those who will object that this doctrine opens the door to loose living (license to sin). Such false conclusions drawn from correct premises are answered in Paul's letters with a definitive *me genoito*, which means "certainly not, of course not, may it never be, no way, absolutely not."

It would be something like someone offering you a little of their cotton candy and you just lift the whole blob off the stick and eat it, or offering a bowl of Blue Bell ice cream and you finish the whole carton, or, God forbid, offering a handful of cashews and you eat the whole jar! That would be sick. Only we are not talking about cotton candy, Blue Bell, or cashews. We are talking about God's incredible grace. To continue in sin just because God by his grace will forgive us is sick thinking. Many concluded it just was not possible to be truly justified and not go on to sanctification. So they began using sanctification as a test of justification. The Reformers were not comfortable with Augustine's claim that a child of God could not know if he were a child of God in this life.

In fact, Calvin followed Melanchthon's mistake when he defined the Greek word *hypostasis* as "assurance" in Hebrews 11:1—"Now faith is the assurance of things hoped for, the conviction of things not seen" (ESV, NASB).[42] This was a fork in the road between the subjective and the objective. Because now people began to examine their faith to see if they had assurance when they believed. It not only led to introspection, but it led to categorizing faith according to its quality. Soon people were talking about "saving" faith and "temporary" faith to explain Hebrews 6. Initially, Calvin thought assurance came from looking to Christ and his promises. But the error of Melanchthon and Luther making assurance part of the definition of faith finally took its toll. It had the effect of taking the eyes of a believer off Christ and onto himself to see if he had the right kind of faith. They began putting their faith in their faith, rather than in Christ.

This was all too subjective for Theodore Beza, who followed Calvin as head of the Geneva Academy. We credit Augustine for bringing

---

42 See *TDNT*, vol. 8, as well as *BDAG* for their explanation of the Greek word used here (*hypostasis*) meaning "reality." Instead of the subjective "assurance," faith is the objective "reality" of the things hoped for. In Hebrews what we can see is always viewed in terms of the shadowy and transitory. It is the heavenly world that is the lasting, eternal reality. Paradoxically, faith is the reality in this world of the things we hope for in the next.

Plato into Christianity, and we credit Thomas Aquinas and Theodore Beza with introducing Aristotle. Aristotle's writings had been lost to the Western church until a cache of his writings was discovered in Spain during the thirteenth century. They were preserved by the Muslims and required a joint effort of Jewish, Christian, and Muslim scholars to translate the Arabic for the Western world.[43] Aristotle was not interested in subjective "forms" or "ideals" in some ethereal world like Plato; he was a scientist interested in the objective evidence before him. Of course, Aristotle was not a Christian, but Beza liked his objectivity. So he said assurance does not come from looking at Christ (especially since Christ might not have died for you—limited atonement); it comes from something much more objective—your fruit.

Thus, whereas Calvin undermined assurance by looking inward to examine the quality of one's faith, Beza switched the focus outward to our fruit production. Now we needed the right kind of fruit, the right amount of fruit, and the right motive for fruit to have any kind of assurance of our justification. End result—loss of assurance across the board for the fruit inspectors, not to mention the fact that they might not persevere to the end of their lives walking with God.

Thus, sanctification became a justification issue. No sanctification? No justification. After escaping the RCC, the pressure was on once again for believers to perform. Even if we say that their performance is by the power of the Holy Spirit (Phil. 2:13), they still **had to** perform. The moment we switch from **want to** to **have to**, we have switched from faith to the flesh—to Neo-Galatianism. Any attempt to deny this is simply playing word games. As Zane Hodges noted:

> Some indeed would claim that discipleship is not a condition for eternal life, but an *inevitable result* of possessing it. But those who so speak are playing a word-game. Whatever is *necessary* to achieve a goal is also a *condition* for reaching it.

---

43   Richard E. Rubenstein, *Aristotle's Children* (New York: Harcourt, 2003).

To call anything an *inevitable* result is to call it a *necessary* result and thus to make it a *condition*. Candor is lacking in those who fail to admit this.

Let's put it plainly. If on-going good works are necessary for reaching heaven, they are also a condition for reaching heaven. Thus, on this view, final salvation is based on faith plus works![44]

Thus, just as the accusation of license in the day of Paul caused problems, so it has since the days of the Reformation. After Beza and William Perkins came the Pietists (Frankl, Spener) who put even more emphasis on sanctification as proof of justification. According to them, Luther got things right with regard to justification. But, as they saw it, a change in the head should result in a change in the heart. There were Lutherans and Calvinists everywhere who were living like hell. The Pietists questioned whether the head could be right if the heart were not. These Pietists influenced a young man by the name of John Wesley. His "warming" at Aldersgate was a sanctification experience through which his heart could be wholly devoted to God and intentional sin completely excised from his life. For the rest of his ministry Wesley emphasized sanctification almost to the exclusion of justification.[45]

The Galatians were "seeking to be justified" when they were already justified! And people have been seeking to be justified rather than just trusting the shed blood of Jesus ever since. Paul clearly states that if we seek to be justified, say through fruit inspection as Beza would have us do, we will fail. And when we fail, does that mean Christ

---

44 Zane Hodges, *Gospel Under Siege* (Dallas: Redencion Viva, 1981), 40.

45 Wesleyan doctrine teaches that all people are justified by the blood of Christ, but each person must claim that justification for it to be effective in his life. So, justification does not come at the moment of faith. It was accomplished as a universal event for all mankind.

failed or that Christ made us sin? Of course not, because Christ freed us from the law. Of course, by freeing us from the law, be it the Law of Moses or the law principle, Jesus was not promoting license. Neither was Paul. As he will say in Galatians 5:13, we aren't supposed to use our freedom as an opportunity for indulgence, but rather to serve each other in love. And here Paul rebuffs the accusation of license with the answer of liberty.

II. ANSWER OF LIBERTY   2:18-21
A. Paul's Old Life Partner—the Law   2:18-19

> For if I build again those things which I destroyed, I make myself a transgressor. For I through the law died to the law that I might live to God.

Paul argues that we have been set free from the law principle. Because neither use of the *nomos* (law) in 2:19 has the specifying article ("the," as in *the* Law of Moses), his use of *nomos* here may well be referring to the law principle rather than the Law of Moses. What is the law principle? It is the performance principle, part of the very essence of legalism. The performance principle tells me I need to perform at a certain level to receive blessings from God in this life. But according to Paul, we couldn't perform for justification, and we can't perform for sanctification.

Peter received a vision from the Lord in Acts 10:11-16 that it was okay to eat some of the things forbidden in the Law of Moses. And he made it clear at the Jerusalem Council (Acts 15) that the heavy yoke of the law should not be imposed on the Gentiles for justification. But now, in Antioch, he is living according to these dietary laws once again, apparently for the purpose of sanctification. Paul wants to make it clear that the Law of Moses was not given for justification or sanctification. Beyond that, the law principle (performance through the energy of the flesh) could not accomplish either justification or sanctification.

It is a strange irony that so many lists are made in order to "seek to be justified" and those very lists, those laws, inflame our flesh and make us transgress all the more. The lists are made ostensibly to tame our sin, but do just the opposite. The way to escape sin is not to reinstate laws or lists. The way to escape sin is to die to the law and "live to God."

The death and remarriage illustration is one Paul will use again when he writes Romans 7:1-4. It is a little difficult to keep up with Paul's illustrations at times. In Romans 7:1-3 it is the husband (the law) who dies, leaving his wife (the believer) free to remarry Jesus. Then in Romans 7:4 it is the wife who dies and is free to remarry Jesus. Here in Galatians it is the wife (the believer) who dies so she can "live to God." Regardless of who is dying, both Romans and Galatians use the death and remarriage analogy to illustrate the new freedom we have after coming to Christ. We were justified without the law, and we shall be sanctified without the law.

B. Paul's New Life Partner—Christ   2:20-21

I have been crucified with Christ; it is no longer I who live, but Christ lives in me; and the life which I now live in the flesh I live by faith in the Son of God, who loved me and gave Himself for me. I do not set aside the grace of God; for if righteousness comes through the law, then Christ died in vain.

The new marriage spouse for the believer is Christ himself. We, the church, are the bride of Christ. To leave Christ and go back to the law was itself unlawful (Deut. 24:1-4). To be **crucified with Christ** is one of the great love scenes in the Bible; more poignant than *Romeo and Juliet*, more passionate than when Heathcliff (Sir Laurence Olivier) heard of Catherine's illness in *Wuthering Heights* and writhed out the words, "Existence after losing her would be hell," our groom (Jesus) laid down his life for his bride (the church), but they were crucified together. This is Romans 6:3-5. Of course, his death was physical and spiritual; ours is just spiritual here and in Romans 6.

"Nevertheless I live"—I much prefer this old KJV translation because it is supportable in the Greek (*de* is a mild adversative[46] and is left out of the NKJV and the ESV) and fits better with the Romans 6 identification of the believer in both Jesus's death **and** resurrection. I died and was buried, but I am raised and I live. "Yet not I, but Christ lives in me." Here, finally, is the **substitutionary life** of Christ. He was my substitute in death for my justification; now he is my substitute in life for my sanctification. I was delivered from the eternal penalty of sin by his death; I shall be delivered from the present power of sin by his life (Rom. 5:10).

Two old illustrations are my favorites for trying to understand the substitutionary life of Christ. One is about a little boy who seemed to love Jesus more than any of the other kids in his Sunday school class. One day his teacher asked him, "Johnny, don't you ever feel tempted to do something wrong?" "Of course," replied Johnny, "but when temptation knocks at my door, I send Jesus to answer." That's it. Johnny got it. When temptation knocks on our doors, we should send Jesus to answer. This approach works on sins of omission as well as sins of commission. What does that mean? Well, it works not just on occasions when sin or temptation knocks at our doors, but it works also when the Holy Spirit is telling us to do something we don't feel we can do.

I hope you are one of those people who never has problems with other people. Bless you. Most of us run into people problems somewhere along the line. These conflicts or misunderstandings can leave deep emotional scars. The negative emotions associated with these scars can raise their ugly heads when we run into these people at church or in the marketplace. Our natural tendency, the tendency of our flesh, is to avoid these people—find another hallway at church or another aisle at the store. But Jesus says the ultimate test of our maturity in Christ is to love those who have hurt us (our enemies—

---

46   *BDAG*, 213a, —"one of the most commonly used Gk. particles, used to connect one clause w. another when it is felt that there is some contrast betw. them, though the contrast is oft. scarcely discernible."

Matt. 5:43-47). That requires us to be proactive instead of reactive. And, for most of us, that requires supernatural power.

So, in a situation where we are called upon by the Holy Spirit to do the right thing but we feel powerless to do it, send Jesus to do it. You say, "Okay, Lord, I know I am supposed to love that person, but I cannot do it. It just isn't in me. What they did hurts too badly. But I know you love them (though I don't know why—uh-oh, is that the flesh talking?), so right now I am asking you to do your thing. Please love them." Then, you walk over to them and initiate—proactive. It's really a beautiful thing when it happens. You sense something eternal is happening, something that will bring glory to our Savior forever and ever.

My second illustration I like to think about with regard to the substitutionary life of Christ is the hand and the glove. The glove lies limp and powerless before the insertion of the hand. But when that hand goes into the glove, all kinds of good things can happen. Just so, we are like the limp glove when it comes to doing eternal things with our fleshly power. We need the hand, which in this case is Jesus. He can empower us to do all things whatsoever he has commanded us (Phil. 4:13). **"Christ lives in me."**

"I live by faith," says Paul. He lives **"in the flesh"** (a reference to his human body as opposed to his sin nature as in Gal. 5:16-21), but he lives **by faith**. He loves to contrast a life of faith with confidence in the flesh (Phil. 3:1-11). When we live by the energy of our flesh (see 3:3), we can never be sanctified. Living by the flesh is to trust in the flesh, in ourselves. Living by faith is to trust in Jesus—"Christ in you, the hope of glory" (Col. 1:27).

CONCLUSION

We were justified by grace through faith, and we will be sanctified by grace through faith. The confusion comes in when justification and sanctification are so tightly wedded that one cannot exist without the other. At the risk of being repetitious, the Calvinistic branch of theology claims a lack of sanctification proves there never was any justification. And the Arminian branch of theology claims a failure in sanctification at the end of one's life negates his or her justification. Both branches wind up in the same place.

Famed Arminian scholar I. Howard Marshall recognized as much in his dissertation:

> If a person is in the former group [Calvinism], he has still to heed the warning: only by so doing can he show that he is one of the elect. In other words, the Calvinist "believer" cannot fall away from "true" faith, but he can "fall away" from what proves in the end to be only seeming faith. The possibility of falling away remains. But in neither case does the person know for certain whether he is a true or a seeming disciple. All that he knows is that Christ alone can save and that he must trust in Christ, and that he sees signs in his life which may give him some assurance that he is a true disciple. But these signs may be misleading.

> It comes down to a question of assurance. Whoever said, "The Calvinist knows that he cannot fall from salvation but does not know whether he has got it," had it summed up nicely. But this can be counterfeit and misleading. The non-Calvinist knows that he has salvation—because he trusts in the promises of God—but is aware that, left to himself, he could lose it. So he holds to Christ. It seems to me that practical effect is the same.[47]

D. A. Carson (a Calvinistic scholar) admits the same when he says:

> Historically, of course, it is a commonplace that some branches of Calvinism have developed their own forms of introversion,

---

47   I. Howard Marshall, "The Problem of Apostasy in New Testament Theology," *Jesus the Savior: Studies in New Testament Theology* (London: SPCK, 1990), 313.

believers constantly examining themselves to see if they were displaying sufficient fruit to justify their conclusion that they were among the elect—thus strangely mirroring their Arminian counterparts who sometimes gave themselves to worrying if they were truly holding on to the promise of God. Thus at their worst, the two approaches meet in strange and sad ways.[48]

Carson is so convinced that true faith will produce works or fruit or perseverance (interchangeable terms in his writings) that he makes perseverance the essence of saving faith. In other words, he makes perseverance part of the definition of true faith: "Hebrews virtually *defines* true believers as those who hold firmly to the end the confidence they had at first (3:6, 14).... Part of the *definition* of saving faith includes the criterion of perseverance" (italics mine).[49] Wow. This is Neo-Galatianism on steroids. With this kind of definition of "saving" faith, when will I know if I have truly believed? The answer is obvious—you cannot until death.[50]

Paul went to great lengths both in Galatians 2:11-21 as well as Romans 4:1-8 to keep faith and works separated and distinct. How sad and anti-Pauline that modern-day interpreters are actually including works in their definition of faith. My, my.

By understanding our justification is by grace, through faith alone,

---

48 D. A. Carson, "Reflections on Assurance," in *Still Sovereign*, ed. Thomas R. Schreiner and Bruce A. Ware (Grand Rapids, MI: Baker, 1995), 268.

49 Ibid., 267.

50 At the end of his article (p. 276) Carson seems to realize the trap he has created, so he pleads for partial assurance for those who are currently persevering. In other words, you cannot have final assurance until the end of your life, but you can have partial assurance if you are persevering today. I am still trying to figure out what partial assurance is.

that we cannot take away from nor add to it by our behavior, we get peace and freedom. We can relax; Jesus paid it all. By understanding that sanctification is the process of living faith daily, and that is the way for us to grow up from being babies to mature Christians, we can understand the enormous waste, loss, and downright silliness to do anything other than live lives crucified with Christ that we might let Christ live through us.

6

CHRISTIAN VOODOO
Galatians 3:1-5

Of course, the title for this section is an oxymoron. Voodoo is from the devil. Christ cannot have fellowship with the devil. But the word "bewitched" (*baskainō*) in Galatians 3:1 does literally refer to witchcraft and magic. It is as though the Galatians had had a spell cast on them.

I have made four trips to Haiti with Walt Baker, who was a missionary there for fifteen years. He was the only white man on the island who could preach in Creole, French, and English. According to him, one of the voodoo practices in Haiti is the creation of zombies. When a person gets out of line, in order to leave a message to others, the witch doctor takes a drug much more potent than cocaine called tetrodotoxin. It is taken from the puffer fish and has paralyzing powers. Extracted from the glands of the fish, it can be turned into a fine white powdery substance. The witch doctor will watch where the target puts his hands. Then he will smear some of this drug on the places where the target regularly touches, knowing that he will get some of this drug on his hands. Once a person touches the ingredient, it takes only a couple of hours before it puts the person who touched it into a drug-induced coma so deep that primitive medicine cannot tell that the person is still alive.

So, not detecting a heartbeat or any breathing, they conduct a funeral service for the person in the coma. They always place the bodies above ground, and the practice is to run from the burial grounds when the service is complete. The witch doctor comes in the night and brings the person to, knowing that the effects of the drug last only twenty-four hours. They then continue to administer smaller doses of the drug and keep the person in a trance-like state and use them as servants. When people see the person they thought was dead walking around, they believe the witch doctor has raised them from the dead, and they are afraid to do anything to anger the witch doctor. These are zombies. Now, if you are like me, all this sounds pretty unbelievable.[51] However, Walt said one man he knew confirmed he could vividly remember his funeral service but could not remember the next eleven years of his life. A zombie walks around in a state of living death.

Paul claims some of his converts had become Christian zombies. They were in a state of living death. That is the power of legalism. And, in a crude way of thinking, they had also become practitioners of Christian voodoo. In magic, the practitioners use their rites and rituals to manipulate the "gods" into doing their bidding or will. Men trying to manipulate supernatural powers—that's magic. And that is also legalism—men going through various rituals or some level of moral performance in order to make God "owe us." Remember, legalism says, "Do, and God will owe you." So Paul is trying to shock his readers out of this very serious error that holds them under its spell.

At this point in his letter Paul leaves his historical defense of his gospel. From three historical vignettes he has demonstrated the truth of justification by faith and sanctification by faith. Now he wants

---

51 Wade Davis, "The Ethnobiology of the Haitian Zombie," *Journal of Ethnopharmacology* 9 (1983): 85-104.

to get theological. Again, he will defend justification by faith and sanctification by faith for both the Jews and the Gentiles. The first five verses of chapter 3 are introductory in which he mentions the sacrifice of the Son and the supply of the Spirit.

I. SACRIFICE OF THE SON   3:1

O foolish Galatians! Who has bewitched you that you should not obey the truth, before whose eyes Jesus Christ was clearly portrayed among you as crucified?

With the word "foolish" Paul is not trying to be rude or to accuse his readers of being undisciplined, uncaring, apathetic, or not trying in their Christian lives. Insincerity is not the problem; insanity is. The only time the word "bewitched" (*baskainō*) is used in the NT is right here. In the secular world it meant "to hypnotize by casting an evil eye." It is as though the teachers of legalism cast a spell on or hypnotize their congregations or readers into their system of spirituality. Here is an example:

> Perseverance, therefore, is the test of authenticity. Scholars will continue to disagree on whether believers can apostatize, but it is hoped that all will agree that believers must persevere to the end to be saved. In this respect there is a remarkable agreement between Arminians and Calvinists.[52]

The above author, Thomas Schreiner, is concluding his commentary discussion of a notoriously difficult section of 2 Peter (2:18-22). He concludes that the language used by Peter to describe the followers of the false teachers sounds as though these followers are genuine believers. But "perseverance...is the test of authenticity." So, since these believers have fallen away, they are not authentic believers. But

---

52   Thomas R. Schreiner, "1, 2 Peter, Jude," in *The New American Commentary*, vol. 37 (Nashville: Broadman & Holman, 2003), 365.

because they are believers, according to Peter, but not genuine believers, according to Schreiner, he must cook up a new name for them. So he calls them "phenomenological" believers.[53] They experienced the phenomena (escape from the pollution of the world) of the elect for a time but proved they were not elect by getting entangled again. (Does this sound familiar? Remember Scot McKnight's treatment of Hebrews 6:4-7?)

But look again at his concluding remark. He concedes that scholars will continue to *disagree* on whether believers can apostatize, but then he says it is hoped we can **all agree** that believers must persevere to the end to be saved. So, on the one hand some scholars will believe that believers can fall away from the faith and at the same time will agree that they cannot fall away from the faith. At this point I feel like saying something vulgar that Luther might say, but I will restrain myself and simply say this is nonsense. I do agree, however, with Schreiner's claim that there is remarkable agreement between Arminians and Calvinists on perseverance to the end of their lives on earth in order to be saved to go to heaven. In this respect both Arminians and Calvinists park their cars in the Vatican parking lot. It is all Neo-Galatianism. But it is as though the devil has cast a spell on these teachers and their followers.

And this is what Paul says about his followers. Someone cast a spell on them. The result (in most manuscripts) of this spell is that his followers do not obey the truth. This shows the seriousness of the error of Galatianism. It does not coincide with the truth. We wonder how this happens, but it is not hard to understand. Many of the teachers of Neo-Galatianism are extremely charismatic. Their personalities act like magnets to fill up their auditoriums. In addition to their charisma, they are extremely gifted as communicators. One such teacher comes to mind. He has no formal training. But he has such an attractive

---

53 This term was actually coined by Scot McKnight of Trinity Evangelical Divinity School in his article on the warning passages in Hebrews.

personality and is such a gifted communicator, sheep flock to listen to him speak. He will even publicly proclaim he doesn't know what kind of mixture of theology he has. But the people don't care. And he feeds the flesh. Remember, the default setting of the flesh is on performance. We instinctively think we must do something to win God's blessings in this life. These preachers tell people how to win these blessings.

The sad thing for Paul is that when he presented his gospel he made sure they had a clear picture of the cross. He painted a picture of the cross. In fact, the word "crucified" (*estaurōmenos*—perfect tense) is written in such a way as to emphasize the completed action of the cross. Completed action. That means *the* sacrifice has been made and completed. No more sacrifice is necessary (Heb. 10). Done—*fini, fait accompli*. Resorting to legalism in its various forms is saying Christ's sacrifice is not enough.

I remember leading a tour of Israel years ago on which a businessman from San Antonio shared his testimony. He said he came from a Neo-Galatian (no need to get specific) church that taught him the sacrifice of Christ was not finished. As a matter of fact, every time he took communion he believed Christ was being sacrificed again. When he heard that the sacrifice of Christ was a done deal and that is why Christ sat down at the right hand of his Father (as opposed to OT priests who never sat down because their work was never finished), he was born again on the spot. Until that moment he had never realized the work of Christ was finished. He thought he had to help fill in what was lacking in the suffering of Christ (Col. 1:24).

Paul is disappointed. He thought he had done a good job of painting a picture of Christ's finished work on the cross. Even Jesus said *tetelestai*, "it is finished." But someone had cast a spell over Paul's converts to make them think otherwise. I love to listen to teenagers and others who have not had much exposure to this Christian voodoo. They are most discerning. They will listen to a certain Protestant teacher who is promoting voodoo and say, "Well, that's just like Catholicism." Or, "I've come out of that stuff and I don't intend to go back." Or, "That's works, plain and simple."

Or here's another one from a foreign country. I was in Kazakhstan teaching a class for seminary students. A very popular Calvinistic teacher had been through this same town (Almaty) three weeks before me. Now, keep in mind that almost all the people who believe in Jesus in Eastern Europe and the former Soviet states are Arminian (they think they can lose their salvation). My students told me these Arminians were running around Almaty praising God because this great Western preacher was preaching the same doctrine they had always believed. But remember, I said this great Western preacher is a Calvinist, a card-carrying Five Point Calvinist. But the Arminians said he was teaching the same thing they teach. Amazing that this great Western teacher cannot see it for himself. As one theologian with two doctorate degrees once told me, "The most Arminian theologians in the world are Five Point Calvinists." It's all the same stuff—Neo-Galatianism.

> Gondor was a great and benevolent king. His kingdom was vast and his people numbered in the millions. All around his kingdom there were pictures of himself and his only son smiling down on his subjects. Then one day out of the dark forest came Maledictor, a man who was the sum of all evil. He took captive the peasants of Gondor and swept them into the forest to work in his mines.
>
> But King Gondor loved his subjects. He wouldn't give them up without a fight. So he sent his only son into the forest to fight Maledictor. The battle was fierce with many casualties. Even the king's son died, but not without freeing the captives. Gondor celebrated the victory by adopting all these freed slaves into his own royal family and giving them a permanent inheritance in his kingdom.
>
> One day Gondor was riding through his kingdom waving and smiling at his people as he passed. But one of them approached him all stooped and bent over from a heavy burden he was carrying. Curious, Gondor stopped as the man drew near.

"Who are you?" asked the king. "I am one of your humble servants," replied the man wearily, as he wiped sweat from his brow. "Well, what are you carrying?"

"These are my works, for which I have labored many years. I hope to remain in your good graces by doing what I can to please you. If it pleases my Lord, I would like to present to you my butterfly collection and over here are my woodcarvings. I hope you like them and that you will accept these humble deeds as only a token of what I hope to do to win your favor in the future."

King Gondor hardly knew what to say. It was obvious from his expression that he was hurt and apparently insulted by the offerings. Finally, he squeezed out this response: "Workman, I find your offerings disgusting and insulting. I sent my only son to fight on your behalf and he lost his life in the process. He died a horrible, gruesome death on your behalf. And now you are going to try to win my favor with butterfly collections and woodcarvings. There is no greater love than sacrificing my only son that I can offer. In return, I don't want your offerings. I just want to be loved. You don't have to earn my favor. You already have it. So just enjoy it. Put down your bag of burdens. Come to me and rest. Let's have a meal together in remembrance of my son and have some fellowship together."[54]

Paul has painted a picture of the completed work of Christ on the cross. Now he mentions the Spirit for the first time in this letter.

II. SUPPLY OF THE SPIRIT   3:2-5

This only I want to learn from you: Did you receive the Spirit by the works of the law, or by the hearing of faith? Are you so foolish? Having begun in the Spirit, are you now being made

---

54   Author unknown.

perfect by the flesh? Have you suffered so many things in vain—if indeed it was in vain? Therefore He who supplies the Spirit to you and works miracles among you, does He do it by the works of the law, or by the hearing of faith?

Although this is the first mention of the Spirit in this letter, he occurs three times in these four verses. Since Paul's primary issue after Acts 15 was sanctification instead of justification, he is going to be telling them just how very important the Holy Spirit is for a victorious Christian life. If works of the law is Romans 7, then works of the Spirit is Romans 8. The law principle brings defeat in Romans 7; the law of the Spirit of Life in Christ Jesus brings victory in Romans 8.

And, ironically, just as we saw in Galatians 2:11-21, believers have trouble being sanctified when they are still trying to maintain their justification or prove their justification (2:17). Paul comes against this same problem in this theological section of his letter (5:4). Their preoccupation with justification gets in the way of their sanctification. That was Augustine's problem that he passed down to us. He never made it to elect status in Manichaeism. Election, therefore, became his great longing and the focal point of his salvation theology (soteriology). To be elect, one must be justified. To be justified, one must endure faithfully to the end of his life on earth = Catholicism alias Calvinism alias Arminianism. Although there are many differences in these three brands of Christianity, one common denominator is perseverance to the end of one's life on earth in order to go to heaven, a teaching that uses an incorrect interpretation of Matthew 24:13 as its primary support, as we have previously discussed.[55]

Paul's argument in Galatians 3:2-5 is simple. If you began by the Holy Spirit, why are you trying to go on in your Christian walk by the flesh? Works of the law did not get you justified, and works of the law won't get you sanctified. "Made perfect" is *epiteleō*, which is a compound word made up of *epi* ("on top of," as in epidermis) and *teleō* ("to finish, to complete"). So the word means "to completely

---

55 See Appendix A in Anderson, *Free Grace Soteriology.*

finish" or "go on to complete maturity." So they began their Christian walk by the power of the Holy Spirit in regeneration. Do they expect to switch the power source now to the energy of their own flesh? How foolish.

Titus 3:5 says the washing of regeneration is not by works but rather by the Holy Spirit. And 2 Corinthians 3:18 says sanctification or the metamorphosis into the image of Christ is done by the Holy Spirit as well. "Supplies" is *epichoregon*, which means "to furnish at one's own expense." God is supplying the power of the Holy Spirit at his own expense. We cannot buy it as Simon Magus was trying to do in Acts 8. And the present tense in this context suggests an ongoing supply. In other words, we cannot exhaust the power of the Holy Spirit.

The mention of "miracles" also points to God as the power source. Certainly the Galatians will remember that the miracles performed in their church came through faith, not the flesh. If we could do some sort of work that would cause God to perform miracles, then truly we would be practicing magic, and God would become our genie. We began the Christian life by "faith," and we must live the Christian life by faith (Gal. 2:20). As George MacDonald well said, "In whatever man does without God, he must fail miserably—or succeed more miserably."[56]

CONCLUSION

Someone cast a spell over these Galatian believers. They had become Christian zombies—the living dead. They were just going through the motions in their walk with Christ. Paul says if we are going to be mesmerized by anything, let's be mesmerized by the cross. If we are going to be put under any spell, let it be the spell of the cross. That's why in Galatians 6:14 Paul says, "God forbid that I should boast except in the cross of our Lord Jesus Christ, by whom the world has

---

56 George MacDonald, *Unspoken Sermons: Self Denial*, www.online-literature.com/george-macdonald/unspoken-sermons/.

been crucified to me, and I to the world."

Someone put it like this: "The cross was Paul's favorite haunt; it is where he liked to hang out." Unfortunately, many seem to think that their first glance at the cross when they trusted Christ as their personal Savior drained the power of the cross like a worn-out battery, when in truth the cross will hold more mystery, more depth, and more power to transform through all eternity than anything else. In football, when a running back makes a nice move and heads into the end zone, we applaud. The cross is God's best move of all time. The cross speaks to every condition of man:

1. **Discouraged.** Look at the Son of Man hanging on the cross, lest you grow weary and not see that the cross is always followed by the crown and that one day you will never be discouraged again.

2. **Fearful.** Look to the cross again, my friend, and see… see a God who loved you so much that he sent his only begotten Son and will surely take care of you now; if he did the big thing, the cross, he will surely do the little things.

3. **Guilty.** Look to the cross. What can take away my sin? Nothing but the blood of Jesus.

4. **Bitter.** Look to the cross, because the basis for forgiving others is the immense, immense debt forgiven us through the cross.

5. **Complacent.** Look to the cross, and you will find that a fire begins to burn in your bones as you see the one who lived the entirety of his life and then gave that life that you and I might have a personal relationship with the living Lord.

6. **Tempted.** Look to the cross. There we crucified the flesh with its passions and desires (Gal. 5:24).

Aleksandr Solzhenitsyn was a Russian intellectual who exposed the Gulag system of forced labor in Russia. His most famous work was *The Gulag Archipelago*, and he won the Nobel Prize for literature in 1970. He was expelled from Russia for being a dissident in 1974, but he returned after the collapse of the Soviet Union in 1994. What is less well known is that he came to Christ through a Russian Jew who also had trusted Christ in a prison camp in Russia. But the suffering in the Gulag continued for him and thousands of others like him.

As the days and weeks and months of forced labor went on, Solzhenitsyn found himself growing very discouraged at times, wondering where God was in the midst of all this suffering. Finally, one day as he was working out in the fields, he decided it was not worth continuing on. He thought he might as well die. So he went over to the side of the field and sat down on a little wooden bench, put his head down, and waited for a Russian soldier to come up. When one of the guards saw a worker with his head down, he would come up, give him one warning, and then use the shovel to bash his head in. It was standard practice.

So Solzhenitsyn waited for his death. He sensed someone coming up behind him, but instead of a soldier, it was one of his fellow workers with a stick in his hand. He didn't say a word to Solzhenitsyn, but just came near him, and with the stick he drew a cross and walked away. As Solzhenitsyn stared at that rough cross scribbled in the earth, his entire perspective changed. He knew he was just one man against the entire Soviet Empire, but at the same moment he knew that the hope of all mankind was represented in that cross, and through its power, he picked up his shovel, went back to work, and inflamed the world.

Never underestimate the power of the cross. It is the best spell you will ever find. Dietrich Bonhoeffer put it this way: "The figure of the Crucified invalidates all thought which takes success for its standard." John Newton is most famous for his immortal song "Amazing Grace." But he wrote scores and scores of other songs. Here is one of them I especially like dealing with the cross:

In evil long I took delight
Unawed by shame or fear,

Till a new object struck my sight,
And stopped my wild career:
I saw One hanging on a Tree
In agonies and blood,
Who fix'd His languid eyes on me
As near His cross I stood.
Sure never till my latest breath
Can I forget that look.
It seem'd to charge me with His death,
Though not a word He spoke:
My conscience felt and own'd the guilt,
And plunged me in despair:
I saw my sins His blood had spilt,
And help'd to nail Him there.
Alas! I knew not what I did!
But now my tears are vain:
Where shall my trembling soul be hid?
For I the Lord have slain!
A second look He gave, which said,
"I freely all forgive;
This blood is for thy ransom paid;
I die that thou may'st live."
Thus, while His death my sin displays
In all its blackest hue,
Such is the mystery of grace,
It seals my pardon too.
With pleasing grief, and mournful joy,
My spirit now if fill'd,
That I should such a life destroy,
Yet live by Him I kill'd![57]

---

57   John Newton, "In Evil Long I Took Delight," http://www.christian globe.com/Illustrations/theDetails.asp?whichOne=c&whichFile =cross (June 15, 2014).

7
CHAIRLIFT CHRISTIANITY
Galatians 3:6-14

Betty and I had two children while we were in seminary, and then ten years later we had two more. Boy, girl; boy, girl. With the ten-year split, vacations were something of a problem. If the older ones liked what we were doing, the younger ones didn't, and vice versa. So we kept trying different things. When the younger two got to be four and two, we decided to go on a family ski trip. We got everyone decked out with gear and headed for the slopes. The older two took off for parts unknown, while Betty and I stayed below to help the younger two.

Mark was four and played around on the bunny slopes for a while. Then he saw the chairlift going up and decided he wanted to do that. I allowed that he might not be ready for that, but he assured me he was. So up we went, and we got off at the first opportunity. Below us was a convergence of green, blue, and black slopes, indicating different degrees of difficulty. So Mark started off going down the blue slope. At that age, they really can't get up any speed, so they just go straight down. No problem. His older sister, Christie, came down and decided to work with him for a while.

All of a sudden Mark slipped over onto the black slope with its many moguls. It was so steep he couldn't stand up. He kept getting up and falling, getting up and falling. I was at the bottom when this happened, so the only way to get to him was to get on the chairlift, go over him, then ski back down. Well, he saw me on the chairlift riding right over him. So he began yelling so loud everyone could hear: "You terrible father. You terrible father. How could you do this to your son?" It was a bit embarrassing, so I didn't look down. Just pretended I had no idea whose obnoxious kid that was.

Of course, Mark was happy to see me when I got to him, but he wouldn't get on the chairlift again. He said he would just walk. So at the bottom he would take his skis off, march up the slope about a hundred yards, and ski down. All morning. Well, he was getting a little better, so I encouraged him to get on the lift with me again to go higher. "Nope." Mark, you don't know what you are missing down here. You will love it up higher, and you'll never get there on your own. You need the chairlift. "Nope."

Now, one problem here, at least in my eyes, is that I had paid for him to have all the rights and privileges of the chairlift. He had a valid ticket—fully paid for. But he spent the rest of our ski vacation on the bunny slopes, never using the chairlift, and never taking advantage of all the rights offered to him by his ticket.

So many of us spend our entire Christian lives on the bunny slopes. We are content to keep marching up the mountain a hundred yards or so to ski down. We will go as far as our own strength will take us. But our heavenly Father wants so much more for us. He would like us in time to go to the top of the mountain. What an incredible view. And he paid for the ticket to give us the right to go as high as the mountain will go. The price he paid not only gives us **the right** to go higher, it also paid for **the power** to go higher as well. Through the Holy Spirit, God has provided a Chairlift to take us to the top. To get there we must have faith in the Chairlift, must get into the Chairlift, and then we must sit back, relax, and trust the power of the Chairlift to get us there. How ridiculous it would look to see someone sitting in a chairlift flapping his ski poles around in an effort to help the chairlift go up the mountain.

As we observed in Galatians 3:1-5, Paul has introduced us to the Chairlift, the Holy Spirit, mentioned for the first time and two more times in these verses. He comes to the Holy Spirit again in 3:14. So Paul very much wants his converts to learn how to avail themselves of the power of the Holy Spirit. It is he who will get them to the top of the mountain. Without him they will spend the rest of their Christian lives on the bunny slopes. There is a degree of fun and enjoyment on the bunny slopes, but the thrill of victory and the exhilaration of jumping a cliff are on up the mountain. Too often it is our own pride that keeps us from going further.

Part and parcel of the pride within us is our stubborn refusal to receive something for nothing. With our default setting on the flesh, we want to earn it, deserve it, or work for it. That is why it is hard for most of us to receive charity—it is a blow to our pride. Miles Stanford wrote, "It is only natural for us to feel that our spiritual walk and service make us acceptable to our Father.... We are making the natural mistake of depending upon condition, instead of position, for our acceptance."[58]

And William Newell said, "To preach devotion first, and blessing second, is to reverse God's order, and preach law, not grace. The law made man's blessing depend on devotion; grace confers undeserved, unconditional blessing: our devotion may follow, but does not always do so—in proper measure."[59]

Paul begins his theological defense of his gospel in Galatians 3:6. He starts with the Jew in this section (3:6-14) and then shows the same principles hold true for Gentiles (3:15-4:7). We will look at the Jew first in 3:6-14. We shall see that God's MO was faith before the law, faith during the law, and faith after the law.

---

58 Miles Stanford, *Principles of Position* (Colorado Springs: n.p., 1967), 4.

59 William Newell, https://archive.org/stream/Romans_Verse_By_ Verse-NewellWR/Romans-CompleteCommentary-Newell- page/ n1/mode/2uph.), 173.

I. FAITH—BEFORE THE LAW   3:6-9

> ...just as Abraham "believed God, and it was accounted to him
> for righteousness." Therefore know that only those who are of
> faith are sons of Abraham. And the Scripture, foreseeing that
> God would justify the Gentiles by faith, preached the gospel
> to Abraham beforehand, saying, "In you all the nations shall
> be blessed." So then those who are of faith are blessed with
> believing Abraham.

In order to defeat the Galatian notion that righteousness comes
from keeping a list, in this case the Law of Moses and its heavy yoke,
Paul moves back in time to Abraham, who was clearly not redeemed
by works of the law; he couldn't be, since the Law of Moses did not yet
exist. He was "saved by faith," as Genesis 15:6 claims.

Of course, the Jews thought they had inherited salvation
genetically, since they were in the physical line of Abraham. But that
which is born of the flesh is flesh; only that which is born of the Spirit
is spirit. We are the spiritual sons of Abraham by faith.

It really couldn't be much more plain, could it? The only
requirement for justification salvation before the Law of Moses was
faith. That was true for Abraham and for the Gentiles. No works were
required by God to justify Abraham, and no works are required by
God to justify the Gentiles. But this brings us to a question concerning
the nature of faith.

THE NATURE OF FAITH

MIND	EMOTIONS	WILL
COMPREHEND	CONFIDENCE	COMMITMENT
the claims of Christ	in the claims of Christ	to the claims of Christ

Most scholars recognize that faith involves the entire inner psyche
of a person: his mind, his emotions, and his will. Some don't want to
go this far. They would say that faith is just a matter of the mind.

I prefer an understanding that includes our emotions and our will. Those who wish to remove our will from the justification equation are unwittingly playing right into the hands of the Augustinians, for it was Augustine who took human choice away, thus turning Christianity into a form of determinism. When we take conscious choice away, we also excise love from the process as well. Our chart shows involvement of the mind, emotions, and will. With our minds we *comprehend* the claims of Christ regarding his person and work; with our emotions we have *confidence* in the claims of Christ; and with our will we make a *commitment* to the claims of Christ.

Many Neo-Galatianists also recognize an involvement of all aspects of the inner self. However, there is a vast difference in how they understand the involvement of the will. One such writer claimed the writings of Louis Berkhof to back up his understanding that with the will a new believer commits to follow all the commands of Christ.[60] This same writer gets most of his gospel from Matthew where Jesus tells us to deny ourselves if we want to be his disciples. Nothing less than an all-out commitment to follow Jesus all the way to physical death, if necessary, will open the gates of heaven, according to this particular author.[61]

I would love to sit by this writer's side and listen to him witness to an unbeliever and explain his understanding of faith: "Go sell everything you have and give the proceeds to the poor, and you can go to heaven" (see Matt. 19:16-22). Since this author himself has not sold all his goods and given the proceeds to the poor, he must have a cop-out, so he claims you just have to be willing to give all your goods away, not actually do it. But is that what Jesus said? I don't think so. He didn't say be willing to. He said do it.

Most people I know prefer to find something a bit simpler from the gospel of John or Romans or Ephesians when they are sharing

---

60 John F. MacArthur Jr., *The Gospel According to Jesus* (Grand Rapids, MI: Zondervan, 1988), 173.

61 Ibid., 179-86.

their faith to an unbeliever. But even more disturbing is when I opened the book by Louis Berkhof ostensibly quoted by the other author. Berkhof does not say anything close to what the other writer claims. It is a total misquote. Berkhof actually said the volitional (will) part of faith is simply a commitment to trust the claims of Christ.[62] That is a whole lot different from a commitment to follow all the commands of Christ. By the way, do you follow all the commands of Christ? No? Uh-oh. How will you ever know if your faith is saving faith? But we will come back to this troubling question, troubling for the Neo-Galatianists, that is. Thankfully, we can rest in the assurance of God's love and grace.

Faith alone in Christ alone. *Sola fide*—that was the cry of the Reformers in the sixteenth century. And that is the cry of Paul to the Galatians. Works were not a requirement for justification salvation before the Law of Moses. Neither were they during the time (dispensation) the Law of Moses was in effect.

II. FAITH—DURING THE LAW   3:10-12

> For as many as are of the works of the law are under the curse; for it is written, "Cursed is everyone who does not continue in all things which are written in the book of the law, to do them." But that no one is justified by the law in the sight of God is evident, for "the just shall live by faith." Yet the law is not of faith, but "the man who does them shall live by them."

It is important here to recognize the quote concerning the just living by faith is from Habakkuk. The reason this is important is that Paul now enters the time period when the Law of Moses is in effect. Abraham lived before Moses, so he could not have been under the Law of Moses. But Habakkuk lived and wrote after the Law of

---

62   Louis Berkhof, *Systematic Theology* (Grand Rapids, MI: Eerdmans, 1939), 503-5.

Moses had been given and before the Holy Spirit was given in Acts 2, signifying the beginning of a new time period (dispensation). Paul wants to make it perfectly clear that keeping the Law of Moses did not justify anyone during the time when the Law of Moses was in authority.

There are several reasons for saying that. For one thing, if one wanted to get to heaven by keeping the Law of Moses, he had to keep the whole law, not just part. The law lovers of Paul's day were probably quoting Leviticus 18:5, which says, "You shall therefore keep My Statutes and My judgments, which if a man does, he shall live by them." Paul agrees, but goes on to quote from Deuteronomy 27:26, which says you must do **all** the things written in the Book of the Law or you will be cursed. He needed to score a perfect one hundred. He has to "continue in all things which are written in the book of the law, to do them." Has anyone ever done that? Don't think so.

Secondly, looking to the Law of Moses for justification was a complete misunderstanding of the purpose of the law. It wasn't about justification at all. It was all about sanctification. It revealed God's standard of holiness. It was about fellowship (an ongoing communion with God), not relationship (our legal status as children born into God's family). The Jews as a nation had a relationship with God established by the Abrahamic covenant. This gave Israel as a nation (not the individuals in the nation) an eternal relationship with God. But she (the nation) had to stay in the land to enjoy that relationship. Enjoying the relationship is what we call fellowship. A father and son have an eternal relationship, but if the son dishonors the father, they won't be having much fellowship (enjoying the relationship).

The Law of Moses told the nation of Israel how to *enjoy* their relationship with God. If they kept the commandments, they were blessed in the land and had fellowship with God. If they did not keep the commandments, God booted them out of the land, meaning they were out of fellowship. If they would repent (Deut. 30), he would bring them back to the land and restore his fellowship with them.

Here Paul says no one ever was or ever will be justified (establish an eternal relationship with God) by works of the law, but one who does the works of the law will "live" by them, meaning they will have a better life here on earth. The Law of Moses was given for sanctification, not justification, for fellowship with God now, not a relationship with God in eternity. The relationship for an individual required faith, but fellowship for an individual (and the nation) required obedience.

III. FAITH—AFTER THE LAW   3:13-14

> Christ has redeemed us from the curse of the law, having become a curse for us (for it is written, "Cursed is everyone who hangs on a tree"), that the blessing of Abraham might come upon the Gentiles in Christ Jesus, that we might receive the promise of the Spirit through faith.

When Paul talks about receiving the promise of the Spirit through faith, he has moved from the period when the Law of Moses was in effect to a new administrative period in God's dealing with men. We call it the Church Age. It began with the giving of the Holy Spirit to baptize believers into the body of Christ (1 Cor. 12:13) and to indwell them on a permanent basis (1 Cor. 6:20). This combined Jews and Gentiles into one new entity, the church, a mystery unrevealed in the OT.

But in order for this to take place, we have to be "redeemed." It is the word *ex* (out of) + *agorazō* (to buy), or "to buy out of." In this context it meant to buy out of the marketplace (the *agora*) where slaves were sold on a regular basis. We were slaves to sin and the devil, but the Father went down to the market and bought us off the slave block with the price of his Son. Thus we can say Christ redeemed us.

Jesus paid the price to lift the curse that was on us because we could not live up to the perfect standard of holiness required to enter heaven. So, he took the curse we deserved. This verse is an important one for our understanding of the substitutionary death of Christ. There are eight different views on the atonement of Christ. The "substitutionary" view is only one of these; however, we believe it is the correct view, partly because of this verse. The word "for" (*hyper*) in this context can mean "on behalf of, for the benefit of" or "in place of." Often in the Greek papyri (documents discovered in Egypt written in biblical Greek that give us great insight into the meaning of words in the Greek NT) the words *hyper autou* were written at the end of a legal document. This meant that one person was signing for another ("in place of him") because the rightful signer could not write. So he found someone to sign for him—a substitute. Christ was our substitute.

Again, the hardest thing in the world for an unbeliever to believe is in the substitutionary death of Christ—Jesus died in our place. But the hardest thing in the world for a believer to believe is in the substitutionary *life* of Christ—Jesus will live his life in us and through us. And he suffered both the curse of physical death and spiritual death in our place so that we could be healed both physically and spiritually.

I have a dear friend who has just entered hospice care after nine years of battling prostate cancer. He has a wonderful outlook on his future "graduation" to live in a better world. And for several months now he has entered into something of an extended epiphany in which he senses joy constantly, 24-7. We have been calling him "Joy Boy Johnny." But those who know him must admit it is hard to watch his physical suffering. This is a tall man (6'6") who only recently weighed 290 lbs., but now weighs about 190 lbs. At one point he had some tumors on his scalp that were eating through his skull on their way to his brain. In the midst of the twelve-hour operation to cut out the tumors and replace them with a 3"x4" flap of flesh from his *latissimus dorsi*, he had a heart attack. He survived that only to face further challenges. You get the picture. But Matthew 8:17 claims Jesus healing people from their physical maladies was a fulfillment of Isaiah 53:4-5. Many want to use this to claim universal physical healing in this life from physical diseases, but Jesus's miraculous healings were just a first fruit of the ultimate physical healing that is to come when our bodies are raised from the dead. There is no guarantee of physical healing in this life. There is the possibility. But even all those Jesus healed physically went on to die physically.

Christ's sacrifice made possible both our physical and spiritual healing. That healing could come on earth for a temporary time (barring the Rapture, we all die physically in time), but it primarily refers to the ultimate redemption of the physical body into a glorified body that will suffer no more.

Scourging was a punishment used by both the Jews and the Romans. The Romans did not limit the number of lashes, and quite often death was the result of the scourging. The Jews limited the number of lashes or stripes to forty. To make sure there wasn't a miscount, they administered only thirty-nine. In *The Passion of the Christ*, directed by Mel Gibson, you can hear the man counting in the background as Christ is scourged.

A cat-o'-nine-tails or *scorpion* was used for most of these scourges. It had long pieces of leather tipped by ragged pieces of iron. When this sharp iron hit the back, it ripped pieces of flesh away. The Jews would administer thirteen stripes to the back, thirteen to the left shoulder area, and thirteen to the right shoulder area. The Romans would beat the back and then simply turn the victim over and beat his chest. Such scourging would usually weaken the victim enough to hasten his death once he was on the cross.

In the case of Jesus, Pilate hoped the Jews would be satisfied with his scourging, so he did not pass the death sentence on the cross until after the scourging. We do not know if Jesus was also beaten along the Via Dolorosa. The text does not say. But we do know that "He Himself took our infirmities and bore our sicknesses" (Matt. 8:17). Both physical and spiritual suffering can be traced back to the Fall of Adam. Ultimately, Christ's suffering, both physical and spiritual, will reverse the effects of the Fall and put an end to all suffering, including death. My friend will be restored to a robust body and a body that will never wear out.

In 2 Corinthians 5:2-3 we read about our future clothing in heaven. After using several different words to describe our current temporal bodies (tent, house, building) Paul says we will be "clothed" (NKJV) or "put on" (ESV) our future "habitation" (NKJV) or "dwelling" (ESV). But this makes no sense. We don't clothe ourselves with a house or a dwelling. We put on clothes. And because we put on clothes, we won't be found naked (5:3). This word they are translating as "habitation" or "dwelling" can be better understood if we think of a nun's habit. It is her getup, her uniform, her clothing.

That is precisely what *oikētērion*, the word translated as "habitation" or "dwelling," means. It is used this way numerous times in the book of Enoch (which, like the papyri, was not inspired but still helps us understand how Greek words were used at the time of Christ). It was used for that piece of clothing that swallows up our mortal bodies and gives us immortality. In Enoch this clothing is described as something gorgeous, beautiful, resplendent. It is this clothing that keeps us from being naked in heaven. I cannot prove this, but it makes sense to me that this *oikētērion* is what covered Adam and Eve in the garden and would have enabled them to live forever had they not sinned. It was not until after they sinned that they appeared naked. The *oikētērion* was taken away and a body that would decay was exposed.

Jesus's physical suffering and spiritual death in our place have made a way for physical suffering and decay to cease and even be reversed. And most importantly, Jesus suffered the spiritual separation from his Father that we deserved. Can anyone say, "Hallelujah!"?

The only requirement for receiving the benefit of Christ's substitutionary death is faith. Paul has shown that faith was the requirement *before* the law (Abraham), *during* the law (Habakkuk), and *after* the law (the Gentiles). Many critics of dispensationalism have wrongly claimed that dispensationalists teach more than one way for salvation—by works during the dispensation of the law and by grace after the dispensation of the law. No way. There was grace before the law, during the law, and after the law. So also with faith. The requirement for the justification salvation of man is always the same—faith. The object of our faith has always been the same—God. The means of our salvation, always the same—the blood of Christ. Only the content of our faith has differed as we move along the timeline of human history. God did not reveal as much to Abraham as he did to David, or as much to David as he did to Peter. His ultimate revelation was Jesus himself (Heb. 1:1). But let it be clearly said, the requirement has always been and always will be the same—faith.

Paul mentions "the promise of the Spirit." Here the interpreter must decide whether Paul means the promise concerning the coming of the Holy Spirit or a promise the Holy Spirit made to us (objective genitive or subjective genitive). We prefer the former. Paul is trying to emphasize walking by faith as opposed to works under the law. In verse 3 he says we began our Christian lives by the Spirit and should therefore go on to maturity through the Spirit, not the flesh. So he brings us back to that thought here: the divine Chairlift. God has both promised and provided the energy or power for a mountaintop experience in the Christian life by the Holy Spirit. It is Chairlift Christianity. As long as we play around at the bottom of the slopes, walking up and down the mountain on our own strength, we will never get very far in our walk. We need to get on the Chairlift and let a Higher Power take us to the top.

CONCLUSION

But if faith is the only requirement for our entrance to heaven, and most branches of Protestantism will make such a claim, what's the problem? Just believe. Ah, yes, but that takes us back to the discussion concerning the nature of faith. What does it mean to believe? Are there different kinds of faith—genuine faith, spurious faith, saving faith, sign faith, head faith, heart faith? Can I believe in Jesus and still not go to heaven?

We have written other works that go into these questions in detail.[63] Let me just state the conclusions of those studies. There are different *quantities* of faith in the Bible, but not different *qualities*. Faith is faith. Jesus spoke of faith as little as a grain of a mustard seed, or of times when the disciples had just a little faith, or of a centurion who had great faith (Matt. 8:10)—but faith was faith.

Of course, faith was tied to an object. If the object was not worthy

---

63 Anderson, *Free Grace Soteriology*, 161-84; David R. Anderson, *Triumph Through Trials: The Epistle of James* (Houston: Grace Theology Press, 2013), 85-113.

of faith, the faith could be very destructive. Faith in the wrong leader like Hitler could be devastating. Faith in thin ice could be life threatening. But faith in a loving God who is omnipotent and omniscient—no problem. Faith also can be tied to different promises. Believing that a mountain can be moved into the sea would get the mountain into the sea, but it would not get me to heaven. If I believe in the right object (God), then I can believe anything he promises. If he promises me eternal life when I believe in Jesus as God who will take away my sins, then belief in those promises will open the gates of heaven.

But to say I must believe in Jesus and then wait around to look at the fruit in my life to see if I had enough faith or the right kind of faith will not only lead to a life of self-absorbing introspection and doubt, but it is not found in the Bible. The salvation of James 2:14-26 is not justification salvation. It deals with our rewards at the Judgment Seat of Christ.[64] The people who believed in Jesus because of the signs he did in John 2:23 were genuine believers.[65] There is nothing wrong with believing in Jesus because of the miracles he did. That is exactly why John wrote about these miracles (John 20:30-31)—so we would believe in him and have life through his name.

It can get to the point that people spend so much time examining their faith to see if it was of the right quality or the right quantity that they wind up putting faith in their faith. That is right back to looking to oneself for assurance of his salvation. Even John Calvin said look to Jesus or you are doomed when it comes to assurance. Look up; don't look in the mirror. Don't worry about your faith; worry about your focus. Peter did not go down in the Sea of Galilee until he lost focus; that is, he went down when he looked down.

When my first two kids were about five and three, I built a tree house for them in the woods next to our home. It was pretty high, about ten feet up, with a trapdoor and a rope ladder. It was great fun

---

64   Anderson, *Triumph Through Trials*, 85-113.

65   Anderson, *Free Grace Soteriology*, 174-83.

for my five-year-old son, but Christie was a little young. She would grow into it. But one day while I was up in the tree house hammering away, I heard Christie down below. She wanted to come up. Well, because she was all of three, I didn't think she would get very far on a rope ladder, so I said okay and went back to my hammer and nails. Next thing I heard was Christie crying. I opened the trapdoor and looked down. Christie had made it up about eight feet. But now she was scared. She wasn't scared at three feet or six feet, but she was at eight feet off the ground.

So I called to her: "Christie...Christie, look up...look at me. I am your father. I love you. Reach up." I extended my arm down a couple of feet. All she had to do was take hold. But she kept looking around and down and crying. So again I said, "Christie, look up. Look at me. I will help you. Don't look down." So she finally looked up, stopped crying, and took my hand. Then I pulled her into the tree house.

Christie's problem was a matter of focus. We must look unto the Author and Finisher of our faith and get on the Chairlift.

8
GOD'S X-RAY MACHINE
Galatians 3:15-29

A ccording to Tim LaHaye in his Left Behind series, a great period of trials and tribulation such as the world has never seen looms in the future for mankind. Those who put their faith in Christ will be snatched up in the air before this time of tribulation begins (the Rapture). Those who don't put their faith in Christ will be "left behind." In this approach, Jesus will return after the Tribulation period and set up a kingdom on earth that will last for a thousand years. Then the New Jerusalem will come down out of the third heaven to a refurbished or a brand-new earth (Rev. 21), and all believers will live out eternity with God in this New Jerusalem.

But many other well-known Bible teachers say, "No. The period of Great Tribulation predicted in the Bible was fulfilled in the first century AD." These same teachers also tell us that Jesus's second coming was in AD 70, when Jerusalem and the nation of Israel were destroyed. Now there remains no more national future for the physical seed of Abraham in God's plan for the future. The physical promises to Abraham are being fulfilled spiritually in and by the church. The church has **replaced** Israel in God's plan for the ages. This is called **replacement theology**.

There is much at stake in how we understand these future things. And Galatians 3:15-29 is one of the primary passages used by replacement theologians to defend their position. It is important that we look at these verses carefully. I am writing in a country influenced by replacement theology. Martin Luther did not see any purpose for Jews after they had rejected the gospel he presented in the second quarter of the sixteenth century, so he said, "Kill them." He thought they were a blight on society; however, he also thought they could be redeemed by the blood. But if they rejected the offer of salvation through Christ, he saw no more purpose for them, so he encouraged the powers that be to kill them.

When Hitler was trying to enlist the support of the German church during the 1930s, he used these writings from Martin Luther in his propaganda against the Jews. How could the German church object if their great founder, Martin Luther, said the same thing Hitler was saying? Any pastor in the "confessing church" (the church opposing Hitler like Bonhoeffer and his followers) was systematically rubbed out of society. Most likely Hitler would have found a way to accomplish his demonic purge of the Jews from Europe without the support of the German church, but while he was still wearing his Christian mask, this replacement theology helped him greatly. Indirectly, replacement theology led to the death of six million Jews.

This is the most egregious of the physical consequences of replacement theology, but the spiritual consequences are even more devastating, if that is possible. You see, when there is no more Tribulation in the future, there is no more Millennium on earth in the future following the Tribulation. This millennial period is the only thing separating the Judgment Seat of Christ (1 Cor. 3; 2 Cor. 5; Rom. 14) and the Great White Throne (Rev. 20). In dispensationalism (the primary if not the only system of theology that defends the future reality of a thousand-year reign of Christ on earth), after the Rapture, believers are judged at the Judgment Seat of Christ to determine, not their destiny with or without God, but their rewards that reveal how much of their lives on earth will go to glorify God and determine their place of service in his kingdom(s). Approximately a thousand years later the unbelievers are raised from the dead and appear before the Great White Throne, not to determine their destiny with or without God, but to determine their rewards on a negative scale (punishment). So, if you are standing at the Great White Throne, you will spend eternity without God. If you are standing at the Judgment Seat of Christ, you will spend eternity with God. Only degrees of intimacy with God (Judgment Seat of Christ) or lack thereof (Great White Throne) are being decided.

But when this thousand-year period is eliminated (amillennialism), the two judgment seats collapse into one judgment seat. If so, it would appear that this single judgment seat is to determine the destiny of those being judged; that is, will they go to heaven or hell? And since all the passages dealing with these judgment seats only mention being judged for one's works, it is very easy to understand how so many people think how we live our lives is vitally linked with whether we go to heaven or hell. Thus, when Augustine propagated this system of replacement theology, a pall of death settled over Western Christianity. Who knows how many millions (billions?) of people have been confused by a faith + works gospel for justification before God.

For example, how would you understand these words from a leading evangelical seminary professor:

Arminians and Calvinists agree that professed Christians **must** continue to the end in three areas if they are to be saved: believing the gospel, loving Christ and other believers, and living godly lives.... Consistently in Scripture, bearing no fruit indicates an absence of salvation. Because disciples cannot bear fruit without abiding in Christ, abiding is the way to bear fruit and is evidence of salvation (Jn 15:4-5).... Jesus threatens those branches that do not abide in him with being cut off from him (Jn 15:2), being thrown into the fire and being burned (Jn 15:6). This speaks not of the loss of rewards but of hell.... Put simply, perseverance in holiness *is essential* for Christians to reach heaven. [emphasis mine][66]

According to this professor, both Arminians and Calvinists agree on everything in the above paragraph. If so, then approximately a billion people are taught that to get to heaven a person *must* believe the gospel, love Christ and other believers, and live godly lives. As soon as we say "must" or "is essential," we are listing requirements, not options. This is **faith + works = salvation**, plain and simple. Another billion professing Christians, the Roman Catholics, are taught exactly the same thing. That's two billion people, and we haven't even counted the Orthodox churches (Greek Orthodox, Russian Orthodox, Eastern Orthodox, etc.).

This particular section will be more theological than any other in this book, but we do it only because we think it is crucial for our spiritual well-being. Galatians 3:15-29 helps us a great deal in determining these issues. Paul is still defending his gospel of justification salvation. He shows how justification is by faith for the Jews in 3:6-14, and now he shows how it is by faith for the Gentiles (3:15-4:7). And 4:1-7 is just an illustration of what he is trying to teach his readers in the previous verses. So, let's jump into 3:15-29 where Paul looks at the promise to Abraham *before* the Law of Moses (3:15-18), the promise to Abraham and its *relationship* to the Law of Moses (3:19-25), and the promise to Abraham *after* the Law of Moses ceased to be in effect (3:26-29).

I. PROMISE BEFORE THE LAW   3:15-18

Brethren, I speak in the manner of men: Though it is only a man's covenant, yet if it is confirmed, no one annuls or adds to it. Now to Abraham and his Seed were the promises made. He does not say, "And to seeds," as of many, but as of one, "And to your Seed," who is Christ. And this I say, that the law,

---

66   Robert A. Peterson and Michael D. Williams, *Why I Am Not an Arminian* (Downers Grove, IL: InterVarsity, 2004), 77-78.

which was four hundred and thirty years later, cannot annul the covenant that was confirmed before by God in Christ, that it should make the promise of no effect. For if the inheritance is of the law, it is no longer of promise; but God gave it to Abraham by promise.

The main point of these verses is that the Law of Moses did not wipe out the promise to Abraham. God's promise to Abraham came *before* the Law, was unilateral (obligating one party to another instead of bilateral—party to party, obligating both parties to each other), and was confirmed (Gen. 17). When God put Abraham to sleep and walked up and down through the severed animals, he was confirming a *unilateral* covenant. In other words, this was not a handshake. It was not an "I'll keep my end of the deal if you keep your end" covenant. It was simply a promise of God to man. Once the promise was made, nothing man did could cause God to break his promise.

Most of the confusion over this revolves around the failure to distinguish relationship and fellowship.

RELATIONSHIP	FELLOWSHIP
POSITION	CONDITION
IN HEAVEN	ON EARTH
ETERNAL LIFE	ABUNDANT LIFE
JUSTIFICATION	SANCTIFICATION
INDWELT BY THE SPIRIT	LED BY THE SPIRIT
SEALED BY THE SPIRIT	FRUIT OF THE SPIRIT
DEATH OF CHRIST	LIFE OF CHRIST
PROVIDED BY THE BLOOD	SUSTAINED BY THE BLOOD
JUDICIAL FORGIVENESS	PERSONAL FORGIVENESS

Relationship deals with our position *in Christ* in heavenly places (Eph. 1:3-14). We were put there by the baptism of the Holy Spirit (1 Cor. 12:13). Nothing we do can ever change our position in Christ. It gives us a forever relationship with God. It puts us into his family that lives forever. But fellowship involves our condition on earth. As Luther said, we may be *iustus* (just) in our position in heaven but *peccator* (a sinner) in our condition on earth, *simul* (simultaneously). Our condition can never affect or change our position. However, our position can affect our condition. By focusing on the truth of God in our position (all that we are and have *in Christ*), it changes our condition to slowly but surely match our position.

Through our relationship with God through Christ we have eternal life, a quality of living that is spiritual and will last forever. It can never be lost. It was given to us as a free gift (Eph. 2:9) when we trusted Christ, and God will never take his gift back (Rom. 11:29). But when we are in fellowship with God, we have an abundant life, which we will define as "enjoying our relationship" with God. And the beautiful aspect of all this is that our eternal life can become more and more abundant as we more and more consistently walk by the Spirit and experience this gift of eternal life. This does not mean our eternal life can get any longer; it just gets better. The quantity does not change, but the quality does.

When the Holy Spirit baptizes us into Christ, he also comes to live in us permanently. He indwells us (1 Cor. 6:19) and gives us the gift of eternal life. Thus, we have all the power we need for a godly life (2 Pet. 1:3), but that power is not unleashed until we are led by the Holy Spirit. When we go our way and he goes his way, his power is quenched in our lives and we grieve him (Eph. 4:30). We are sealed by the Holy Spirit as a mark of ownership (Eph. 1:13) and protection whether we are sinning or not, but we only enjoy the fruit of the Holy Spirit when we walk with him (Gal. 5:16ff.). In this way we experience the reality of the eternal life that he gifted us.

Our eternal relationship with God is accomplished through the death of Christ (Rom. 5:8-10), but our current fellowship with God is accomplished through the life of Christ (Rom. 5:10). He was our substitute in death; he also wants to be our substitute in life; "not I, but Christ" (Gal. 2:20 KJV). Our relationship with God was provided by the blood of Christ, and our fellowship with God is sustained by the blood of Christ (1 John 1:7).

When we trusted Christ to forgive our sins, we received judicial forgiveness in the courtroom of heaven. The gavel of God came down, so to speak, and God said, "Declared righteous," or, if you prefer, "Not guilty." In heaven he forgave us for *all* our sins—past, present, and future. It is this last aspect (future sins) that was not understood until the Reformation. And it is this future forgiveness that is the basis for our eternal security. If our *future* sins are forgiven, what sins could we possibly commit in the *future* that would jeopardize our eternal life with God? So in contrast, when we sin in our present condition on earth, it is a personal matter, not a judicial matter. I must go to God and ask his forgiveness (1 John 1:9) in order to regain my fellowship with him. It is a temporal-personal matter, not an eternal-judicial matter. Fellowship is what allows me to enjoy and realize the eternal life that is my gift. But I must always remember, my condition cannot affect my position.

Now all these NT concepts are found in God's relationship and fellowship with Israel. An eternal relationship with Israel as a nation (her position) was established by the Abrahamic covenant. But fellowship (her condition) was another matter. When Israel sinned in her condition, it did not affect her position as the chosen wife of God, but it did affect her fellowship. So, the Law of Moses was designed to help restore the sinning nation back to fellowship. It worked for individuals as well. The Law of Moses told Israel how to behave and please God and show him that he was loved (Deut. 8). So the sacrificial system was established to make a way for fellowship forgiveness when Israel did sin.

Here in Galatians 3:15-18 Paul makes it clear that the Law of Moses did not set aside, annul, nullify, abrogate, rescind, cancel—whatever word you want to pick—the promise (covenant) given to Abraham. The Abrahamic covenant and the Mosaic covenant had different purposes. The Law of Moses was never designed to give an eternal relationship to Israel. They already had that eternal relationship as God's gift to Abraham by faith. But the Law of Moses was designed to help Israel enjoy that relationship through fellowship with their God, which required faithfulness to the law.

Well, Paul anticipated their questions about the law. If we have the promise to Abraham, what purpose does the Law of Moses serve? He answers that for them in Galatians 3:19-25.

II. PROMISE AND THE LAW   3:19-25

What purpose then does the law serve? It was added because of transgressions, till the Seed should come to whom the promise was made; and it was appointed through angels by the hand of a mediator. Now a mediator does not mediate for one only, but God is one. Is the law then against the promises of God? Certainly not! For if there had been a law given which could have given life, truly righteousness would have been by the law. But the Scripture has confined all under sin, that the promise by faith in Jesus Christ might be given to those who believe. But before faith came, we were kept under guard by the law, kept for the faith which would afterward be revealed. Therefore the law was our tutor to bring us to Christ, that we might be justified by faith. But after faith has come, we are no longer under a tutor.

Notice the opening question: "What purpose then does the law serve?" Here are three purposes for the Law of Moses:

1. **To reveal—our sinfulness.**

   Paul says he would not have known sin if it were not for the law (Rom. 7:7). The law reveals God's standard of holiness. Concomitantly it reveals our sinfulness. When we juxtapose our lives with his standard of holiness, we come up short; we fall short of the glory of God (Rom. 3:23). This helps us see our need for a Savior. In the Sermon on the Mount, Jesus raised the bar higher than even the Law of Moses. He called for perfection (Matt. 5:48). As he took holiness from the external to the internal, everyone listening must have seen his or her personal inability to fulfill the required standard.

2. **To guard—our fellowship.**

The law was given to help maintain fellowship. God gave Abraham an irrevocable covenant. That's relationship. But to *enjoy* the covenant *blessings* (fellowship), Abraham had to stay in the land promised in the covenant (Israel). Every time Abraham tried to leave the land, God got him back. Then Isaac tried to leave the land (Gen. 26:2-6), but the Lord appeared to him and told him not to leave the land. When Jacob left to find a wife, the Lord appeared to him in a dream and told him he would bring Jacob back to the land of Israel so God could fulfill his promises to Abraham through the seed of Jacob (Gen. 28:13-15). Finally, the sons of Jacob left the land and wound up as slaves—people not enjoying the Abrahamic covenant. Relationship, but no fellowship.

So God decided to spell it out for them. At Mt. Sinai he made a covenant with them for the purpose of fellowship (Ex. 23:7-8). Part of that covenant was to get back to the Promised Land. But that generation of Jews did not have the necessary faith to battle the giants in the land. So they never got to enjoy the full blessings of the relationship they had with God through the Abrahamic covenant. Forty years later, God gave Israel another chance. Deuteronomy was to show them how to live in the land and enjoy it. But when they chose to serve other gods or just be disobedient in general, God would take them out of the land. If they repented, in time he would restore them. Unfortunately, they were unfaithful, so here came the Assyrians. They were unfaithful again, so here came the Babylonians. They were unfaithful again, so here came the Greeks. They were unfaithful again, so here came the Romans. So, one purpose of the law was for fellowship.

Listen to the words of the high priest on the Day of

Atonement in accordance with the required confession in Leviticus 16:20-21. He offered two prayers. The first was personal confession for himself and his family:

I beseech you, O Lord;
I have sinned, rebelled, and transgressed against you,
I, and my household;
I beseech you, O Lord,
Grant atonement for the sins,
and for the iniquities and transgressions
which I have committed against you,
I, and my household,
As it is written in the Torah
of your servant, Moses:
for on this day
atonement shall be made for you,
to purify you from all your sins—before
the Lord you shall be purified.

The second prayer offered by the high priest was for the entire nation:

I beseech you, O Lord;
Grant atonement for the sins,
and for the iniquities and transgressions
which the entire house of Israel
has committed against you,
As it is written in the Torah
of your servant, Moses;
For on this day
atonement shall be made for you,
to purify you from all your sins—before
the Lord you shall be purified.[67]

---

67 Chaim Richman, *The Holy Temple in Jerusalem* (Jerusalem: The Temple Institute, 1997), 55, 59.

Because the nation of Israel already had an unbreakable relationship (which implies positional forgiveness for the nation), there is a basis for forgiveness in her condition, which is required for fellowship. We say again: the nation had and still has a secure position with God, a relationship that will last forever (all this is contained in the covenant with Abraham); but for any given generation of Jews to enjoy the blessings (fellowship) of their position within the Abrahamic covenant, they had to be in the land and keep the Mosaic covenant (faithfulness).

It is very important to see that an eternal relationship with God for the nation does not guarantee an eternal relationship for the individuals in that nation. This is where many of the Pharisees got confused. They thought that just because they were the physical seed of Abraham that each individual in the nation was guaranteed a place with God forever. Not at all. As seen in the last section (Gal. 3:6-14), God deals with individuals based on their faith or lack thereof.

3. **To tutor—us to Christ.**

    Paul says the law was like a tutor to bring us to Christ. In fact, that is precisely how I saw my need for a Savior. I had been successful at most of the things I had tried either academically or athletically. Then I read the Bible for the first time when I was seventeen. When I came to Exodus 20 and the Ten Commandments, in my arrogance and pride I decided to keep them for thirty days. No special reason. Just wanted to prove to myself I could do it if I wanted to. I failed miserably and saw that I could not stop sinning even when I tried as hard as I could. So, I asked for Jesus's forgiveness and asked him to be my personal Savior. God literally used the law (in this case the Ten Commandments) to bring me to Christ. It revealed my sinfulness and my need for a Savior from sin, which was obviously a barrier between God and me. And my realizing that was a good thing.

In 2001, I broke my hip while skiing in Colorado. It was a crack of the femoral neck. Such a break can be surgically repaired if the surgery is done within twenty-four hours of the accident. Otherwise, the chances of healing are only about 20 percent. The doctors kept delaying my surgery in lieu of more serious cases. Then when the surgery was done, the doctor messed up, so he had to do it again. Chances of success were slim. Three years later I was having a lot of pain, so I went to an orthopedic surgeon I knew from my days at Rice University. He took some X-rays and showed them to me. Sure enough, the femoral head (the ball in the joint) had died and was slowly caving in. Instead of a ball, I had a hemisphere. He said I needed to get that out as soon as possible.

Well, that was bad news. I didn't like what that X-ray machine had revealed. I thought, *I'll just go down there with a sledgehammer and smash that X-ray machine. See if it ever gives me bad news again.* Wouldn't that have been stupid? They'd have carried me away to a hospital from which I might never have returned. Of course, the X-ray machine had just revealed an internal problem that needed fixing. The X-ray machine couldn't fix the problem, and the X-ray machine hadn't caused the problem. The X-ray machine had shown me the need for a surgeon to repair the problem. The law is God's X-ray machine to bring us to the Divine Surgeon.

To summarize, justification (imputed righteousness) was never the intent or goal of the Law of Moses (Gal. 3:11). The promise of blessing (Gen. 12:1-3) to all the nations of the world was that justification would be by faith in his Seed, Jesus Christ. And when

Christ came, he fulfilled the requirements of the law and brought an end to the Law of Moses (Rom. 10:4). The law was for fellowship, not relationship. So we have seen the promise to Abraham *before* the law and the promise as it *relates* to the law, but what about the promise *after* the law?

III. PROMISE AFTER THE LAW   3:26-29

> For you are all sons of God through faith in Christ Jesus. For as many of you as were baptized into Christ have put on Christ. There is neither Jew nor Greek, there is neither slave nor free, there is neither male nor female; for you are all one in Christ Jesus. And if you are Christ's, then you are Abraham's seed, and heirs according to the promise.

Christ is the great Barrier Buster. In him there is neither Jew nor Greek, slave nor free, male nor female. He broke down all castes, all distinctions, and all racial barriers. Surely some of the greatest satanic twists of all time have been the killing done in the name of Christ: Aryan supremacy, the KKK, the Crusades, and the Inquisition.

Paul argues that through our faith in Christ we are baptized into Christ and belong to Christ. And if we belong to Christ, we must be Abraham's seed. Since we are not the physical seed of Abraham, we must be the spiritual seed. This makes us heirs of the promise given to Abraham. One promise—all the nations of the earth will be blessed through his Seed.

Notice it does not say "promises," plural. We are not heirs of all the promises given to Abraham. It is primarily based on this verse that many theologians teach that the church has replaced Israel in God's plan. Since Paul says we in the church are the spiritual seed of Abraham and are an extension of the promise given to Abraham, they claim the promises to Abraham must be fulfilled spiritually instead of physically. This is a classic non sequitur, meaning one concept does not logically follow from the concept preceding it. Just because one of the promises was going to be fulfilled spiritually does not mean **all** the promises would be fulfilled spiritually. More than one promise was given to Abraham, two of which could **not** be fulfilled spiritually.

1. **Land.** This was a physical promise. God gave the land of Israel to the nation of Israel as an everlasting possession (Gen. 17:8). This could not be fulfilled spiritually.

2. **Seed.** This was a physical promise also. Abraham couldn't have a great nation from his progeny without physical seed. This was clarified in Genesis 15:5 and 17:6-8 in which the physical seed and the physical land were to be everlasting; it is an everlasting promise that could not be set aside or nullified by the Law of Moses. This promise could not be fulfilled spiritually.

3. **Blessing.** Abraham was to be a blessing to all the families of the earth. This required a physical Seed. It is a good thing the Seed promise (Christ Jesus) was not merely fulfilled spiritually, without a physical body. But this was also a spiritual promise ("blessing") and through this spiritual promise *the Seed* (Jesus) would make us the spiritual seed of Abraham. But this does not cancel out the essential physical promises to Abraham, which will also be fulfilled physically in the millennial kingdom.

There was a covenant with Abraham with multiple promises before the Law of Moses. These promises to Abraham were not set aside by the Law of Moses. And one of the three promises to Abraham was still being fulfilled after the Law of Moses (the blessing to all the families of the earth). So we would agree with Tim LaHaye. God is not finished with the physical seed of Abraham or a certain piece of land in the Middle East (Israel). And you have to wonder, don't you, if God is finished with the physical seed of Abraham and the physical land of Abraham, why on earth all the fuss over that little sliver of land two thousand years after the death of Christ? It appears that something is afoot, Dr. Watson.

CONCLUSION

1. **Justification** is by faith without works of the law for the Gentile as well as for the Jew.

2. Any **performance** system of morality will ultimately reveal our sinfulness.

3. God still has a **plan** for the **physical** seed of Abraham (the Jews).

4. Those who are not the **spiritual** seed of Abraham will be **left behind**.

Promises, promises. Promises are great motivators. If the kids start acting up on the way home from church, just promise them you will take them to Dairy Queen for some ice cream if they will settle down. But you better keep your promises. It reminds me of the couple who rarely went out with just each other for a date because it was hard to find a babysitter who could corral their kids. Well, they just had to get out, so they took a risk with a new gal.

With fear and trepidation the couple returned home. They opened the door and the babysitter had a big smile on her face. How did it go? "Great. No problem." Incredulous, the parents asked the girl how she had done it. "Oh, it was easy," she said. "I just promised them in the morning you would buy them a new pony."

Human promises seem made to be broken far too often. Not God's promises. And he promises eternal life to anyone who believes in his Son, Jesus Christ, and his work on the cross to take away their sins. He also promised if you do not take advantage of this window of opportunity to believe in Jesus…you'll be left behind.

9

ADOPTION PROCEDURES
Galatians 4:1-7

After three arduous and failed attempts to adopt here in the States, my daughter Christie and her husband, Scott, decided to go to Russia. The procedures were difficult and expensive, but doable. The first step was to make a trip to Russia to visit the orphanages to see if they could find a child they wished to adopt. At the time (2002) it cost $25,000 for the first child and $5,000 for the second. So, Scott and Christie decided to go for two. After choosing a boy and a girl from different orphanages but just two months apart in age, they were ushered into a courtroom where the judge [68]read the medical rap sheet on each child. They let it be known that these children were up for adoption because they had medical issues and were not wanted by either their parents or the state.

Of course, the adopting parents had no way of knowing if the medical issues were real or trumped up to give the orphanages a legal

---

68   www.helprussianorphans.com/statistics.htm, accessed on September 11, 2014.

sanction to put the children up for adoption. However, after hearing the issues, the prospective parents then flew back to their home country to decide if they wanted to go on with the adoption. They had to wait about a month, enough time for their emotions to subside so they could make a rational decision. Thus, if any medical issues did pop up later, the Russian government could always say, "We told you so."

Well, according to the Ascent Russian Orphan Aid Foundation, during their first year out of the orphanage 50 percent wind up pregnant, prostituted, or turn to crime (boys join the mafia and girls become prostitutes), 40 percent become addicted to alcohol or drugs, 40% are homeless and unemployed, and 10 percent commit suicide. Knowing that the two children they had picked out would not have much of a chance in life, if they lived to "graduate," Scott and Christie decided they had the opportunity to bring salvation to these kids on two levels: physically and spiritually. So they adopted them, brought them to America, and now the children, Drew and Grace, are eleven years old.

Personally, I have learned so much about God's love for us through being a sideline participant in the adoption of my grandchildren. The passage before us says that all of God's children (except One) are adopted. And God has his own unique adoption procedure. It behooves us to take a look at what this means for us who are his adopted children. We will see that we were slaves in the past (4:1-3), are sons in the present (4:4-6), and will be heirs in the future (4:7).

I. SLAVES—IN THE PAST   4:1-3

Now I say that the heir, as long as he is a child, does not differ at all from a slave, though he is master of all, but is under guardians and stewards until the time appointed by the father. Even so we, when we were children, were in bondage under the elements of the world.

It is hard to decide which of the law codes (Roman, Greek, or Syrian) Paul has in mind as he writes this. It does not fit any one perfectly, but then illustrations rarely fit perfectly. It appears closest to the Roman laws, which would make sense because Galatia was a Roman province. The main point of the illustration is that just as slaves have people over them telling them what to do, so also an heir has guardians (until age fourteen) and stewards (until twenty-five) over him telling him what he can and cannot do.

In this illustration, "when we were children" is hard to understand because it sounds like we were the children of God and thus in the forever family. But in Paul's analogy we don't enter God's forever family until our adoption in 4:5. Until that adoption we are not redeemed. So in 4:1-3 he describes our enslavement as non-Christians to "the elements of the world." Scholars have debated the word for "elements" (*stoicheia*) for centuries. The suggested meaning I prefer is "principles of the world" or "worldly principles." One of the universal principles of the world is the law principle, or what I call the performance principle. In some way, shape, or form most of us grow up under this principle.

Sometimes this principle first pops up in our upbringing. Many parents do not distinguish between acceptance and approval. The parents subjugate their children to the performance principle in order to win the love of the parents. This gives rise to the second-born syndrome in which the second born in the family is the most competitive. Because he is not as big or strong as his older brother or sister, he must fight and scrape for the attention of his parents, which he translates into love. He grows up thinking he has to perform at a high level in order to be accepted (loved) by Mom and Dad. Often these people are very driven to succeed in life, only to find out that their stellar performance still isn't good enough for the acceptance of their father.

Wise is the parent who distinguishes between acceptance and approval. This parent makes sure his children know they are 100 percent accepted no matter how they perform. These children will always be loved by their parents no matter how well they do in school or athletics or business. But approval is another matter. Though the child who becomes a drug addict or a criminal may still be loved by his parents, he would not have their approval.

If the law principle (the performance principle) is not learned in the home, it usually is picked up pretty quickly in school. We learn early on whether we belong in the Blue Bird reading group or the Red Bird reading group. Do we get picked first or last at recess for whatever game is being played? How we feel about ourselves (self-esteem) is tied directly to how we perform. If we perform well, we feel good about ourselves. If we perform poorly, we feel bad.

Unfortunately, when we become Christians, depending on how long we have used performance as our drug of choice, we bring the performance principle into the Christian life with us. In the world, we performed for our parents, for our teachers, for our coaches, for our bosses, and so on. Why not perform for God? That is the essence of legalism. Expressed somewhat simplistically, legalism says, "Do, and you will be blessed." On the other hand, God says, "You are blessed; therefore, do."

Again, to go back to our physical family, the children who seem to grow up with the fewest internal scars and who also perform to the best of their abilities are those who know they are unconditionally (no performance) loved (accepted) by their parents. They don't have to worry about their performance to know they are loved, so they are able to relax and perform at a higher level, should they choose to do so.

I well remember a girl in my Algebra II class in high school. She and I were fighting it out for the top grade in the class. Whenever I would beat her on a test, she would cry. I was just fourteen, three years before I became a believer in Jesus, but I felt sorry for her. I couldn't figure out what would drive her so hard that she would cry over a math test. It wasn't like she was flunking. Then someone told me her father was a math professor at Vanderbilt in my hometown, Nashville, Tennessee. He had made it clear to her that she **had** to be number one. Apparently, she felt she had to perform to win her father's love (acceptance).

Nevertheless, I too became a performance addict, both in school and athletics. Winning was my drug. It took away my personal pain of feeling insecure and insignificant. If I could win, then maybe my parents would love me more. If I could win, then maybe I was somebody. Although the performance principle may be a basic principle for success in the world, it is a formula for defeat in the Christian life. It took me years to learn that the performance principle is one of the beggarly elements of this world and has nothing to do with being accepted by God.

Now it is true that we want to be approved by God, if we are healthy Christians. The healthy child wants the approval of his parents. No problem. And good parents are lavish in their praise when their children do well in their various activities. My eleven-year-old grandson plays the piano and takes karate lessons. Even though I am not one of his parents, he always wants to know if I will be there when he has a recital or a test to move up a level in karate. And even during his performance (piano or karate) he will steal a glance in our direction (his family) to see if we are watching. This is all good and healthy as long as he knows we love him completely no matter how well he performs.

Well, doesn't God do the same? At the cross he poured out his unconditional love. We cannot earn this love. Faith alone in Christ alone. Our performance cannot win his love or lose his love. But approval is another issue. He will set up the Judgment Seat of Christ to give us our approval rating. Every faithful servant would love to hear him say, "Well done, good and faithful servant." That's not acceptance; that's approval.

The Neo-Galatianists have this all turned around. They believe they must perform for God's acceptance (relationship), not for his approval (fellowship). Again, the Arminians believe they must perform (be good and faithful) until the end of their lives or they lose their justification salvation (acceptance into heaven). And the Calvinists believe they must perform (be good and faithful) until the end of their lives or they never had justification salvation. *Instead of making their performance (being good and faithful) a condition of approval, they make it a condition of acceptance. That is a disastrous difference.*

Someone will surely ask, "But aren't you just shifting the

performance principle from acceptance to approval? You can still feed your addiction to performance by performing to get rewards at the Judgment Seat of Christ instead of to get into heaven." Great question; glad you asked it. Jesus anticipated that very question in the minds of his listeners right after a lesson on rewards given to his disciples.

Peter has just asked what he and his friends would get out of leaving everything to follow Jesus (Matt. 19:27). Jesus promises a reward. Peter and company will get to sit on the twelve thrones ruling over the twelve tribes of Israel in his millennial kingdom. Jesus goes on to motivate everyone who sacrifices to follow him with the promise of future rewards. Aha. He can just sense the competitive juices begin to flow in his disciples. After all, the disciples were eaten up with the performance principle like most of us, if not all of us. They wanted to know who would be the greatest among them (Luke 22:24). So Jesus tries to clarify the doctrine of rewards a bit by telling a parable, the parable of the vineyard (Matt. 20:1-16).

We remember from the parable that some workers were only in the vineyard an hour but they received the same wages as those who had borne the heat of the day and had worked all day. Those who had worked all day were mad at the owner of the vineyard who had hired them. Why? Because they had worked harder and longer than those who had worked for just an hour but got the same wages. You see, they thought God *owed* them more than those who had worked less. That is why they were mad. They were legalists. They thought they had put the owner in debt to a certain level of wages but that God did not *owe* the same amount to those who did not *deserve* it because they had not worked as long or as hard (heat of the day).

There is your tip-off that these people were caught up in Galatianism before there was Galatianism. However, Galatianism did exist before Galatianism because Galatianism is just one form or another of legalism. The legalist thinks God owes him for his good works and gets mad when God does not give him what he thinks he's owed. A very successful pastor decided to leave the ministry. He suffered from burnout and other issues. In trying to restore him (Gal. 6:1) to usefulness, I just listened to him pour out his anger for about six months. Then I looked him in the eye and said, "You know what your main problem is? You're a legalist." "A legalist? How can you say that? I've preached through Galatians three times." "I don't care. You are still a legalist. It's obvious." "Why is that?" "Because you are mad at God. You can't get mad at God unless you think he owes you and hasn't paid up. You have done all these things for God's kingdom and your marriage isn't what you expected, your children are not what you were expecting, your elders don't show you the respect you think you deserve, and you think God hasn't come through for you. That's why you are mad at him." I am glad to say that was many years ago. He has since repented and has returned to ministry.

The parable of the vineyard is telling us that even rewards are a matter of God's grace. Paul made it clear in Romans 4:4 ("Now to him who works, the wages are not counted as grace but as debt") that grace and debt do not go hand in hand. The focus in Romans 4 is on justification salvation. Those who plug works into the justification equation think God owes them (debt). But we can never put God in our debt. He doesn't owe us at the gates of heaven, and he doesn't owe us at the Judgment Seat of Christ.

Most of us define God's grace as an "undeserved favor." So when we say that rewards are a matter of grace, we are saying that we cannot show up at the Judgment Seat of Christ and tell God he owes us because we have been such good and faithful servants. He can give to me or you or anyone else whatever he wishes. Now God does promise to reward the faithful believers, as he stated just before the parable of the vineyard. But the point of the parable is that we cannot tell him how much he owes us. We cannot put him in our debt. If he gave us nothing, he would be untrue to his promises. But we must leave the "how much" up to him. As mentioned in the parable, he did not go back on any promise to the workers in the vineyard. It's just that by his grace he chose to give some workers more than others thought those workers deserved. It is the whole "deserved" concept where we get mixed up. The works that count forever have been done by the power of God anyway (Phil. 2:13). And the victory we have over the flesh is by the power of the Holy Spirit, not our flesh. That is why our rewards ultimately reflect on him and bring him glory. Nevertheless, he has graciously offered rewards to us as a healthy and positive motivation. Who does not want to bring glory to his Savior? But because these rewards are according to grace, we can never demand of God that he reward us. Like Moses, we remind God of his promise to reward us. His gracious promise allows us to earn rewards. But because these rewards are according to grace, we can never tell him what we **deserve**. We **deserve** nothing.

A huge part of God's grace in offering us rewards is the immense fulfillment that attends his approval. Jesus says of us as parents that we, being evil, want good gifts for our children; how much more the heavenly Father? If children can be driven to extreme behavior to attempt to gain the approval of their human parents, does that not demonstrate the immense fulfillment available to us through the mercy of God in giving us the approval of a life well lived? It should provide us extreme motivation, not because we can in any way control God, or cause him to owe us, but because God loves us and *wants* to bless us. What sane person would not want to sell all he or she has and purchase this pearl of great price?

Paul understood completely that although he was the "chief of sinners" he was completely accepted by Jesus. Totally, unconditionally. But Paul was driven to gain Christ's approval. He refused payment as an apostle, and part of the reason (2 Cor. 9) was so he would not abuse his authority and find himself "disqualified" from winning the prize— which is nothing other than the approval, the recognition, of Jesus. Heaven was not the prize: rewards were the prize. Paul also says in 2 Timothy 1:12, "For this reason I also suffer these things; nevertheless I am not ashamed, for I know whom I have believed and am persuaded that He is able to keep what I have committed to Him until that Day." Paul has made a heavenly deposit and is convinced it will still be there for him. And yet, although he has faith that God will reward him, he never says anything about being "owed." In fact, with respect to his good friend Onesiphorus, he asks for "mercy" with respect to Jesus's reward. Paul understands that every reward and approval of God is an act of his mercy. He owes us nothing. Rather, God graciously promised. We simply are asked to believe in his generosity and "make deposits."

So in our past life before Christ we were in bondage. We were slaves to the principles of this world, one of which is the performance principle. Now Paul will explain to us God's adoption procedures, that is, how we became sons in the present.

II. SONS—IN THE PRESENT 4:4-6

But when the fullness of the time had come, God sent forth His Son, born of a woman, born under the law, to redeem those who were under the law, that we might receive the adoption as sons. And because you are sons, God has sent forth the Spirit of His Son into your hearts, crying out, "Abba, Father!"

One reason Paul says Jesus was brought to earth when he was is that it was the "fullness of the time." There are many reasons why scholars believe the time of his birth was the fullness of the time. One is what we call the lingua franca, which simply means there was a common language around the Mediterranean world and to the East through which the gospel could travel quickly. About three hundred years before Christ, Alexander the Great conquered most of what was considered to be the civilized world. In his opinion there were no more worlds to conquer. And because he thought Greek philosophy was a superior approach to life, he forced every land he conquered to learn Greek.

In fact, one of the world's leading NT scholars did his dissertation on the languages spoken in Israel at the time of Christ.[69] It was his thesis that all of Israel was bilingual at the time of Christ. Everyone spoke Aramaic (brought back from Babylon) and Greek (brought in by one of Alexander's generals and the generations that followed

---

69 Martin Hengel, *Judaism and Hellenism* (Philadelphia: Fortress, 1974).

him). Although English is becoming the lingua franca of the modern world (probably so the gospel can spread like it did in the first century AD), fifty years ago the language, racial, and national barriers were greater than at the time of Christ.

Now we come to the adoption procedures.[70] In Rome a child under age seven was called an *infant* (Latin) or *nēpios* (Greek), a **babe**. From then until age fourteen a male was an *impubes* (Latin) or *teknon* (Greek), a **child**. At puberty he became a *filius* (Latin) or *huios* (Greek), a **son**. Although he could sit at the family council, he could not conduct the affairs of his estate, including the exercise of property rights, until age twenty-five. But even at twenty-five he was still under what the Romans called the *patria potestas* (paternal power, power of the father).[71] This meant that his natural father had authority over the son until the father died[72]—*except* in the case of adoption.

To finalize adoption, the natural father took his son to the marketplace and sold him three times to the prospective father. A father could sell his children to pay off his debts, but he could also buy them back twice after paying off his debt. But with the third sale his *patria potestas* was broken, and the child was no longer obligated to his natural father in any way;[73] he was adopted "for good."[74] Such adoptions could take place at any age. In fact, Nero became emperor of Rome through adoption by Claudius. Since Claudius had no heir

---

70 These procedures are taken from Anderson and Reitman, *Portraits of Righteousness*, where Paul relies heavily on Roman law. Since Galatia was a Roman province when Galatians was written, Paul is probably relying most heavily on Roman law; although, he may have been influenced by Greek law and Syrian law as well.

71 Max Kaser, *Römisches Privatrecht*, trans. Rolf Dannenbring (Durban, South Africa: Butterworth, 1968), 61.

72 Ibid., 256-57.

73 Ibid., 258.

74 Ibid., 264.

to his throne, he simply chose to adopt one of his favorite generals. When an adoption took place, there were four consequences:

1. The adopted son lost all rights in his previous family, and his natural father lost all rights over him.

2. In the new family the adopted son gained rights equivalent to blood relatives (this is only true of *Roman* adoption, among the various cultures in the Bible).

3. His previous life record was wiped out, including any debts.

4. He began a new life with a new name, new rights, and new status.

So, how does Paul apply this to the Christian life? Every unbeliever has a father just as every believer does. Paul says that all non-Christians are by nature children of wrath (Eph. 2:3). Their spiritual father is the devil. But when a non-Christian receives Christ, he is born into a new family with a new Father, God, and all four consequences of Roman adoption also apply:

1. Our former father (Satan) has lost all his rights over us, and we have no obligation to obey him.

2. We have rights in the new family on an equal basis with the only begotten Son himself.

3. The record of our old life with its debt of sin has been completely wiped out.

4. We have begun a brand-new life in a new family with a new status as new creatures.

One more key feature of Roman sonship completes Paul's analogy to the "obligation" of Christian maturity. A Roman son was under the care of a **tutor** (compare Gal. 3:24-25; 4:2) who trained him in morals and education and served as guardian and executor of his estate until age fourteen. At fourteen the child underwent a ceremony in which he was given the *toga virilis*—the apparel of manhood. A **curator** now took the place of the tutor, but his role was similar. The son could exercise a few legal rights and was allowed much more freedom but was still under the authority of the curator, who provided counsel and protection and administered the boy's property. Finally, at age twenty-five, the boy was considered a full-fledged son who could exercise full rights and privileges. No more tutors or curators; although, he was still under the power of his father.

Paul draws on all this imagery in the passage before us. The believer's "biological father" (in Adam) was the devil, who had absolute *patria potestas* over him. His tutor and curator were the flesh, which trained him in self-sufficiency, self-gratification, and the performance principle. As an unbeliever, he was obliged to obey the flesh, but through adoption he was transferred into a new family. Our Father in heaven paid the price to buy us out of the marketplace, which ended the *patria potestas* of the devil, the old father. Now we are under a new Father, the Father of our Lord Jesus Christ. While Jesus is our Father's only *begotten* Son, we are his *adopted* sons. As such, we no longer have any obligation to our former tutor or curator, the law or the flesh. Now we have a new tutor or curator—the Holy Spirit—whom God the Father has appointed as our protector, teacher, guide, and counselor. In sum:

IDENTITY	FATHER	TUTOR/CURATOR
Old: in Adam	the devil	the law/the flesh
New: in Christ	God	the Spirit

The redemption price paid in the marketplace (see Gal. 3:13) was the blood of Christ. It was the ultimate price—an infinite price to cover any number of sins. It was this price that made our adoption possible.

According to the Roman adoption ceremony, a child never had the privilege of calling his father "Father" until he was placed as a son.[75] And that privilege is what we see in verse 6: Abba, Father. The word "Abba" originally meant "Daddy." It was a term of endearment and intimacy,

---

75   Anderson and Reitman, *Portraits of Righteousness*, 178.

one of the first sounds a baby would make in the Aramaic language. But in Galatians 4 it is not the little child who says "abba." The Aramaic word "abba" would not mean much to the Galatians, who spoke Greek. Why then does Paul include this term "Abba" in the text? If we look at the use of this word in Scripture, we find that it is a term of *privilege*.

Never once in the OT does an individual address God as "Father." In fact, nowhere in the known literature of Judaism before the coming of Jesus Christ do we have any Jew calling God his own Father. Finally, in the NT we have Jesus addressing God as "My Father" some twenty times. Only once does Jesus call his Father "God," and that was on the cross when he said, "My God, my God, why have you forsaken me?" On the cross Jesus became the sin offering for us, separated from his Father, bearing our judgment. The close, intimate fellowship between the Father and his Son was broken for the first time since eternity past; so instead of addressing his Father with deep intimacy, Jesus calls him "God." Every other time it is "My Father." In fact, some 170 times in the NT he speaks of "the Father" (150 times) or "my Father" (20 times).

In the special case of John's gospel, Jesus mentions the Father over a hundred times, but none in Matthew and only three times in Mark. This is because John always reserves the term *huios*, son, for Jesus in his gospel. Nowhere in John's gospel do we see other Christians being called the sons of God. They are only called children, little children, believers, or disciples. The term "son" was reserved for Jesus. And it is only Jesus who addresses his God as Father.

In the Garden of Gethsemane it was Jesus who cried out in prayer, not as a baby, but as a dependent son, "Abba, Father." It is noteworthy that "abba" occurs only one time in the Gospels and that is from the lips of Jesus in the garden. We suggest, then, that "abba" was a term of great intimacy on the part of a mature son with intimate fellowship and dependence on his father. This is the intimacy Paul has in mind in Galatians 4:6, as opposed to John's gospel where "children" are in view. Here, then, we see the mature son calling his Father "Abba" after he is placed as a son, adopted, being led by the Spirit of God (5:18)—just as Jesus himself was "appointed" or "placed" as a Son by the Father when *he* was empowered by "the Spirit of holiness" (Rom. 1:4).

This is the adoption in view in Hebrews 1, with its attendant royal inheritance—a *reign over the world to come* (Heb. 2:5-9). The OT basis for this inheritance is a *reward* covenant, known as a "covenant of grant."[76] When a servant showed exemplary faithfulness, his lord might choose to reward him by adopting him and giving him a piece of land. In the adoption ceremony the lord would say, "Today I have begotten you; you will be a son to me, and I will be a father to you." It is this OT cultural practice that the NT authors have in view: Jesus came to earth as a Suffering Servant, but he ascended as a Son (Rom. 1:3-4)[77] and received as a reward the *inheritance* of a faithful Son (Heb. 1:4-14), along with his "companions" (*metochoi*, Heb. 1:9, 14). Thus, Paul can also say that his companions *share* the Son's intimacy with the Father, as well as his inheritance, for they too fulfill their "obligation" as faithful, adopted "sons of God" who are led by the Spirit in the face of suffering (see Rom. 8:12-17).

Therefore, although we were slaves in the past and are sons in the present, we shall be heirs in the future.

III. HEIRS—IN THE FUTURE   4:7

Therefore you are no longer a slave but a son, and if a son, then an heir of God through Christ.

In this verse God reveals to us that every one of his children is an heir. Later in Galatians we learn that there are heirs in different spheres, and still other passages (Col. 3:24; Matt. 19:27-30) reveal that heirship can be at different levels according to our faithfulness. At the base level every child is an heir. All it took to become an heir is

---

76   Moshe Weinfeld, "The Covenant of Grant in the Old Testament and the Ancient Near East," *Journal of the American Oriental Society* 90 (April-June 1970): 184.

77   Martin Hengel (*The Son of God* [Philadelphia: Fortress, 1976]) has argued that there are actually *three* phases to the sonship of Christ: before the earth, on the earth, and after the ascension.

all it took to become a child, or in this passage, a son—faith. Every child of God will inherit a glorified body, full forgiveness of sins, presence with God forever, and much more. But faithfulness brings an even greater inheritance. Suffering for Christ brings the reward of coinheritance with him (Rom. 8:17).

Inheritance is a very apt analogy to help understand why eternal life can be a free gift and yet there is still motivation for faithfulness. The unfaithful son, by Roman law, was not kicked out of the family, but he could be disinherited. So a child of God is always a child of God, but he could lose most of his inheritance, his reward. Second John 8 reads: "Look to yourselves, that we do not lose those things we worked for, but *that* we may receive a full reward." Our rewards and our inheritance are the same thing (Col. 3:24). Our inheritance can be increased or decreased according to our faithfulness or lack thereof.

It is interesting that a feature of the *reward covenant* (e.g., referenced in Heb. 1) was usually a piece of real estate. When the adoption ceremony took place, the former servant was given a piece of land as part of his reward. We must remember that Adam was called to take over a piece of real estate—planet earth. Because of his unfaithfulness, he lost his first chance at doing so. He was given another chance after expulsion from the garden. He failed again. Noah was given a chance (Gen. 9:1-7). He failed. So, from man's perspective, God came up with a new plan. He would create another Adam who would be faithful and would take dominion over (inherit) the earth— the Second Adam, Jesus Christ.[78] This is exactly what we see going on in Hebrews 1. The Suffering Servant has been faithful to complete his mission. At the ascension he is adopted as a son and receives part of his inheritance (reward). It is a piece of real estate called planet earth. He reigns from heaven today but will actually take physical dominion

---

78 The second person of the Godhead was not created. To be God he had to be eternal. But Jesus Christ was created, that is, the God-man. The human side of Jesus was created in Nazareth and birthed in Bethlehem. Thus, we can say that Jesus Christ was created.

over the earth when he sets up his kingdom and rules from Jerusalem for one thousand years.

But here's the cool thing. Jesus wants to lead many sons to glory (Heb. 2:10). The faithful Son (Heb. 1-2) is looking for many faithful sons (Heb. 11-13) to share (Heb. 1:9; 3:1, 14) in that kingdom reign (Matt. 19:27-30) and glory. Part of God's desire for his children is that they "stake their claim" in Christ's future kingdom and thus fulfill his original desire and destiny and purpose for mankind. That is part of being an heir in the future.

So there we have it—from slaves to sons to heirs.

CONCLUSION

Things were pretty miserable for my grandchildren when they lived in the orphanages in Russia. The Russian government at the time they were adopted spent less than a dollar a day on these children for food and medical care. To say the least, there was a lot of neglect. Both kids had rickets because they rarely saw the sun. They were pretty much left in their cribs all day to cry. They had never seen a man. Bonding is a problem for most of these kids because without parents to love them and consistently nurse them, they have no sense of belonging. Needless to say, they enjoyed a better life after adoption.

But one day my granddaughter, Grace, reached into a fire and got burned. It hurt. She cried. However, wouldn't it be foolish for her to go to her parents and say, "I want to go back to Russia. I don't like it here. I got burned"? You too, as a Christian, may have gotten involved in the Christian life of faith and gotten burned. But how foolish to say to God, "Okay, I tried this faith thing and look where it's gotten me. I've gotten burned. I want to go back to living under the performance principle. I want to go back to the orphanage of the law."

That is exactly what the Galatians were doing, and that is exactly what the Neo-Galatianists of today are doing as well—trading the joy of a *thank-you* life for the burden of a *have-to* life. Falling from grace back into bondage. From liberty to law.

10

THE DANGER OF DRIFTING
Galatians 4:8-20

I can never forget the day I sat in a seminary classroom and the professor asked us to look at the man on our left and then the man on our right. Then he said, "Two out of three of you will not be in full-time ministry twenty years from now." In those days they did not let you into seminary unless you declared your desire to be a full-time minister. Today I wonder if that professor's estimate was low. One of the great dangers in the Christian life is drifting away from our initial devotion to Jesus. And if men who have committed their entire lives to follow and serve him are in danger of drifting, then what about the rest of the sheep in God's flock?

The book of Hebrews talks about the danger of drifting in 2:1. It gives us the picture of a boat tied to a dock, but for whatever reason its tether becomes loose and it drifts away. Nothing sudden. Just a slow, steady drift. All of us have known someone who ended up with a terrible substance abuse problem that began innocently, with just a mild usage. This is the way of sin, to gain a foothold, then gradually move us away from the road to life toward death.

Too often this is the case in the spiritual world. The Bible contains many warnings about the danger of drifting in the spiritual life. It seems that one of the dangers of drifting is to petrify, to develop a heart of stone. A heart of stone is filled with the cement of legalism—just going through the motions. It is when Christ becomes routine and worship becomes robotic. Instead of being the overflow of a grateful heart, our praise and adoration settle like rust on the bottom of empty, worn-out hearts with only faint echoes of the excitement and joy of a forgotten era in our walk with Christ.

Paul fears for his converts in Galatia. Their devotion has turned into duty; their turbulent desire into tedious discipline; their unbridled joy into a boring journey. So in Galatians 4:8-20 Paul warns his readers about the danger of drifting.

This is a transitional section. In his theological defense of his gospel, Paul defends justification by faith and sanctification by faith. He has just finished his defense of justification by faith, so now he transitions into his defense of sanctification by faith. Most of the time in Western Christianity when we say "saved," we mean what Paul calls justification, the moment in time when we put our complete trust (faith) in Christ as our Savior. That opens the gates of heaven. But much of the time when the NT says "saved," it is talking about sanctification.[79] And Paul's gospel includes the good news of deliverance from the power of sin (sanctification) as well as deliverance from the eternal penalty of sin (justification). Justification is by faith at a moment in time (Rom. 4:3), while sanctification is by faith moment by moment, over a long period of time (Rom. 1:17—"from faith to faith"; "the just shall live by faith"). Both are by faith.

Yes, this is a transitional section, but it is a long transition—thirteen verses. He brings up the problem in 4:8-11 and then gives us the solution in 4:12-20.

---

79   See Anderson and Reitman, *Portraits of Righteousness* for a fuller explanation of the word "saved" in Romans 5:9-10.

I. THE PROBLEM—GOING BACKWARD 4:8-11

> But then, indeed, when you did not know God, you served those which by nature are not gods. But now after you have known God, or rather are known by God, how is it that you turn again to the weak and beggarly elements, to which you desire again to be in bondage? You observe days and months and seasons and years. I am afraid for you, lest I have labored for you in vain.

Paul most likely refers to the Gentiles here in their pagan worship before they believed the gospel. The pagans were known for their graven images, or making gods out of rocks and wood. Rocks and wood are created things. If something is created, then it cannot be the Creator. The creator is always greater than that which he creates. So before these new believers received Christ, they were often worshipping created things, which by definition could not be gods. They were not gods by their very nature.

But now these Galatians do know God. The word "know" here is used twice. It speaks of an intimate relationship with God, a love relationship. But Paul stands mystified. To him it is unthinkable that his converts would experience the spiritual freedom of a love relationship with Jesus but choose to go back to a life of spiritual slavery to legalism. It would be like being married to Mel Gibson the Patriot and dumping him to marry Arnold Schwarzenegger the Terminator. Who in her right mind wants a love relationship with a deadly robot?

The Galatians have been duped into thinking that some days are holier than other days. Here is where we see the law lovers coming in to influence the Gentile Galatian converts. They were convincing them to keep the Law of Moses in order to be saved (sanctified). And so they were teaching them the importance of holy days. Keeping the Sabbath day holy was one of the Ten Commandments. You will remember that it is the only one of the Ten Commandments not repeated in the New Testament. That is one of the reasons we do not worship on Saturday. But this particular commandment was elevated in the Jewish social life so that much of their social structure was organized around keeping the Sabbath day holy. It is as though they worshipped the Sabbath more than the Savior.

So what are some of the things that cause believers to drift?

1. **Riches.** Jesus says riches are deceitful. How? Well, for one thing, they can deceive us into thinking we are better than other people, something the Bible calls pride. And pride cuts off the faucet of grace (James 4:6). Without grace we cannot progress in our walk with God. Another way riches can deceive us is to make us feel secure so that we don't need to depend on God. That is a spirit of independence, another look of pride.

2. **Bitterness.** This bitterness is usually toward a family member or friend who let you down. Or it could be a Christian leader who let you down. Now this person follows you around like a ball and chain. Your mind periodically drifts back to him, the hurts resurface, and you find yourself reviewing the situation and imagining how you could get even.

3. **Fear.** Obviously, fear can be paralyzing—especially the fear of following God. This happened to the Israelites at Kadesh-Barnea when the spies went into the land. Ten of the twelve scared the wits out of the people. This led to drifting (Heb. 2:1), hardness of heart (Heb. 3-4), stunted growth (Heb. 5:12-14), and divine discipline (Heb. 6; 10). Hebrews warns us that it all begins by drifting.

4. **Disillusionment.** This is often caused by trials and suffering. Most people don't sign up for suffering unless they are one of the apostles or Dietrich Bonhoeffer or Eric Liddell. So when it comes, it does not fit into their paradigm of what the Christian life is supposed to be all about. I recently spoke at a conference on "Suffering—the Gift No One Wants." After one of the talks, an elderly

woman came up to me and mentioned her granddaughter who had died of a disease at age twelve. She said she and her daughter, the child's mother, had prayed fervently for God's healing. It did not come. The grandmother I was talking to had not ceased going to church and believing in God. But her daughter had. She had completely turned away from her faith. Until we realize that suffering of all stripes (deserved because of our sins or undeserved, whether innocent like a child's disease or because of righteousness like the persecution of a missionary) is part of the normal Christian life, we are prime candidates for disillusionment.

5. **Legalism.** There is comfort and security in legalism. It can be measured and quantified. There is a routine. There is tradition. It is what we are used to. Usually there is repetition: Lord's Supper, Lord's Prayer, Book of Common Prayer, a certain service, a certain row, a certain seat. William James said, "Sow a thought, reap an action; sow an action, reap a habit; sow a habit, reap a destiny." If I were to adapt this for legalism, I would say, "Sow an action, reap a routine; sow a routine, reap a ritual; sow a ritual, ruin a relationship." No doubt some routines are good. But the danger of repeating any routine is that it can become a legalistic ritual, and rituals can easily ruin relationships.

Any of the above can lead to drifting, and many more. But regarding drifting, they all have one thing in common. The drifting is usually imperceptible along the way. It is usually very slow. But all of a sudden, a person wakes up, looks around, and says, "How did I ever get here?" If nothing else is said about drifting, let it be said that Christianity is not some sort of ritualistic routine of keeping rules; it is a dynamic relationship with the living God. So we have identified the problem; what is the solution?

II. THE SOLUTION—GO FORWARD 4:12-20

A. By Remembering Your Former Joy 4:12-16

Brethren, I urge you to become like me, for I became like you. You have not injured me at all. You know that because of physical infirmity I preached the gospel to you at the first. And my trial which was in my flesh you did not despise or reject, but you received me as an angel of God, even as Christ Jesus. What then was the blessing you enjoyed? For I bear you witness that, if possible, you would have plucked out your own eyes and given them to me. Have I therefore become your enemy because I tell you the truth?

Here Paul gives us a couple of hints to help us stop drifting or, better yet, never start. First of all, he reminds the Galatians of the joy they used to have in their Christian lives—how in spite of his own physical infirmities (stoned once and beaten eight times for his faith: five times by the Jews and three times by the Romans—2 Cor. 11:23-25), they received him as though he were an angel or Jesus himself. And they would have plucked their own eyes out and given them to him if it would have helped him. Some think his infirmity dealt with an eye disease or problem resulting from his stoning. At any rate the Galatians had so much love for Christ and for Paul his messenger, they would suffer themselves if it could help.

In the midst of this reminder of their early fervor for Christ, Paul mentions their "joy" (NIV 1984; probably better than "blessing" of NKJV and NASB). Paul wants them to remember the joy they had in their early years as Christians. Like the Ephesian church of Revelation 2, the Galatians had lost their first love. To recapture their first love, John tells the Ephesian church to return to their first works, that is, start doing the things you were doing when you were madly in love with Jesus. Quite often feelings follow actions.

I well remember what got my motor racing when I was a new Christian. It was when I went with a bunch of college kids to Balboa Beach and Newport Beach in California to learn how to share my faith. Jimmy Williams (Probe Ministries) and Bill Counts and Hal

Lindsey (the Three Musketeers of Campus Crusade for Christ at the time) took us out to beaches, dumped us off with clipboards and copies of "The Four Spiritual Laws" to share our faith. I had tried this once my first year at Rice, and it was a disaster. But then I had had no training. These guys trained us and turned us loose. I was amazed. Nobody kicked sand in our faces, and about half the people prayed right there on the beach to receive Christ. I was never the same.

But sometimes as a pastor I found it hard to get with unbelievers. I had to go create the opportunities to share. But it still worked. When I got a little ho-hum in my walk, all I had to do was go knock on some doors or visit a hospital or a jail and share Christ with hungry people to get excited again.

Willard Harley picked up on this principle of "doing the first works" in his marital counseling. He surveyed the thousands of couples over the years and found they spent an average of fifteen hours per week in a meaningful relationship with each other while they were engaged (movies and TV did not count—no talking). Years later, when their marriages got in trouble, they averaged spending one hour together per week, alone, having a meaningful relationship (which means talking). He encouraged them to go back to what they were doing when they were in "love." Well, with kids and businesses to run, it was hard for most of these troubled couples to get back to fifteen hours a week, but they did find when they hit the ten-hour mark, their marriages had improved dramatically. They had just stopped spending time together alone.

Was there a time in your Christian experience when you spent more time alone with God than you do today? If the answer to that question is yes, then be careful; you may be drifting but can't see it. Remember your former joy. Go back to doing what you were doing when your relationship with Jesus was vibrant and alive.

So this is the first step to prevent drifting or to stop drifting in one's spiritual life—remember your former joy and do the things you were doing that brought joy. The second step is to remember your future goal.

B. By Remembering Your Future Goal　　　　4:17-20

They zealously court you, but for no good; yes, they want to exclude you, that you may be zealous for them. But it is good to be zealous in a good thing always, and not only when I am present with you. My little children, for whom I labor in birth again until Christ is formed in you, I would like to be present with you now and to change my tone; for I have doubts about you.

Before spelling out the goal of our Christian lives, Paul makes a crucial observation about how we get sucked into legalism. It is through our desire for approval. The legalists are doing what legalists always do, creating an exclusive club of conformity from which to exclude any Galatians who would not conform. No one likes to be excluded. God built into us a desire for approval. Every person will seek it. The question is, approval from whom? Of course, God wants us to seek it from him. Paul wants the same thing for his spiritual children. But the Judaizers seek to exclude the Galatians from fellowship unless they conform to their lists of rules.

This is how it always works. There is a list. If you do not conform to the list, you get chastised and threatened with exclusion. You must conform, at least outwardly. It is a perverse substitute for true approval that can only come from God, who can judge the thoughts and intents of the heart. Paul instructed the Corinthians to "judge nothing before the time" and said he did not even judge himself (1 Cor. 4:1-5). That is because Paul completely entrusted all that he did unto "that day." And that is what he wants the Galatians to continue to do. And while they are trusting, God is moving them along toward his goal for their lives.

Paul uses some unusual imagery here. He portrays himself as a pregnant mother giving birth to his converts. He refers to the pain he endured while he journeyed forward to share the good news with them and to birth them into the faith. But he says the birthing process did not stop with their new birth as Christians. Now he continues in birth pangs while another birthing process is going on within his converts. Now the Galatians are pregnant themselves. That which is being formed within them is nothing other than Christ himself. The gestation period will take years, but the ultimate goal is that Christ or rather Christ-like character be formed in them. Christ-likeness—that's the goal.

It helps to stop spiritual drift or stagnation or even backsliding if we remember the goal of our faith. As Paul tells the Colossians, it is to present every man "perfect" in Christ Jesus (Col. 1:28). In Bill Gothard's course "Basic Institute in Youth Conflicts," which was going around the country decades ago, his workers would hand out little pins for us to wear. These pins had a bunch of letters and no words on them: PBPGINFWMY, which stood for "Please Be Patient; God Is Not Finished with Me Yet." It was a good reminder of two things: (1) all Christians are a work in progress; and (2) the goal of this process is to make us like Jesus. It helps to prevent drift if we remember where we are going and that we won't get there overnight.

The goal of the Christian life *is not* to get to heaven when we die. If that is our goal, then there isn't much to do but to wait around until we die. Naturally, spiritual lethargy and living for this world will set in. We are on a mission. It is to become like Christ through a life of daily faith. He is to be formed in us. But we cannot do that without doing what Christ did:

He fed the poor.
He healed the sick.
He preached the gospel.
He discipled men and women.
He spent time with his Father.
He had a global vision.
He ate meat others knew not of.
He expected miracles.
He endured suffering.
He became a servant.
He was obedient.
He respected authority.

He spent time in prayer.
He seized the day.

Either we are going forward or we are going backward. Legalism does not fuel the fire. Legalism throws cold water on our relationship with Christ. Duty says we *have to*; devotion says we *want to*.

Have you ever noticed how couples who have loved each other for decades actually start to display the same mannerisms and facial expressions? They have spent so much time gazing at each other and admiring each other that they begin to reflect each other. They think so much alike they can finish each other's sentences. That's the way it is in a love relationship. Paul doesn't want legalism to rob his children of that joy and that kind of love. It is lost by substituting the mundane duty of routine for the excitement of the relationally romantic.

CONCLUSION

People are drawn to love relationships. We all want to be loved. Genuine love will impact a life forever. I had two living grandmothers while growing up. One I called Grandmother and the other Grammie. Grandmother was from a successful, upper-middle-class family. She was witty, attractive, and proper. Grammie's husband died suddenly, leaving her penniless. Her children had to support her in her latter days. Grandmother always sent a card and a check on my birthday. Grammie didn't have any money, but she would write a nice letter and Scotch tape a dollar bill to the letter.

Grandmother never invited me or any of her grandchildren from my family to come to her home for a week to visit. But when I was hit by a car at age three, Grammie came to live with us for six months while she nursed me back to health. Grandmother would give me a perfunctory peck on the cheek when she saw me. Grammie read my favorite book at age six (*Peter Pan*) scores of times while she scratched my back.

When I got married, I drove with my new wife over a thousand miles so she could meet one of these two women before she died. *I wonder which one.* Both of these women passed on, and I cried at the funeral of one of them. *I wonder which one.* I knew without doubt that one of these women loved me. *I wonder which one.* When I was the ripe old age of eight, I decided it was time to run away from home. I didn't get far, but guess where I was going? Love draws all of us.

As the world looks on, cold, sterile orthodoxy does not draw them. But love does. Neo-Galatianism sucks the love and the life right out of our relationship with Christ. It's duty instead of devotion, rules over relationship, *have to* versus *want to.* The Christian life becomes more of a *job* than a *joy.*

11

A DECLARATION OF INDEPENDENCE

Galatians 4:21-5:1

Some time ago an ad appeared in a local newspaper for a reward offered to anyone who would kill an American, any American. Purportedly, the ad was placed by a Pakistani. Strangely enough, an Australian dentist decided to respond. Here is what he wrote:

> An American is English, or French, or Italian, Irish, German, Spanish, Polish, Russian or Greek. An American may also be Canadian, Mexican, African, Indian, Chinese, Japanese, Korean, Australian, Iranian, Asian, Arab, Pakistani or Afghan.
>
> An American may also be a Comanche, Cherokee, Osage, Blackfoot, Navaho, Apache, Seminole or one of the many other tribes known as native Americans. An American is Christian, or he could be Jewish, or Buddhist, or Muslim. In fact, there are more Muslims in America than in Afghanistan.

The only difference is that in America they are free to worship as each of them chooses. An American is also free to believe in no religion. For that he will answer only to God, not to the government, or to armed thugs claiming to speak for the government and for God.

An American lives in the most prosperous Land in the history of the world. The root of that prosperity can be found in the Declaration of Independence, which recognizes the God given right of each person to the pursuit of happiness. An American is generous. Americans have helped out just about every other nation in the world in their time of need, never asking a thing in return. When Afghanistan was over-run by the Soviet army 20 years ago, Americans came with arms and supplies to enable the people to win back their country!

As of the morning of September 11, Americans had given more than any other nation to the poor in Afghanistan. The national symbol of America, The Statue of Liberty, welcomes your tired and your poor, the wretched refuse of your teeming shores, the homeless, tempest tossed. These in fact are the people who built America.

Some of them were working in the Twin Towers the morning of September 11, 2001, earning a better life for their families. It's been told that the World Trade Center victims were from at least 30 different countries, cultures, and first languages, including those that aided and abetted the terrorists.

So you can try to kill an American if you must. Hitler did. So did General Tojo, and Stalin, and Mao Tse-Tung, and other bloodthirsty tyrants in the world. But, in doing so, you would just be killing yourself. Because Americans are not a particular people from a particular place. They are the embodiment of the human spirit of freedom. Everyone who holds to that spirit, everywhere, is an American.[80]

As I sit here writing in Germany, I cannot keep from thinking about the people who died here so we could be free. A week ago a friend and I visited Buchenwald, the concentration camp near Weimar, the old headquarters of the Weimar Republic. This is where many of the medical experiments were performed, where Dietrich Bonhoeffer was sent for two months before going to the prison where he was hanged, where more gypsies were killed than Jews. When Eisenhower saw this hellhole, he went down the road to Weimar and made the German citizens march through the piles of naked corpses stacked up for the crematorium so they could see what was going on right under their noses.

Yes, man appears to possess an indomitable drive for freedom. The specter of death cannot scare away the desire to be free. Ironically, however, men and women who will fight to the death for physical freedom lay down their spiritual arms faster than an Iraqi soldier in Desert Storm to become spiritual slaves. From the American Revolution to the French Revolution to the Bolshevik Revolution in Russia, men cry, *"Freedom!"* But when the one who roars like a lion (1 Pet. 5:7) opens his mouth, Christians surrender without a whimper.

It was as true in the early days of the church as it is today. Paul marveled that his Galatian converts had so quickly abandoned the good news of spiritual freedom he had preached. His new converts gave up their spiritual freedom in Christ faster than a lone man facing Alexander the Great's entire army would surrender. Paul can hardly stand it. So he pens Galatians, the Magna Carta of Christian liberty. And in Galatians 4:21-5:1 we read his Declaration of Independence for Christians.

---

80 "Australian Dentist Explains What an American Is," a12iggymom's blog, accessed August 12, 2014, http://a12iggymom.wordpress.com/2011/05/31/australian-dentist-explains-what-an-american-is/.

GALATIANS
"The Gospel of Grace"

In Galatians 4:8-20 Paul gives us a transition away from his theological defense of justification to his theological defense of sanctification. His gospel includes the good news of deliverance from the *power of sin* (sanctification) as well as deliverance from the eternal *penalty of sin* (justification). I repeat: justification is by faith at a moment in time (Rom. 4:3), and sanctification is by faith over a period of time (Rom. 1:17—"the just shall live by faith" from "faith to faith").

146

Here in 4:21-5:1 Paul uses a rare teaching device to help us understand the facts of freedom. He uses an allegory. It is a method of comparison seldom found in Scripture. When he wanted to make a comparison of similar things, Jesus used figures of speech called similes, metaphors, or parables. The simile made a like comparison by using the words "like" or "as"—the kingdom of God is like a mustard seed. The metaphor does the same thing as a simile only it does not use the words "like" or "as"—Peter, you are a rock. The parable does the same as the similes and metaphors, but it is longer. Nevertheless, a parable has only one main point or comparison or correspondence, not several. The allegory also makes a comparison, but it has several points of correspondence.

One of the early problems in hermeneutics (the science of interpretation) was to turn parables into allegories. Origen of Alexandria was a champion at this. He saw a point of correspondence in every character in the parable of the good Samaritan. Because of this allegorical approach, he strayed far from the plain meaning in many passages of Scripture.

We have said all this to help us understand this allegory. We know it is an allegory and not a parable because Paul tells us so— the word for "symbolic" in 4:24 is *allēgoroumena*. You can tell just by trying to pronounce the word that we are speaking of an allegory. Thus, we should look for several points of correspondence, not just one as in a parable. Paul uses this allegory to give an illustration of our independence (4:21-31); then he makes a declaration of our independence (5:1). Let's look at the illustration.

I. ILLUSTRATION OF OUR INDEPENDENCE 4:21-31

Tell me, you who desire to be under the law, do you not hear the law? For it is written that Abraham had two sons: the one by a bondwoman, the other by a freewoman. But he who was of the bondwoman was born according to the flesh, and he of the freewoman through promise, which things are symbolic. For these are the two covenants: the one from Mount Sinai which gives birth to bondage, which is Hagar—for this Hagar is Mount Sinai in Arabia, and corresponds to Jerusalem which now is, and is in bondage with her children—but the Jerusalem above is free, which is the mother of us all. For it is written:

"Rejoice, O barren,
You who do not bear!
Break forth and shout,
You who are not in labor!
For the desolate has many more children
Than she who has a husband."

Now we, brethren, as Isaac was, are children of promise. But, as he who was born according to the flesh then persecuted him who was born according to the Spirit, even so it is now. Nevertheless what does the Scripture say? "Cast out the bondwoman and her son, for the son of the bondwoman shall not be heir with the son of the freewoman." So then, brethren, we are not children of the bondwoman but of the free.

Here are the various points of correspondence:

ABRAHAM	
ISAAC	ISHMAEL
SARAH	HAGAR
FREE	BOUND
FAITH	FLESH
ABRAHAMIC COVENANT	MOSAIC COVENANT
JERUSALEM ABOVE	JERUSALEM BELOW
SPIRITUAL SEED	PHYSICAL SEED
FREE FROM THE LAW	BOUND TO THE LAW

This illustration is very confusing if we forget that Paul is not tracing actual history; he is using people and places in history to be symbols in his allegory. He uses Hagar, an Egyptian woman, as a symbol of Mt. Sinai, the Mosaic covenant, and the city of Jerusalem in Israel. Historically, of course, Hagar had nothing to do with Mt. Sinai, the Mosaic covenant, or earthly Jerusalem.

Ironically, however, Paul uses the bondwoman, Hagar, as a symbol of the physical seed of Abraham who are still in bondage to the Law of Moses given at Sinai. Paul is saying these legalists *of the flesh* came forth from the *earthly* Jerusalem and were wreaking havoc in the local churches of Galatia.

In contrast, Paul uses Sarah as a symbol of freedom and claims his Galatian converts are the spiritual seed of Abraham and hence children of Sarah, children who are heirs of the promises to Abraham, children of the free woman.

Perhaps no people who have ever lived have left us a better example of the irony of a people who would die for physical freedom while surrendering willingly to spiritual slavery than certain sects among the Jewish people. In AD 70, Titus, son of the Roman emperor, had destroyed the Jewish revolution in Jerusalem. The Zealots, so named because of their zeal for the law combined with their willingness to fight for it with guerrilla warfare as their forefathers, the Maccabees, did, tried to take over the rebellion against the Romans in Jerusalem in AD 66. But after the Romans won, the Zealots did not give up. They headed for Masada, which comes from the Hebrew word for "fortress." This rock fortress, rising thirteen hundred feet above the southern part of the Dead Sea, had been used for protection by Jewish people since the time of David. Herod the Great, perhaps the most paranoid political leader of all time (he had the children in Bethlehem killed and six of his own sons) until Joseph Stalin, spruced Masada up for his own use.

Here the Zealots fled from the Romans, who sent the powerful Tenth Legion to encircle Masada. They set siege and used ten thousand Jewish slaves to build a four-mile wall completely encircling the high fortress. Since there was no drinking water nearby for the Roman soldiers, they forced the slaves to make a continuous round trip of twenty miles to Ein Gedi to bring them water—for three years.

You can still see the path these Jewish slaves left as you stand on the northern end of the fortress.

But inside Masada they had their own water, crops, and even livestock. Year after year the Romans camped around this great fortress, the last symbol of Jewish freedom. Nine hundred sixty-seven men, women, and children were alive the night before the Romans broke through the western wall by building a ramp six hundred feet long. But when they took the wall, their hollow victory was overshadowed by what Josephus, the Jewish historian, called "the courage of their resolution, and the contempt toward death which so great a number of them had shown." All but seven of the 967 people had committed suicide or been killed voluntarily by the heads of their families, respectively. Two women and five children hid in a cistern to tell the tale.

Ironic. The Zealots. Men and women who would rather die physically than become Roman slaves, but men and women who voluntarily gave their spiritual lives to be slaves to the Law of Moses, a burden Peter the apostle said was too heavy for the most dedicated of Jews to carry (Acts 15:10). Christ has set us free.

Enough of Paul's illustration of our independence. Now he makes his declaration.

II. DECLARATION OF OUR INDEPENDENCE 5:1

Stand fast therefore in the liberty by which Christ has made us free, and do not be entangled again with a yoke of bondage.

Paul declares that we are free in our *position*; therefore, we should stand free in our *condition*. Christ has set us free from the law; therefore, don't get ensnared by the law again. How foolish that would be!

What would we say about a man who was released from prison but a few months later knocked at the prison gates and asked to be recommitted? **Astonishing!** And what would we say about a slave who was bought from a tyrant by a merciful master and set free only to voluntarily return to his old tyrant to be used and abused? **Incredible!** And what would we say about a person who was raised from the dead only to go back to the owner of the cemetery and beg to be reburied? **Insane!** Our response to these physical incredulities is only surpassed by Paul's marvel that his converts, who have been set free from bondage to the law, have returned to be shackled by it once again.

So here Paul **cries, "Freedom!"** It is his declaration of independence for Christians. So how do we become so easily trapped in legalism?

1. By neglecting the more important values of godliness (Matt. 23:23-24).

Here we find that the Jews tithed mint, anise, and cumin (spices—Jesus condoned this practice) but neglected the more important matters of the law like justice, mercy, and faith. Here Jesus notes a hierarchy of values. Some things are more important than others. Quite often people focus on the little things that are easily measurable because they are already failing in the more important things. A man might be proud of the fact that he doesn't drink or smoke or chew, but then he goes home and beats his wife and kids.

Mercy is one of the toughest on the list. That's why Jesus said to the Pharisees after they criticized his disciples for picking corn on the Sabbath, "Go and learn this. God desires mercy and not sacrifice." The interesting word in that verse for me is the word *learn*. Apparently, mercy doesn't come easily for us. We must learn how to have mercy. Our own self-righteousness causes us to be very hard on those we think less righteous than ourselves. We tend to be very harsh on people who violate our personal taboos while at the same time pride is staring us in the face every time we look in the mirror. Can you think of something God hates more than pride? Not according to his hate list in Proverbs 6. Pride is at the pinnacle of problems God hates. We better learn mercy. God will judge us without

151

mercy some day if we have been unmerciful to others (James 2:12-13).

2. By putting more emphasis on external cleanliness than internal cleanliness (Matt. 23:25-28).

I read about a police officer in Galveston, Texas, who was known for having the cleanest boat around. Galveston is right on the Gulf of Mexico, and many people live there because of their love of the water. The unusual thing about this policeman was that he went through the effort to wash *and* gunk (cover it with a protective, slimy goo to keep it from rusting from the salt water) his boat every time he took it into the water. Gunking was very time-consuming and not necessary every time the boat was used. Come to find out this same policeman had been pilfering from the impounded marijuana stored at the police station.

One of the signs of obsessive-compulsive disorder is an inordinate preoccupation with external cleanliness, seen especially in the repetition of hand washing. This kind of focus on cleanliness on the outside usually indicates dirt (unresolved guilt) on the inside. Isn't it interesting that the Pharisees often required washing of the hands seven times before eating? That did not come from the Bible. And Jesus says on the inside they are full of dead men's bones. First John 1 says joy comes from a clean conscience, and 1 Timothy 1:5 says without a clean conscience we cannot love other people.

3. By a judgmental spirit rooted in an attitude of superiority and pride (Matt 23:29-30).

What causes a judgmental spirit and spiritual pride? The same thing that causes a focus on external cleanliness: a dirty conscience. A dirty conscience beats us up with more vengeance than a haymaker from Mike Tyson or former world heavyweight boxing champion George Foreman in his heyday could. It is hard to live with a dirty conscience, but it is easier if we can compare ourselves to others whom we believe are more sinful than we are.

What do these words remind you of?

This administration has proved it is utterly incapable of cleaning out the corruption which has completely eroded it, and reestablishing the faith of the people in the honesty and morality of their government employees. The investigations which have been conducted to date have only scratched the surface. For every case that is exposed, there are ten which are successfully covered up, and even then this administration will go down in history as the "scandal a day" administration. Typical of the moral standards of the administration, that when they are caught red-handed with pay-off money in their bank accounts, the only defense they can give us is that they won the money in a poker game, or a crap game, or they hit the daily double. A new class of royalty has been created in the United States, and its princes of privileges and payoffs include the racketeers who get concessions on their income tax cases, the insiders who get favored treatment on government contracts, the influential peddler with his key to the White House, the government employee who uses his position to feather his nest. The tragedy, however, is not that the corruption exists, but that it is defended and condoned by the President and his administration officials. We have had corruption defended by those in high places. If they don't admit that corruption exists, how can we expect them to clean it up?[81]

---

81   Richard M. Nixon, http://www.u-s-history.com/pages/h1948.html.

These words were spoken by Richard Nixon in 1951 concerning the Truman administration. They came back to haunt him as he resigned in disgrace for covering up illegal political activity.

4. By getting sucked into the performance principle (Gal. 4:3).

The more years we spend under the performance principle (I must perform well in order to overcome my sense of insecurity and worthlessness), the harder it will be to break the addiction. Of course, many times Jesus breaks addictions instantly. In other cases, it takes time. My experience with this one is that I am a recovering performance addict, and will be the rest of my life. That means I must always be on guard for ways my flesh feeds on performance to take away my pain. One "stiff drink" of performance can set my addiction going again.

Of course, we have to remember that the desire to perform for approval is built into us. At the Judgment Seat of Christ we want God's approval. We want him to say, "Well done, good and faithful servant." But performing to gain acceptance is different than performing because we know we are accepted. Those who perform for acceptance tend to live miserable lives because they never know if their performance has been good enough to be accepted. Even worse is to perform to gain approval from men in order to prove to myself that I have acceptance from God. This creates the twisted impossibility of controlling God through controlling other people, neither of which will ever happen. No wonder it makes us so miserable when we try to do it.

However, when a child knows he is unconditionally loved because he has unconditional acceptance as a member of the family, that child is free to perform for approval instead of acceptance. He knows he is accepted and loved whether he performs well or not. Such unconditional acceptance only motivates him to perform at a higher level. As Titus 2:11ff. claims, grace actually **teaches** us how to live godly lives in this present age. The law doesn't do that; grace (unconditional acceptance) does.

CONCLUSION

Why do people want to be free? Obviously, because slavery breeds misery. As I mentioned earlier, in 2001, I broke a hip while skiing in Colorado. Because the hospitals were so crowded, the operation was delayed and was not successful. Over a three-year period, the repaired hip caved in slowly and died. Thus, in 2004, I had it replaced. I went into surgery directly after leading a tour of Paul's Journeys in Greece and Turkey. After the operation I was feeling pretty good, so I told Betty there was no need for her to spend the night in an uncomfortable bed in the hospital. So she went home about 4:00 p.m.

I hadn't had anything to eat for a long time, so I started getting a headache. I don't get them often, but I keep some Imitrex in my bag for those occasions. Problem was, I couldn't move. So when the nurse came in, I asked if she would get me my bag so I could get the Imitrex. She said, "No." She didn't speak English very well, so I asked again. "No," she said. "Why? It was prescribed by my personal physician." She said, "He is not in charge here." Whoaaaa. All of a sudden my pain increased. Why? Because she laid down the law.

Well, the pain from the operation was slowly increased as the anesthesia left my system (an epidural), so I lined up my vials of pain medicine I had kept from other operations: hydrocodone, oxycodone, and something else I can't remember. Good stuff. But my nurse came in and took them away. "What are you doing? That's mine." "Can't have it." Now I was really under the law, and guess what? I was getting mad. After all, I was hurting. *Do you feel my pain? I **deserve** some pain medication. I paid good money for this operation, and now this hospital **owes me** a little consideration.*

Unfortunately, the anger was compounding my headache. I don't do well with headaches. They are usually followed by nausea. So, no food for twenty-four hours, no pain medicine, plus a headache led to vomiting. All over the bed. So, these little nurses came in and spent about twenty minutes at 2:00 a.m. trying to get me off the bed so they could clean it up. Finally, the job was done, but both my head and my hip were hurting. They turned out the lights and left. It was cold. I couldn't sleep because I was on Mediterranean time. Around 3:00 a.m., I started sweating even though it was cold. I was under the law and miserable.

It got so bad I drenched the sheets in sweat. This was not right. I shouldn't have been sweating like this when I was this cold. I turned on the lights. The sheets were covered with blood. I hadn't been sweating. The IV had pulled out, and I was bleeding all over the bed—one pint. Fortunately, I had prepackaged two pints of my own blood before the operation. Another half hour to get me off the bed, clean things up, and turn out the lights. But my headache was still there, so at 6:30 a.m., guess what? Yes, I barfed all over the bed again.

Finally, at around 7:30 a.m., my surgeon's assistant was making his rounds. "Things okay?" I didn't have the energy to tell him all that had gone on, so I just asked him if he could get me some pain medication. In my other operations I had had a little pump next to my bed so I could self-medicate, but not here. "You haven't had any pain medication since the operation?" No. "Well, you can have it every four hours—all you have to do is ask for it." My, my, my. I wasn't under the law at all. I was free to have pain meds all that time. I just didn't know it. What we had here was a failure to communicate. Suddenly, I was free, and with freedom came a measure of joy.

12

SEVEN DANGERS OF LEGALISM

Galatians 5:2-12

How would you like to spend your whole life running the wrong way? On January 1, 1929, Georgia Tech played UC Berkeley, in the Rose Bowl. Roy Riegels was the captain of the UC Golden Bears and a first-team all-American. Midway through the second quarter Riegels picked up a fumble by Tech. He was just thirty yards away from scoring for his team. But he got disoriented and ran sixty-nine yards in the wrong direction. His own teammate caught up with him and tried to turn him around, but by then the Georgia Tech players had caught up with him and tackled him at the one-yard line. He was so humiliated by his mistake that his coach and teammates had to plead with him to play the second half.

The play led to a safety in favor of Georgia Tech, who won the game 8-7. The two-point safety made the difference. Roy spent the rest of his life (d. 1993) known as "Wrong Way Riegels." In 2003, a panel from the College Football Hall of Fame and CBS Sports chose

Riegels's "Wrong Way Run in the Rose Bowl" as one of the six "Most Memorable Moments of the Twentieth Century."[82]

According to Matthew 7:21-23, many who have served in the name of Christ (preached in his name, cast out demons in his name, done miracles in his name) will be surprised when he says, "I never knew you"—*wrong way*. These will not enter the kingdom of heaven, which is speaking of unbelievers that will not get into heaven.

But you are a believer. You have assurance of your salvation based on the promises of God. Is it possible to show up at the Judgment Seat of Christ (just for believers) and have him look at you and the angels and say, "Here stands Wrong Way [**your last name**]"? That's what very well may happen to every believer caught up in Neo-Galatianism—*wrong way*. It is the wrong way to live the Christian life. It is a *have-to* life rather than a *thank-you* life. Let's now look at seven dangers of legalism (Neo-Galatianism).

I. A LEGALIST FORFEITS THE SUBSTITUTIONARY LIFE OF CHRIST (5:1-2).

Stand fast therefore in the liberty by which Christ has made us free, and do not be entangled again with a yoke of bondage. Indeed I, Paul, say to you that if you become circumcised, Christ will profit you nothing.

We quote 5:1 again to underscore the fact that in verse 2 Paul is addressing those whom Christ has set free. He claims these people were set free by the cross, but now they are drifting back into works. They were not justified by works. But now they are seeking to be sanctified by works of the law rather than by the works of faith (and some of them who are already justified still think their justification depends on their good works—5:5).

The word "profit" (NKJV) or "value" (NIV) or "benefit" (NASB)

---

82   "Roy Riegels," Wikipedia, accessed August 12, 2014, http://en.wikipedia.org/wiki/Roy_Riegels.

is *opheleō*, which, according to BDAG, means "to be useful, beneficial, or profitable." So Christ was "beneficial" for getting these believers into the Christian life (saved in the justification sense), but not for living the Christian life (sanctification). Christ was profitable for getting them into heaven, but he is of no profit (use) at all for living a godly Christian life. Why? Because the Neo-Galatianist is trying to do it by the flesh.

Let us remember Galatians 2:20: "I am crucified with Christ: nevertheless, I live; yet not I, but ***Christ lives*** in me" (KJV). What is the hardest thing for a nonbeliever to believe? The substitutionary **death** of Christ (this gets a person justified). And what is the hardest thing in the world for a believer to believe? The substitutionary **life** of Christ. This gets a person sanctified. When we forfeit the substitutionary **life** of Christ (Christ lives in me), we are on our own to try to live the Christian life. Impossible. We will have failure for breakfast, defeat for lunch, and depression for dinner. Or we will just become good actors and self-deceived.

II. A LEGALIST LIVES A HAVE-TO LIFE INSTEAD OF A THANK-YOU LIFE (5:3).

> And I testify again to every man who becomes circumcised that he is a debtor to keep the whole law.

The word "debtor" implies a have-to life. The NIV translates it "obligated," as does the ESV. The word is *opheiletēs*, which means "one under obligation" (BDAG). Could the text be clearer? A Neo-Galatianist is a debtor. He is obligated to be good. If this isn't a have-to life, I don't know what is. This is not a want-to life or a thank-you life. Trust me. It won't be as enjoyable.

I'm writing in Germany right now in a beautiful retreat center near Hanover. While eating dinner last night, one of the young people (twenty years old) wanted to practice his English. So he told me he plays three musical instruments: flute, piano, and violin. I asked how long he had been playing. He said he began with the flute at age six, then added piano at nine, and violin at fourteen. Then I asked which one he enjoyed the most. He said the violin. I asked why. He said because his parents hammered away about the piano: "You *must* play the piano." So he hated it. "But I chose to play the violin. I was free not to play it, but I wanted to play it, so it brings me the most joy." That's it. On average, people living a have-to life do not enjoy their Christianity as much as those living a thank-you life.

And notice the legalist is not allowed to pick and choose which laws he would like to obey. He can't just choose the Ten Commandments. The Torah included moral, civil, and ceremonial laws. If someone wanted to obey part of the Law of Moses, he **had to** keep the entire Law of Moses. The law was a seamless garment (see James 2:1-13). We have Neo-Galatianists in America today who want to impose just part of the Law of Moses, either on their followers so they can become sanctified or on our federal government. They miss this point. If we are going to go back under the Law of Moses, Paul says we have to go all the way (sacrificing animals again?).

III. THE LEGALIST LIVES A "LOW" LIFE (5:4-6).

You have become estranged from Christ, you who attempt to be justified by law; you have fallen from grace. For we through the Spirit eagerly wait for the hope of righteousness by faith. For in Christ Jesus neither circumcision nor uncircumcision avails anything, but faith working through love.

Ruth Paxson once wrote a book entitled *Life on the Highest Plane*. It was about a life of liberty as opposed to a life of law. The higher plane was the life of liberty. To live a life of law was life on a lower plane. That is what Paul is getting at here. He contrasts a life of grace and a life of law. To live a life of law is to have fallen from the higher plane of living, the life oriented around grace. He also contrasts a life of works (circumcision) and a life of faith ("righteousness by faith... faith working through love").

Two errors of Neo-Galatianism are apparent from this verse. First are those who take the Arminian approach and think to "fall from grace" means to lose one's salvation. By taking "fallen from grace" out of context, they understand the phrase to mean fall from a state of grace. If one dies in a state of grace, according to this approach, he gets to go to heaven. But if he falls from this state of grace because of sin in his life, he will go to hell, according to Arminianism.

But this is all completely foreign to the context. The issue is living under the law as a way of sanctification or living by grace. At this point in Paul's epistle the primary error deals with sanctification (Gal. 3:3), going on to maturity through the flesh. But this leads us to the second error apparent from this verse. Many of the people confused about sanctification are also confused about justification. And this is exactly what happens when the Millennium is removed from our understanding of the prophetic future (eschatology). Both judgment seats (the Judgment Seat of Christ and the Great White Throne) collapse into one judgment seat before which both believers and unbelievers appear. They are judged for their works simultaneously like the sheep and goats (Matt. 25:31ff.). Some go to heaven; some go to hell. No wonder people are confused about the gospel. Nowhere does it say the people at these judgment seats are judged for their faith or lack thereof. No wonder the church taught for twelve hundred years that we get to heaven through meritorious works.

Confusion in one area of theology leads to confusion in another area. That is why I like to say systematic theology is spreadsheet theology. If we change one column, it can easily affect other columns in our theology as well. Confusion over sanctification can lead to confusion over justification. Just as in Galatians 2:17 these people are still trying to be justified. That's what the verse says.

"*Attempt* to be justified" (NKJV) is "trying to be justified" (NIV) or "seeking to be justified" (NASB). This is what is called a conative present by Greek grammarians, which just means the subject of the sentence is attempting to do something but can't get there.[83] The word

---

83   Daniel B. Wallace, *Greek Grammar Beyond the Basics* (Grand Rapids, MI: Zondervan, 1996), 535.

"attempt" is in italics in the NKJV text because it is not actually in the Greek text. Neither is "seeking" or "trying." Because Paul has said no one can actually be justified by keeping the law (2:16), he would contradict himself if he implied here that someone could be justified by keeping the law. Hence, we think this is an example of the conative present. But enough grammar. What does all this have to do with Neo-Galatianism?

A lot. The subject here is really sanctification. In 5:1, Paul says Christ has freed these people. But because they have confused sanctification and justification, many of them who are justified are trying to maintain their justification by their works or trying to prove they are justified by their works. There you have it—Neo-Galatianism. Shall we say it again? The Arminians think they must have good works until they die or they lose their salvation; the Calvinists think they must have good works until they die or they never had salvation. And the Roman Catholics have always taught they must have good works in order to complete their justification (a process that begins with infant baptism and continues until death).

Some will say, "Well, you just condemned 99 percent of professing Christians." No, I haven't. Heaven or hell is based on what we believe, not on what we do. I have no way of knowing what someone believes; neither do you. Belief is internal. We can see the fruit; only God can see the root. Only he can judge the heaven or hell issue because only he knows what is in the heart of a person. I suspect there are believers who will be part of the bride of Christ from most groups who name the name of Christ. But no human really knows. But to get there, no matter what group you come from, your justification comes by faith alone in Christ alone. Of course, this includes all the OT saints, Tribulation saints, millennial saints—all must enter the gates of heaven through the blood of Christ. His death was retroactive for all who lived before the cross and forward acting for all those who have lived or live or will live after the cross.

What we can know is that Paul is concerned about a group of his converts who very quickly slipped into Galatianism, which he calls a different gospel than the one he preached to them (1:6). The good news (gospel) that Paul preached actually included both justification and sanctification (Rom. 1:16-18). These people had gotten both issues mixed up to the point that works of the flesh permeated both doctrines. Now, if this could happen to the Galatians who are just a couple of years or so removed from Paul's preaching, what about us? According to F. Torrance in his doctoral dissertation, by year AD 100, salvation by grace through faith was completely missing in Christian literature until the Reformation.[84] Apparently, Neo-Galatianism had its roots in the first century and had taken over by the second.

This really shouldn't surprise us. Every morning I wake up, my default setting is on the flesh, which in my case means performance. My flesh wants to perform for acceptance and for approval—from God and from people. It is a symptom of my own sense of insecurity and insignificance. And my flesh never loses its power. It cannot be reformed. It is not getting weaker. This concept is part of the legalistic system of self-reformation, or reformation through works of the law. I am getting better and better because I am keeping these rules in the sight of men.

But the gospel of grace knows no such sham. We realize the flesh is as bad today as it was the moment I believed. So we don't try to reform it. Neither did Paul. He tried to recognize it and chose not to walk in it. Someone has suggested that all religion tends toward legalism. That means me. It means you. It means my church and your church, my brand of Christianity and your brand. Neo-Galatianism is something of which we all need to be wary. We should expect to find it everywhere. Why? Because the flesh is everywhere. Country western singer Garth Brooks is not the only one with "friends in low places." Neo-Galatianism is a "low" life.

Paul wants to make it perfectly clear that justification is by faith ("righteousness by faith") and sanctification is by faith ("faith working through love"—see Rom. 1:17, "from faith to faith"). The

---

84   Thomas F. Torrance, "The Doctrine of Grace in the   Apostolic Fathers" (doctrinal dissertation, Basel, 1948).

"righteousness by faith" mentioned is most likely a reference to the imputed righteousness of Christ that comes by faith alone in Christ alone (Rom. 4:3).[85] This righteousness is the perfect life of Christ credited to us in our accounts in heaven when we trusted him as our Savior. But when Paul mentions "faith working through love," he has shifted from our position in heaven to our condition on earth. Here he is referring to sanctification. We are justified by grace through faith, and we are sanctified by grace through faith.

IV. THE LEGALIST FORFEITS THE HOLY SPIRIT TO FOLLOW MEN (5:7-8).

You ran well. Who hindered you from obeying the truth? This persuasion does not come from Him who calls you.

Neo-Galatianism does not come from reading the Bible and following the Holy Spirit. It comes from reading men who write about the Bible and following their teachings. Or preachers. Jesus never put anyone under the law; it takes men to do that. I love to use what I call the twelve-year-old test when teaching the Scriptures. Twelve-year-olds are smart. Their brains are almost fully formed. They can think well.

So, when faced with a controversial passage, I like to ask twelve-year-olds what they think it means. They get it right (right from my perspective, of course) 90 percent of the time. Why? Because the plain meaning of the text is usually the right meaning. We have to be educated out of the truth, or the plain meaning.

I once had a commercial airline pilot come to my office with some questions about dispensationalism. So I took him to the only verse in the whole Bible I need to convince me of dispensationalism—Daniel

---

85 Though this could be the righteousness of sanctification (see Anderson and Reitman, *Portraits of Righteousness*, 35-36), the near use of the verb "attempt to be justified" in 5:4 leads us to believe Paul is referencing imputed righteousness here.

9:24, which begins, "Seventy weeks are determined for your people and for your holy city." Now if I asked a twelve-year-old what people Daniel meant in this verse, if he or she had any Bible background at all, the twelve-year-old would say, "The Jews." And the holy city of Daniel? "Jerusalem." But not my well-educated friend. He said "your people" meant all the people of God for all time. The holy city? Why, that is the New Jerusalem of Revelation 21-22, of course. He went on to tell me the church was everywhere in the OT post-Moses. My friends, I assure you he did not get that understanding from reading the Bible. He got that from reading what other men have written about the Bible. And after a while, it gets pretty easy to tell which men someone is reading just from the phrases he uses. Again, you have to be educated out of the obvious.

Paul knew this new "persuasion" was not from God.

V. THE LEGALIST IS OFTEN CHARACTERIZED BY CRUST AND CORROSION (5:9).

A little leaven leavens the whole lump.

Leaven, or yeast, would spread its way throughout a lump of dough. So legalism may start slowly, but before long it can take over one's entire Christian life or church or parachurch organization.

VI. THE LEGALIST WILL BE HELD RESPONSIBLE FOR THOSE HE INFLUENCES (5:10).

I have confidence in you, in the Lord, that you will have no other mind; but he who troubles you shall bear his judgment, whoever he is.

It is no small thing to lead others astray with unbiblical doctrine. James 3:1 actually discourages people from teaching with the reason that the teacher will receive a stricter judgment. Now we all know that church people and the world hold religious leaders up to a higher standard than their own. As one church member told me, "I like my preacher to be a little more holy than I am." Wonder where he got that?

But the context of James 3:1 is the Judgment Seat of Christ. That is what he has been talking about since 2:12 (see *Triumph Through Trials* by this author). So I would suggest that the teacher receives a stricter judgment at the Judgment Seat of Christ. But that doesn't seem to jibe with James 2:1 and Romans 2:11. The former tells us that it is wrong to treat people differently (show partiality), and the latter verse says God does not show partiality. He treats us all the same. Yet James 3:1 claims teachers are treated differently—they receive a stricter judgment. How do we explain this?

May I suggest that teachers receive a stricter judgment because each of us is judged according to the light we have been given (Matt. 13:10-15). Because a teacher must spend a lot of time in the Word of God in order to teach it, he or she receives more light than most. The teachers are responsible for that light and will be judged accordingly. The greater the light, the stricter the judgment.

Thus, it is a dangerous thing to promote Neo-Galatianism. To whom much is given much is required (Luke 12:48). Each one of us will be judged based on the talents we are given. The guy with one talent in Matthew 25 was not judged for having only one, but for not putting that talent at least with the bankers. And those who divide the Word of God have the greatest responsibility of all. Second Timothy 2:15 speaks of **rightly** dividing the word of truth to be approved and not ashamed (at the Judgment Seat of Christ).

VII. THE LEGALIST NEUTRALIZES THE CROSS (5:11-12).

> And I, brethren, if I still preach circumcision, why do I still suffer persecution? Then the offense of the cross has ceased. I could wish that those who trouble you would even cut themselves off!

"Offense" is the word *skandalon*, which means "stumbling block" and is obviously the word from which we get *scandal*. What was the stumbling block of the cross? That Jesus paid it all. The penalty we deserved for our sins was completely paid for by his death on the cross. There is nothing left for us to do but accept what he has already done for us.

The legalist neutralizes this message by saying that I too **must add to** what Christ has done by being a good person or performing works of the law. By saying, "I must now do this," we mollify the idea that the cross was sufficient. This is an offense **to** the cross and to God because it says his offering was not enough to open the gates of heaven. It also says there is not enough power in the "crucified life" (see Gal. 2:20) to live a victorious Christian life.

Larry Moyer of EvanTell likes to tell congregations there are three types of people in the world who want to go to heaven: (1) Those who say you can go to heaven by being good. But if that is true, says Moyer, then Christ didn't have to die, did he? (2) Those who think you have to believe in Jesus but also have to live a good life. But if that is true, then Jesus did not do enough, did he? (3) Those who believe Jesus paid it all.

I have gone with evangelistic teams around my neighborhood (about five hundred homes). Most of the people in this subdivision claim to be churchgoers. But of those who claim to go to church regularly, 80 percent of them say we get into heaven by believing in Jesus and living a good life. That is Neo-Galatianism with regard to justification. Where did they get this misunderstanding? Not from the Bible.

Now there is a subversive way most teachers of legalism explain this deception of good works or a good life to reach heaven. "I am not doing the good works; God is. God does the good works through me so that they are his works, not mine." This sounds pious. However, the problem is that neither Paul nor any other NT author makes such a false distinction between good works done by us or by God through us. The contrast is always between faith and works. Again, we are leaving the plain meaning of Scripture to be educated out of the truth.

CONCLUSION—HOW CAN I STOP LEGALISM IN MY LIFE?

1. **Flip the power switch—from the flesh to faith (5:5-6).**

   The flesh operates through my power; faith operates through God's power.

2. **Flip the motive switch—from the law to love (5:6).**

   It's the difference between a have-to life and a thank-you life.

3. **Flip the expectation switch—from your kingdom to God's kingdom (5:5).**

   The hopes of the legalist are in this world; so are his disappointments.

Michael Eaton tells the story of his own pilgrimage through the dark and discouraging catacombs of Reformed theology in his book *No Condemnation*, based on his dissertation "A Theology of Encouragement—A Step Towards a Non-Legalistic Soteriology." Though steeped in the writings of Reformed scholars, he found very little joy in his own Calvinistic church in London. In fact, he found most of the members of his church to be "narrow-minded, introspective and pharisaical."[86] "Why," he asked, "was it that the Reformed tradition seemed to consist of an ossified legalism, a crippling introspection, and a harshness of spirit that seemed nothing like the Jesus of the Bible?" He traced the problem back to their Reformed theology. But he didn't stop there. As he studied Arminianism, he discovered the same crippling lack of assurance of salvation he noticed among the Calvinists. In describing the Calvinism of Asahel Nettleton, a powerful evangelical preacher in nineteenth-century America, and John Fletcher, an Arminian friend of John Wesley, he wrote:

---

86 Michael Eaton, *No Condemnation* (Downers Grove, IL: InterVarsity, 1995), 5.

These great men exemplify a theological problem that has troubled evangelical churches and preachers since the 17th century, if not before. On the one hand, Nettleton's doubts related to the *genuineness* of salvation. On the other, Fletcher said no Christian could be absolutely sure about the *permanence* of their salvation. Nettleton's teaching has been popularly summarized in the phrase "Once saved, always saved"—but he was not quite sure that he was even once saved! John Fletcher taught "Once saved, maybe lost"! I find neither doctrine very encouraging. In fact, both seem rather terrifying. My certainty of salvation is Jesus. My trust is in him. But am I to believe, with Nettleton, that my salvation may not be genuine, and that what I think is salvation may turn out delusive? If so, I shall spend all my life wondering whether I am really saved or not. Or am I to believe with Fletcher that my salvation may not be permanent and I have to work hard at keeping it? If so, I shall live my life in the fear that perhaps I shall not keep going.[87]

It wasn't until Eaton discovered the freedom and power of the substitutionary **life** of Christ that he was able to let go of the necessity to perform for his salvation—either to keep from losing it or to prove that he had it. Like Roy Riegels, Eaton had spent most of his Christian life running the wrong way. Fortunately he turned around and found the joy of his free salvation while still in midlife. Let's not spend our entire Christian lives running the wrong way and not find out until the Lord comes.

---

87   Ibid., 3-4.

13

BALANCING THE CHRISTIAN LIFE
Galatians 5:13-18

S ome of you will recognize this title from a book written by Charles Ryrie with the same name.[88] We hear a lot about the balanced Christian life, but it is difficult to find and even more difficult to recognize when you are there. Howard Hendricks used to say, "The balanced Christian life is that midway point we pass as we swing from one extreme to the other." If we can agree that Jesus was the only one who ever lived a balanced "Christian" life, then we can also agree that all of us are out of balance in one way or another.

Nevertheless, the balanced Christian life is still something we should seek. In a general sense, we tend to drift into one of two errors regarding Christian behavior: law or license. Martin Luther described the early years of the Christian life as a drunken man trying to ride a horse—he is always falling off on one side or the other. He either falls on the side of legalism or on the side of license. The first is living

---

88   Charles C. Ryrie, *Balancing the Christian Life* (Chicago: Moody Bible Institute, 1994).

according to a law system, while the second is living according to our lusts. Obviously, neither is a balanced Christian life.

However, it might be said that Galatians 5:13-18 goes far beyond mere balance. In this passage Paul shows us how to live a life that is transcendent, and even brings heaven to earth.

GALATIANS
"The Gospel of Grace"

From the outline above we can see that we are well into Paul's theological defense of sanctification by faith. The focus is on our freedom. He has illustrated the facts of our freedom (4:21-5:1) and indicted the foes of our freedom (5:2-12). The foes of our freedom are the Neo-Galatianists, the legalists. They have fallen off the horse on the side of the law, a self-imposed standard by which they can put

God in debt for blessings, either in this life or the next. Of course, God has promised to bless us in many ways. The error here is to put him in a box and tell him he must bless us because of our good behavior. Legalism is just another way of finite, fallen beings trying to harness the omnipotence of an infinite, perfect Being for our benefit. He well may choose through his sovereignty to bless us in the way we want, but we can never say, "God owes us." We can never put him in debt; that is, he is never obliged to bless us in the way we want.

Now Paul wants to address the other side of the horse: the problem of license. License is using our freedom in Christ to indulge our fleshly appetites. That is a *perversion* of freedom. He addresses this perversion in 5:13ab. Then he explains the purpose of freedom (5:13c-15) and the provision for freedom (5:16-18).

I. PERVERSION OF FREEDOM   5:13ab

> For you, brethren, have been called to liberty; only do not use liberty as an opportunity for the flesh.

Some have called Galatians a "little Romans" because so many of the truths of Galatians, which was written first, are expanded in Romans. The great truths of freedom from our sin nature and legalism are expanded in Romans 5-8, so we can use those chapters to help us here in Galatians.[89]

In Romans, as in here in Galatians, Paul felt compelled to correct a temptation to imbalance that inevitably arises when he emphasizes our freedom from the law. The temptation is to accept God's grace and live "like hell." This would be like getting back on the horse after a fall into legalism only to fall off the other side of the horse into license (living according to our fleshly lusts). What a perverse response to God's grace. As previously discussed, it is insane, crazy,

---

89   Again we refer you to *Portraits of Righteousness* by Dave Anderson and Jim Reitman. It is an exposition of progressive sanctification in Romans 5-8 from a free grace perspective.

nuts to go back into slavery after having been delivered from slavery, or get reburied after having been delivered from death. But the reason this is an important topic to Paul is because, unlike what the Galatians have come to believe, Paul emphasizes that we *can* abuse our freedom. Because that is what freedom is; freedom is the ability to make choices. Slaves are not free because their master makes their choices for them.

We can use our freedom for license, to fulfill the flesh. Likewise, we can use our freedom for legalism, which also fulfills the flesh, just in a different way. But now, this is where we depart from simply "balance." We aren't trying to balance a little legalism with a little license. No, Paul wants us to deny the flesh, either legalism or license, and choose something else altogether: he wants us to live a substitutionary life.

"Opportunity" (NKJV, ESV, NASB, NRSV) is *aphormēn*, literally "the starting point or base of operations for an expedition." It can also mean "occasion" or "excuse." Isn't that ironic—that freedom could be the base of operations for the flesh, or even its excuse? Yet we see it all the time. It would seem that the church at large stays one level above the world in terms of morality. Fifty years ago, there was a stigma attached to a woman who had a baby out of wedlock. No longer. In some segments of American society, the majority of children are born out of wedlock. There used to be a stigma for living together out of wedlock. No longer. Practically every church has couples in their congregation who live together but are not married. Homosexuality used to be viewed in churches as unacceptable behavior. Now there are entire churches for homosexual people and weddings performed in church for homosexual couples. One of my church members had a sister who was under church discipline. Why? Because she had an affair with a female organist in a church for homosexuals in San Francisco while she was already married to another woman. Can you unravel that one? Even divorce used to carry a stigma. No longer. The divorce rates among professing Christians and society at large are about the same.

The man Lot is an interesting study along these lines. He wasn't even supposed to be in Israel because Abraham was not supposed to take his relatives with him from Ur of the Chaldeans. But when Abraham offered Lot his choice of places to live in Israel, he chose the fertile lands of the Jordan Valley. He was free to pitch his tent whenever he pleased in the lush valley. He pitched his tent toward Sodom. Every morning he walked out of his tent and Sodom was right in front of him. The lust of the eyes drew him to Sodom. He became one of its leaders.

Lot was not a believer? Well, how do you interpret 2 Peter 2:7-8 where it uses the word "righteous" three times to describe him? It even describes his soul as righteous (*dikaios*). And he "tortured" (imperfect tense, speaking of ongoing action) his righteous soul day after day as he exposed himself to the wicked deeds of the culture in which he lived. This kind of internal torture is often the war going on inside of a believer (Gal. 5:17; Rom. 7:14-24). Yet when he entertained angels and the homosexuals wanted to break the door down to sexually abuse them, Lot offered his virgin daughters to them in place of the angels. Wait a minute. Say it isn't so, Lot. We think, *How could you?* There had to be some flawed understanding here. Perhaps Lot had not had a course on angelology. The angels probably could have taken care of themselves, you think?

Somehow in Lot's system of ethical relativity, offering his own daughters was better than offering the angels. Heterosexual sin was better than homosexual sin (the angels appeared as men) in his eyes. So, apparently Lot thought what he was doing was okay, or at best the lesser of two evils. His morality was one step or one notch above the society in which he lived. Could there be a general principle here? The church seems to stay one notch above the world in terms of its morality.

As long as we are at least one notch above the world, we can look down on the world and feel good about ourselves. But as the morality of the world sinks lower and lower, that means the morality of the church sinks lower and lower with it—just one step above. This is using our freedom as an occasion for the flesh. You have to wonder what some of the early Puritan settlers to America would think if they could wake up in our current culture. Many of them had fallen off the horse on the side of legalism, but no doubt they would think a good portion of the church in America today has used their freedom to indulge the flesh (license).

Well, if this is the perversion of freedom, what is the purpose of freedom?

II. PURPOSE OF FREEDOM   5:13c-15

But through love serve one another. For all the law is fulfilled in one word, even in this: "You shall love your neighbor as yourself." But if you bite and devour one another, beware lest you be consumed by one another!

C. S. Lewis says through a character in *The Great Divorce* that we are most like our Maker when we are exercising our freedom to make choices.[90] Now Paul shows us the basic choice for living we have as humans: whether to bring harmony into the portion of the world we inhabit, or division and death. Which will it be?

One choice we have is to "bite and devour one another." Legalism certainly does this, as we have clearly shown. But so too does license. Destruction of our bodies with drugs and alcohol? Devastation of trust in relationships through sexual immorality? Destruction of a society through corruption and violence? All these things create division and destruction. The alternative choice is the transcendent one, and for that we need the substitutionary life. And that is to love our neighbors as ourselves.

It is a life of love that brings peace and harmony into our world. This brings not biting and devouring, but forgiveness and reconciliation. Love does not bring destruction to relationships, but healing.

Here is another irony: we are *free* to *serve*. The noun form (*doulos*) of this word for "serving" was often used of a slave. In other words, we are to use our freedom as an opportunity to become slaves and in doing so will be setting ourselves free, free of the death of the sin

---

90   C. S. Lewis, *The Great Divorce* excerpt, accessed August 13, 2014, www.merelewis.com/CSLgd0Xchooseitwillhaveit.html.

nature. The Savior did not take us off death row to live a life of self-indulgence; rather, he set us free to live a life of self-sacrifice in serving others. This is the substitutionary life. This is the life of Christ, who came not to be served, but to serve.

It was Phillips Brooks who said, "No man in this world attains to freedom from any slavery except by entrance into some higher servitude. There is no such thing as an entirely free man conceivable."[91]

We will serve someone or something. Only God is absolutely free of any other authority. In Romans 6, Paul teaches we will serve either our sin nature or Jesus—one or the other. So in Galatians 5, we will be a slave of either our flesh (sin nature) or Jesus. And if we choose to serve Jesus, he tells us to serve each other.

Agapē is a word almost exclusively found in Christian literature from the world of Greek writings. Could that be because its source, at least the in its biblical examples, is usually God? And it is generally characterized, though not exclusively so, by a attitude of selflessness or actions of service. It is, as we shall see, a fruit of the Holy Spirit, and Romans 5:5 says the love of God (divine love) is poured out in our hearts by the Holy Spirit. But what is this kind of love? There are many passages that describe it (1 Cor. 13:4-6; Rom. 5:5-10; 1 John 4:16-18). Perhaps the best one-word synonym in English is "selflessness." It might be defined as "seeking God's desire for the other person." So the "look of love" will be different depending on whom I am trying to love. If I am loving someone who does not know Christ, I am behaving in such a way as to help make him or her thirsty for Christ (God's desire for them is that they receive Christ). If I am loving someone who is a Christian but not walking with the Lord, I will behave in such a way as to help him or her come back into fellowship with God. If I am loving someone who is already walking with the Lord, loving him or her will mean to not do anything to cause that person to stumble in his or her walk but, on the contrary, to help that person continue in his or her walk.

---

91   Phillips Brooks, *Perennials*, Sermon Illustrations, accessed August 13, 2014, www.sermonillustrations.com/a-z/f/freedom.htm.

At any rate, this divine love is not self-centered; it is Christ centered. If we are living the substitutionary life of Christ, then it stands to reason we will be choosing a life of complete dependency in the same manner Christ lived while on earth. If I just use my freedom to indulge in the flesh, then it is a very self-centered focus, which of course leads to slavery to my own appetites. God set us free to help other people, that is, to love them. We serve them through love. So it is not just what I am free *from* (the sin nature and legalism); it is also what I am free *for* (to love). As I exercise this freedom through the substitutionary life of Christ, I enjoy freedom from slavery to my sin nature, something I was freely given in my position in Christ when I was justified, but something I only enjoy in my condition as I am being sanctified.

According to Larry Crabb, most couples who get married are "in love," but they don't know how to love each other.[92] By that he means most couples in America, whether Christian or non-Christian, are drawn together by their hormones (*eros*) and their emotions (*philē*) but do not yet understand the selflessness of *agapē*.

I know when I got married, I loved Betty and thought I was a pretty good guy. But after a few years of marriage, I realized I was a self-centered jerk. I had fallen into what Crabb calls the "tick on the dog" syndrome. Ticks, of course, spend most of their lives sucking blood or looking for blood to suck. It is a very self-centered existence. According to Crabb, most couples come to the altar like two ticks, each looking to suck blood out of the other. By this he means both the groom and the bride have the expectation that their new mate will meet their needs better than anyone they have ever met. Why else marry the other person, right?

The problem with that approach to marriage is you have two ticks and no dog. It is a marriage of manipulation. If one of my goals in marriage is to get my needs met, then when I am not

---

92   Larry Crabb, *The Marriage Builder* (Grand Rapids, MI: Zondervan, 2013).

reaching my goal (my needs aren't being met), I start manipulating my mate to meet my needs. Essentially, Crabb claims each partner is doing the same thing. So at the beginning of marriage (most, not all), both partners are manipulators. But manipulation is not *agapē*. Manipulation is self-centered. It's all about me, you know. *Agapē* tries to meet the needs of the other person. God's desire is that Christian marriages become marriages of ministry instead of marriages of manipulation.

As we grow in Christ, we walk by the Spirit more and more consistently. As that happens, we spend more and more time serving others rather than ourselves. In marriage, that means I am more seeking to meet my wife's needs than my own. As that happens, husbands and wives can enjoy *eros*, *philē*, **and** *agapē*—serving one another through love. Jesus summed all this up for the Pharisees (Matt. 22:34-40) when he condensed the first four commandments of the Ten Commandments into "love God" and the last six commandments into "love your neighbor as yourself." Love is others centered. Loving God and loving your neighbor are not self-centered.

As a husband and his wife make the choice to "in love serve one another," they literally grow together as one. The result is that our primary desires in life (harmony, acceptance, and approval) become reality in experience because we are living the substitutionary life. And even if our spouse or the person we are loving does not respond, the substitutionary life provides the peace that passes understanding, as Paul demonstrates in his own life. Even as his spiritual children (the Galatians) are testing him, Paul's example of love in this epistle is stern but given for the best interest of these people he loves.

Now the opposite of loving your fellow Christian is to "bite" (*daknō*—literally "the bite of a snake"; its only use in the NT) and "devour" (*katesthiō*—literally "to swallow a smaller animal" or "to tear to pieces and swallow" as the lions ate the Christians). The result of those sins of the tongue is destruction (*analoō*—total destruction as in a fire; see James 3:6-8; Prov. 6:16-19). The tongue is a WMD (weapon of mass destruction). Every church is full of them. These weapons must be under tight security or the whole church will blow up.

The problem with this wonderful standard of love set forth for us by Jesus is that we are incapable of acting accordingly. Our sin nature is just too selfish to ever cooperate with a life of selflessness (*agapē*). Why, then, would God command us to do something we cannot do? If God commanded it, we can't be held accountable if we don't have the power to do it. But we are accountable—it is appointed unto man once to die and then the judgment. Therefore, we must be able to fulfill these commands, said Pelagius. Wrong. We simply do not have adequate strength to live the Christian life. That is why God had to make a provision for us to have any hope for victory in this lofty life to which we are called.

III. PROVISION FOR FREEDOM   5:16-18

> I say then: Walk in the Spirit, and you shall not fulfill the lust of the flesh. For the flesh lusts against the Spirit, and the Spirit against the flesh; and these are contrary to one another, so that you do not do the things that you wish. But if you are led by the Spirit, you are not under the law.

This has to be one of the great promises of the New Testament. There are two key words: "walk" and "Spirit." The victorious Christian life is better described by the word "walking" than by the word "working." Of course, the two are not mutually exclusive. Anyone who is walking by the Spirit will also be working for God's kingdom. But since we have said the Holy Spirit is the key to victory in this chapter, perhaps we should distinguish "walking by the Spirit" from some of his other ministries, which are often claimed to be the means by which we find victory.[93]

Some say we must be baptized by the Holy Spirit for power. Usually these groups believe in two baptisms of the Holy Spirit: one

---

93   Anderson and Reitman, *Portraits of Righteousness*, 142.

by the Holy Spirit to put us into the body of Christ (the universal church) and another in which Christ baptizes us with the Holy Spirit for power.[94] Unfortunately for that view, Ephesians 4:5 tells us there is only "one baptism," and because of the context of the body of Christ (Eph. 4:11ff.), this "baptism" cannot be referring to water. It is the baptism of/by the Holy Spirit, and there is only one baptism of the Spirit.

Others will tell us that it is the filling of the Holy Spirit, which gives us power for victory. If so, then Paul was remiss in not mentioning such an important key in two of the greatest victory chapters in the New Testament: Galatians 5 and Romans 8. Nowhere do we find any mention of filling by the Holy Spirit in these two chapters. In the two instances where the Greek word *plēroō* is used (Eph. 5:18ff. and Acts 13:52), it is a group worship experience. And in all the instances where the Greek word *pimplēmi* is used, the recipient(s) of the filling did not confess any sins to get the filling, nor did they commit sin to lose the filling. The filling in these cases (John the Baptist, Zacharias, Elizabeth, the Upper Room, Peter, and Paul) was for a special witness and had unmistakable physical effects. It came on the person for a short period and was gone.

However, in the great victory chapters (Gal. 5 and Rom. 8) we find the words "walk" and "led." From our perspective we walk with or by the Spirit; from his perspective he is leading us (Gal. 5:17). The following chart contrasts the differences in these three ministries of the Holy Spirit.

BAPTIZING	LEADING	FILLING
1 COR. 12; ROM. 6	ROM. 8; GAL. 5	LUKE 1; ACTS 2; 4; 9
Indwelling	Enabling	Intoxicating
Permanent	Progressive	Periodic
Fact	Faith	Feeling

---

94 Melvin E. Dieter, et al., *Five Views on Sanctification* (Grand Rapids, MI: Zondervan, 2011), 103-36.

From this we can see that the baptizing ministry of the Holy Spirit is an **indwelling**. It is a **fact** whether the new believer knows it or not. And this indwelling is **permanent**, since we are sealed until the day of redemption (Eph. 4:30).

But the leading ministry of the Holy Spirit is an **enabling**, which gives us victory over the lusts of the flesh. And it is **progressive**. In other words, as we grow in Christ, we log more and more time walking by the Spirit. This is a ministry in which we must exercise our **faith**, for there are times the Holy Spirit will lead us into the desert, as he did Jesus (Luke 4:1). At those times we probably will not be feeling good. Nevertheless, since we are being led by the Holy Spirit, we can enjoy the fruit of the Spirit whether we are in jail, in the desert, or on the mountaintop.

As mentioned, the filling ministry of the Holy Spirit seems to come at the sovereign discretion of the Holy Spirit himself. The filling is for a special ministry and is not expected to last hours or days on end until we knowingly sin. Peter was filled in Acts 2 and filled again in Acts 3, but there is no record of his sin between Acts 2 and 3 that would have taken the filling away, only to be restored again by confession of that sin. No, this ministry of the Spirit is **periodic**. He sovereignly chooses when and where and for how long to fill a believer. It lasted long enough for the special witness (usually preaching or evangelism or encouragement). The person filled did not have to take this ministry by faith. He knew something special was happening; he could **feel** it. In some cases it was **intoxicating** (interesting that observers in Acts 2 thought the people filled by the Holy Spirit were drunk). But this ministry by the Spirit was never described as the key to a victorious Christian life. And putting together formulas by which we can get the Spirit to fill us smacks of man manipulating God, or what we call magic. Another observation: he only fills those he is leading, and he only leads those he has baptized.

A supernatural standard of righteousness requires supernatural enablement to fulfill that standard. And God made a way. He provided the Holy Spirit to enable us, but only as we walk by him will we not fulfill the lusts of the flesh. Our problem, obviously, is the flesh. The fact that this involves more than the physical body is apparent from the list in 5:19-21, which includes many problems not sourced in just our bodies. Things like jealousy, envy, hatred, and anger are not physical. So in Galatians 5 we suggest the flesh is what Paul calls our *he hamartia* in Romans 6-8, our sin(ful) nature. This sin nature is like a bottle factory, and the list includes the different types of contents produced by the factory to fill the bottles.

Here we are told that the flesh "lusts" against the Spirit and the Spirit against the flesh. The word translated "lusts" in this verse in noun form refers to "a desire, a longing, or a craving." The NRSV may have the best translation here: "What the flesh desires is opposed to the Spirit, and what the Spirit desires is opposed to the flesh." There is opposition here—a struggle. The result is that we so often wind up doing the very things we do not want to do. Does this sound like the last half of Romans 7? It should, because this one verse summarizes the Romans 7 struggle pretty well. There is a battle going on, a war inside the Christian.

In fact, the very presence of this battle is a pretty good indication that someone *is* a Christian. I once had a man come into my office with serious doubts about whether he was a Christian. I tried to give him assurance from the promises of God, our main source. "Do you believe the promises?" "Yes." "Okay, that should settle it. Why do you think you are not a Christian?" He went on to describe his thought life, which was so sordid he did not think someone could be a Christian and have thoughts like that. "Do those evil thoughts bother you?" "Oh, yes." "Then, that means there is a real fight going on, which means something is inside you fighting against these bad thoughts, right?"

Unbelievers have the same thoughts, perhaps worse, but whatever internal battle they might have will not rise to the level of the battle that includes the Holy Spirit. You have this epic struggle precisely *because* you are a believer. It is because the Holy Spirit lives inside and "lusts" for you (see James 4:5) that your conscience is more sensitive than during your non-Christian days, and now you are aware of the internal battle.

I've had seminary professors who specialize in the Greek NT tell me that a true Christian couldn't have that kind of battle going on, especially one in which there is ongoing defeat. "Pretty dismal view of the Christian life, isn't it?" one of them asked me. Well, yes, because the flesh is dismal. That, I believe, is Paul's whole point in Romans 7. Trying to progress in one's sanctification through the flesh (Gal. 3:3) will lead to one defeat after another until one cries out, "O wretched man that I am! Who will deliver me from this body of death?" (Rom. 7:24). This is not the cry of an unbeliever. It is the cry of the Christian who, as James D. G. Dunn suggests, longs to be in a better world where this kind of struggle is gone forever. According to Dunn, any Christian who denies the reality of this kind of struggle at some phase of his Christian life either has a conscience so seared he no longer struggles or he is self-deceived.[95]

The flesh acts like the law of gravity pulling our good intentions down. It acts as a continual force. When we come against the flesh in our own strength, it is only a matter of time until our energy is depleted. What we need is a power greater than our own and one that cannot be depleted. In *Portraits of Righteousness* I have illustrated that higher power as the law of displacement. I start tying helium balloons to a ten-pound weight I am trying to hold parallel to the ground, and at some point the law of displacement (helium is lighter than air) will kick in and the balloons will hold the weight up or actually take it away. That is what it is like to rely on the law of the Spirit of Life in Christ Jesus (Rom. 8:2). God has provided a law higher than the law of sin and death that the flesh uses to pull us down. It is the law of the Spirit of Life in Christ Jesus. And the Holy Spirit uses this higher law to lift us up and give us our victory. Through him Paul can claim that we will not fulfill the lusts of the flesh.

Now we are accustomed to thinking of the word "lust" as a bad word. So two questions come to mind: (1) How can the Holy Spirit lust; and (2) what are the Holy Spirit and the flesh lusting *for*? "Lust"

---

95 James Dunn, "Romans 7:14-25 in the Theology of Paul," *Theologische Zeitschrift* 5 (September/October, 1975): 268, 272.

here indicates a passionate desire. The reason we tend to associate "lust" with bad things is that our flesh (our first actor) is so dominant in our lives that we tend to be dominated by passionate desires for fleshly things of the world. But the Holy Spirit and flesh are not lusting for worldly things. They are both lusting *against* one another for the *same thing*. And that thing is you and me.

This inner battle involves the whole man—body, soul (the mind, emotions, and will), and spirit. My friend, who thought he might not be saved because of this inner battle (who should have been comforted in his salvation *because of* the inner battle), experienced this battle in his thought life in pictures, words, and conversations. This is primarily our mind engaging with the flesh and the Spirit in a debate. The flesh puts up an image, makes an accusation or a promise, then urges action. The Spirit responds with a Scripture, a bit of truth, repeats a promise, then urges the opposite action. The mind evaluates. The emotions react. The emotions demand I do something. My will then decides what, in fact, I will do. Will I act in accord with the flesh? If I do, I am "walking" according to the flesh. If I act according to the Spirit, I am "walking" according to the Spirit.

I have a friend who testifies his life in Christ was transformed when he began to understand this dynamic, that the voice of the flesh was not actually *him*. It is a foreign agent of the devil's world residing within, desiring power over him. Romans 7:17 states it, speaking of sin, "It is no longer I who do it, but sin that dwells in me." But because of the substitutionary life of Jesus, it has no power unless he *grants* the power, through his will.

My friend began to speak with his flesh (usually in his thoughts, but sometimes out loud) as though he were speaking to a monster locked in a cave in his house, begging to be let out. Once he realized that the flesh used his voice, knew how to trigger his emotions, but was not actually him, and that he was a new creation and could live the substitutionary life, he was never the same.

Note that verse 18 says that you do not do what you wish. This battle typically results in two things: (1) we do something; and (2) we wish we had not done it. This is nothing less than the Spirit telling us our default setting is on the flesh. The dominant "do" is from the flesh. But, praise God, the dominant "wish" or desire is from the Spirit. This is, once again, evidence that we now have the inner power of the Spirit to live the substitutionary life. Our main desire is to follow the Spirit.

So how do we recognize our dominant "do" is the flesh but not exercise that first impulse?

We think it bears repeating that the great key is to understand this inner battle raging for control of our soul (our mind, emotions, and will). If the flesh controls our mind, emotions, and will, we will be its slave. The flesh knows how to manipulate our emotions to demand *action*, and the flesh knows how to speak with us to make false promises as to how that action will benefit us. "Lash out with your tongue and put that person down and you will feel vindicated," or, "Lie now and you will not have to feel embarrassed." It is vital to understand that our first impulse is to "do" what the flesh urges.

That means it is vital to recognize that, while the emotions provide the very valuable and God-given function of telling us *action is demanded*, we have a will that can act independently of emotions when we are being led by the Spirit. We can stop and ask one of the most important prayers we can ever pray, and one you can pray often every day, "God, what would you have me do?" In this way we can elevate the "wish to do" coming from the Spirit, who "lusts" for us to follow him, above the flesh who "lusts" for us to follow the world. This is the substitutionary life of Christ.

From our perspective, when we choose with our will to follow the urging of the Spirit, we are **walking** with the Holy Spirit. From his perspective, he is **leading** us. When verse 18 says, "But if you are led by the Spirit, you are no longer under the law," Paul leaves out the article (*the*) before "law" in the Greek text. It is there in English because we need it to make sense of the statement. But by leaving it out, he indicates he is not referring to *the* Law (the Torah), but rather to a *law principle*, which is the performance principle—our default system. It is this compulsion to perform by our own strength that throws us into the Romans 7 or Galatians 5:17 struggle. Walking by the Spirit or being led by the same takes us out of that struggle.

But how? How do we walk by/in/with the Spirit? This takes us back to the word "led." We cannot walk by the Spirit unless we are led by the Spirit. But being led by someone requires a conscious choice. I have tried more than once to take dance lessons with my wife. It just never has worked out for us. It is not Betty's fault. She has made a conscious choice to follow my lead. I'm just a lousy leader when it comes to dancing. Thankfully the Spirit is a great leader. So in our conclusion let's take a look at what is involved in our choice to be led by the Spirit.

CONCLUSION

1. **Yield.** I need to yield my life to the sovereign control of the Spirit. In Galatians 5:25 where Paul discusses walking by the Spirit and living out the fruit of the Spirit, he will use a word for "walk" that is different from the one he uses in 5:16. In 5:16 he uses *peripateō,* while in 5:25 he chooses *stoicheō* to help fill out the picture of what it means to walk by the Spirit. The first word means "to walk around." In fact, the philosophy students who followed Socrates around a walking path he used to teach via his Socratic method (dialogue) were called the peripatetics because they walked around in a circle with their teacher. The second word means "to march." This adds something helpful. A military unit cannot march as a unit if its members do not follow the commands of the leader. If the Holy Spirit is going to lead us, we do need to follow his commands. That would seem to go without saying, but it is surprising how many times believers think they are living a Spirit-led life when they are violating clear, nonambiguous commands from the Holy Spirit in Scripture. So we need to both listen and learn, as well as obey what we hear.

2. **Pace.** I cannot be led by the Spirit if I don't walk with him at his pace. When I get ahead of him, I may choose

the wrong path and lose his protection. When I get behind him, I am resisting his call, and friction begins. Quite often we come to forks in the roads in our lives. The Spirit will tug but not push. He will encourage but not force. In fact, one meaning of the word *Paraclete*, the word Jesus used for the Holy Spirit in John 16:7, is "one who encourages." Precisely because he does not force, he can be resisted. Who could resist an omnipotent Being if he chose to force his desires on us? And the awful thing about the Spirit is that he will let us have our own desires if we want them badly enough. That leads to trouble. So, if we want to walk with the Spirit or be led by the Spirit, we need to do what he asks now and let him lead our next steps when the time comes.

3. **Focus.** Romans 8:5 speaks of a mind-set: "Those who live according to the flesh *set their minds* on the things of the flesh, but those who live according to the Spirit, *set their minds* on the things of the Spirit." I have heard championship-caliber athletes describe how they have been so in sync with their coach that they had one mind. The player knew exactly what the coach wanted, and that made it easier to execute the game plan. I have heard Olympic horse riders describe the same sense of harmony with their horses. After years of riding together, rider and horse seem to understand each other to the point that the horse kind of knows what is coming next and is responsive to the slightest touch from its master. Perhaps that is what it is like to have one's mind set on the things of the Spirit. After years of filling one's mind with the thoughts of the Spirit (Scripture), it is easier to sense the leading of the Spirit and be responsive to his nudges.

4. **Direction.** If the company commander tells the company to about-face and the company does not obey, then the company commander will be going one direction while

his company goes another. We can be pretty sure that our Company Commander is going in the direction of Matthew 6:33—"Seek first the kingdom of God and His righteousness." That is the direction the Spirit will be leading us. But Peter didn't see it that way. He told Jesus he was going in the wrong direction—to Jerusalem. "Not good for your health, Lord." From those words Jesus knew that Peter was going the wrong direction. He rebuked Peter by saying Satan was speaking through him at that moment and that his words revealed that he (Peter) was more concerned about his personal kingdom than God's kingdom. If our lives are built around building our own kingdoms instead of God's kingdom, you can be pretty sure we are not being led by the Spirit.

This is so hard for us. May I say it again: the hardest thing in the world for the Christian to believe is the substitutionary *life* of Christ. "Christ lives in me" (Gal. 2:20) and "walk in the Spirit" are two different ways of saying the same thing. The disciples did not understand why Jesus was going to leave them. How on earth was he going to fulfill his promises to them if he left? But he explained to them in the Upper Room that if he did not go away, he could not send the Holy Spirit to them to enable them to live the Christian life.

John the Baptist predicted that one would come after him who would baptize people with fire and with the Holy Spirit. The disciples asked Jesus forty days after his resurrection if he was going to restore the kingdom to the Jews at that time. He told them not to worry about when he would restore the kingdom but rather go back into Jerusalem and pray for the coming of the Holy Spirit. One of the signs of the Messiah was that he would send the Holy Spirit. After his ascension Jesus did exactly that. And the disciples were never the same, right? Each found power for a victorious Christian life through the power of the Holy Spirit.

So, what we used to try to do out of *duty* we can now do out of *disposition*. Our makeup has changed. Every Christian has the

Holy Spirit living inside of him to empower him to lead a victorious Christian life (1 Cor. 12:13; Rom. 8:9).

Rene Morrison was a football star in high school and college. He grew up in St. Louis going to Catholic elementary, junior high, and high schools. He said he lived a life of fear of God and the nuns. "The nuns tried to scare the hell out of me," claimed Rene. As he got older, he became more of a disciplinary problem. But the nuns had a punishment commensurate with every offense. He grew to hate them and hate God. After college, Rene got married, but he didn't want to have anything to do with Christianity ever again.

Rene became a successful salesman in the oil-field world of Houston, Texas. He had several children, some of them scholarship athletes. Rene was a faithful father, but he never took his children to church. He didn't want them exposed to the fear with which he had been raised. Then a change occurred in his family. His wife, Penny, became a believer. She began regular Bible studies and went to church. But not Rene. No way. Finally, after attending the church I pastored for several years, Penny talked Rene into coming—once. "I'm going to stand at the back the whole time. If just one man tries to hug me, I'll never go back." Rene was a man's man. And he stayed in shape by lifting weights five days a week at the downtown YMCA. None of this emotionalism for him.

But Rene heard a message he had never heard before. He heard some good news. He heard about a love he did not have to earn and could never lose. He heard that Jesus proved his love for Rene while Rene was still sinful by dying for Rene. Rene believed and was born again. Then he said, "When you go to Israel again, I want you to baptize me in the Jordan." We did. And as our group stood before the Western Wall, Penny shared how she had put a piece of paper in the wall ten years before praying that her husband would become a Christian. Tears were flowing as we watched Rene give his wife a big hug. Rene even hugged me and said, "If you ever have anyone wrestling with fear, send them to me."

When we got back to Houston, Rene shared his testimony with our entire church. A year later he was having trouble swallowing.

A month after that, he had gone from 230 lbs. to 200 lbs. A month after that, he went from 200 lbs. to 170 lbs. and died of esophageal cancer at age sixty-two. As he lay on his deathbed, he told me, "I have absolutely no fear. Thank you for telling me about a God for whom I don't have to perform."

14

FOCUS ON THE FRUIT
Galatians 5:19-24

One of the Grimms' fairy tales tells of a beautiful girl named Rapunzel who lives with a wicked witch in a drab and dingy tower. The old witch is holding Rapunzel captive, and to keep the girl "in her place," the wicked witch does two things. First, she removes all the mirrors from the tower so Rapunzel cannot see what she looks like. And then the old witch tells Rapunzel repeatedly that she is ugly. In fact, the witch says to her, "Rapunzel, you look just like me."

Since there are no mirrors in the tower, poor Rapunzel believes she is as ugly as the witch. She can't see how beautiful she really is, so she remains a prisoner in the tower—a prisoner of her own supposed ugliness. The witch believes that if Rapunzel is convinced she is ugly, she will never try to escape.

Then, one bright day, Prince Charming comes riding by on his white horse, just as Rapunzel is leaning out of the tower for a breath of fresh air. Their eyes meet, and it is love at first sight.

"Rapunzel! Rapunzel! Let down your hair," the prince cries out. And she does just that: she lets her long, flowing hair down from the balcony, and Prince Charming, using her hair like a rope ladder, climbs up into the tower.

As they gaze at each other lovingly, Rapunzel sees a clear reflection of her own face in the glistening eyes of her prince. In the mirror of his eyes, Rapunzel sees for the first time that she is beautiful. And in that moment, she is set free! Free from the witch! Free from the tower! Free from the past! Free from the feeling that she is ugly! Then Prince Charming takes Rapunzel into his arms. They parachute onto his horse and ride happily off into the sunset.

Who knows what the Grimm brothers thought the witch represented. But in Christianity the witch could easily represent the devil or in Galatians 5:19-23 the flesh. For the flesh is as ugly as it gets. If the works of the flesh listed in Galatians 5:19-21 were dots on a page, and you could connect the dots, you'd get a pretty good picture of the flesh. Each time we fall prey to the flesh, the devil or one of his minions is there to whisper in our ear how ugly we really are.

Do you ever hear a little voice whispering in your ear about what an ugly person you are? How could a real Christian have thoughts like you are having? The things you think about other people and the anger built up inside of you are rotten. Therefore, the little voice says, you must be a rotten person.

Although this kind of thinking comes from the devil, two of his main hooks he uses to stir up this pot of repulsive gut-rot are the flesh and the law. The flesh is evil, but the law (whether the Law of Moses or the Law of Christ) is good. But *flesh + law = legalism*. The law actually stirs up the flesh until we become more sinful than before we were aware of the law (see Rom. 7:7-12). Of course, there is nothing wrong with the law. Our internal flaw is the flesh. We need to learn how to have victory over the flesh so we can enjoy the fruit of the Spirit. But how? We want to examine the works of the flesh in 5:19-21 and then the fruit of the Spirit in 5:22-23. Then we will look at our freedom by the Spirit in 5:24.

I. WORKS OF THE FLESH 5:19-21

With all of these works there is some sort of attraction or compulsion. Usually it is a short-term pleasure. Hebrews 11:25 speaks of the "passing pleasures of sin." Nevertheless, there are long-term losses. We want to look at both.

A. Short-Term Gains 19-21a

Now the works of the flesh are evident, which are: adultery, fornication, uncleanness, lewdness, idolatry, sorcery, hatred, contentions, jealousies, outbursts of wrath, selfish ambitions, dissensions, heresies, envy, murders, drunkenness, revelries, and the like...

1. **Sexual Sins**

   - **Adultery**—this word is not found in 2 percent of the manuscripts we have of the NT. As a general rule I follow the Majority Text edited by Zane Hodges and Art Farstad, which represents approximately 98 percent of the extant manuscripts. This just refers to sexual immorality of married people.

   - **Fornication** = *porneia*, which is any kind of sexual immorality, not just sexual relations between unmarried people. As a pastor, it was amazing to me how many people thought adultery was wrong because it is one of the Ten Commandments but everything else was okay.

   - **Uncleanness**—this word is often listed right along with other sexual sins such as in Ephesians 5:3; Colossians 3:5; and 2 Corinthians 12:21. Apparently there is no end to the deviant sexual behavior human beings can dream up. This addresses the attitude as well as the action of immorality.

- **Lewdness**—this word is found not only in 2 Corinthians 12:21 but also in Romans 13:13 in tandem with the word from which we get *coitus*. It literally meant "bed" but became a euphemism for sinful sexual intercourse.

- **Idolatry** = *eidololatria*. This word is coupled with "covetousness" in Ephesians 5:5 and Colossians 3:5. Because it is found right in the midst of these passages on sexual sins, and because part of the covetousness mentioned in the Ten Commandments (Ex. 20:17) included coveting another man's wife, we think this word is also in the realm of sexual sins. I would suggest sexual addiction. It is making an idol of sex to the point that a person cannot be satisfied with a relationship with one person. The sexual addict will sometimes have encounters with over a hundred partners, whether heterosexual or homosexual. Unfortunately, when they attend SAA groups, they often hook up with other members of the group. There are probably many forms of this sin that fall short of actual physical encounters. Perhaps the worse thing available to feed these addictions since the turn of the century has been the Internet. Many a marriage has blown up in divorce over addictions to the cafeteria of options on the Internet.

The sex drive creates powerful desires in our body, and the flesh knows how to channel those desires into its "lust" for us. The flesh promises pleasure, which undoubtedly is true for a time. But unlike pleasures of the Spirit, which bring life and peace, the various pleasures derived from expressing sexual desires in a sinful manner offer short-term gains, but as with all sin there are also short and long-term losses. Since the pleasure of sin does not last, it wants more and more. And the travesty of pursuing pleasure through the flesh is that rather than fulfilling our desires we become enslaved to them. We call this addiction. But there are other negative impacts of sexual sin in this life, and they are nothing new. An example comes from Malachi 2 when the Israelites were trading in their older Jewish wives for younger Gentile models. This angered the Lord greatly. He claimed they were dealing treacherously with the wives of their youth.

The word for "dealing treacherously" is *bgd* in Hebrew. I bring this out only to expand on its meanings: adultery with foreign gods, adultery with foreign women, adultery in general, unfaithfulness to a covenant.

The Israelites wanted to know why God was not pleased with their worship. He said, "Because the Lord has been witness between you and the wife of your youth, with whom you have dealt treacherously; yet she is your companion and your wife by covenant" (Mal. 2:14). The context speaks of the marriage covenant, so "dealing treacherously" most likely refers to being unfaithful to the marriage covenant.

Then Malachi goes on to explain that it is spiritually dangerous to be unfaithful to one's first wife by divorcing her and marrying another. He says when God formed Eve, he had plenty of the spirit of life left over to make more wives for Adam, but he chose not to do so. He breathed the spirit of life into just one. Why? He wasn't just trying to make a bunch of fornicators to propagate the human race. God was trying to solve the problem of loneliness, something that existed in the garden before the fall of man.

Loneliness is an amoral problem. Loneliness existed in

the human race before sin. God's first attempt at solving the problem was through marriage. That's why Malachi says she is not only the wife of your youth, she is also your "companion," which is *kbr* in Hebrew. This word means "united, joined, knit together" as an adjective. As a noun it means "partner, companion, or associate." Our spouse is God's primary answer to loneliness.

Having many wives does not solve the problem of loneliness, at least not for the women. Suleiman the Magnificent had hundreds of concubines. The hope of one of these concubines was to be selected at least once a year to spend time with Suleiman. Talk about a lonely hearts club. But even a man with multiple wives cannot achieve the total intimacy envisioned by God for one husband with one wife. Jealousy among wives, if nothing else, would be a barrier to such intimacy.

The beauty of one husband married to one wife is that their intimacy can increase as long as they live. After forty-six years of marriage, my wife and I are closer than ever. One of the reasons is that we are slowly losing our minds, which is another way of saying we can't really remember the things about each other that used to bug us so much. And we find new ways to be intimate.

Years ago we couldn't figure out why old couples often did not sleep in the same bedroom. Then awhile back we discovered why—snoring. I can crack plaster. I took an associate pastor with me to Israel some time back. He was my roommate, and the poor guy would go out into the hall and lie on the floor in order to get some sleep.

Well, my dentist finally made a snore guard for me. It's that thing that keeps your jaw from falling down at night, which in turn allows your tongue to fall back and produce snoring. But it works so well, my beautiful wife decided she wanted one. She doesn't really snore—just purrs. But she got one anyway, and just last month we enjoyed a new form of intimacy—we had our first kiss with our snore guards in! Talk about romance! Yeah, baby. Anyway, back to Malachi.

Now Malachi inserts a big *therefore* and says to "take heed to your spirit" two times (2:15, 16). Apparently, there is some sort of spiritual union that takes place when a man and woman come together. First Corinthians 6:18-20 suggests we do damage to our spirits when we have sex with someone who is not our spouse. The Holy Spirit lives in our human spirit. He says having relations with someone who is not one's spouse does not glorify God with our bodies or with our spirits. I am not sure we understand all this, at least I don't, but there is a strong warning here: take heed to your spirit.

The phrase "take heed" comes from *shmr*, which usually means "to set up a guard" as in one who would protect the town or fortress from outside enemies. Somehow being sexually pure helps us guard our spirits from damage. Perhaps it relates to the ego boundary we will discuss shortly.

So the category of sexual sins is all about us inflicting damage and pain upon ourselves for a promise of pleasure that will turn into slavery, death, and self-destruction. That's bad enough, but there is more. What about people problems?

2. **People Problems**

So far, we might be able to make a case that Paul intends "flesh" to equate to our human body in Galatians 5. But the next list makes it definitively clear that Paul is talking about our sin nature. Though we might relate the sexual sins to just the human body, you can't do that with people problems. No, best to understand the flesh as our sin nature here. These sins are pretty self-explanatory, so we won't dwell on them.

- Hatred

- Contentions

- Jealousies

- Outbursts of wrath

- Selfish ambitions

- Dissensions

- Heresies = *haireseis* = divisions, factions, splits

- Envy

It's interesting that James 3:13-18 describes the same type of behavior and indicates that many of these people problems come from wisdom that is demonic. Fancy that—demonic words from Christians. We have already seen that Peter became an instrument of Satan by focusing on the things of man rather than the things of God. If it can happen to Peter, it can happen to any of us. In fact, I would suggest to you that the most demonic words you will ever hear may well come from other Christians (Matt. 16:22-23). Of course, when the devil (or demons) get together with our sin nature (the flesh)—watch out! The world is still Satan's realm, for a while longer, and the flesh is connected with the world. See the importance of this internal battle? There is no sitting on the fence!

3. **Improper Use of Drugs**

- **Sorcery**—this is the word from which we get *pharmacy* (*pharmakeia*). Though "magic, secret arts, or sorcery" may be the meaning here, in this context (drunkenness and orgies follow), it may well refer to using drugs in ritual worship or at wild parties (see below).

- **Drunkenness**—this is the Greek word *methai*. Could it be the Turks (Galatia is in central Turkey) were the first to use crystal meth? Just kidding. The word is associated with drunkenness in both its verbal form and noun form.

- **Revelries**—the ESV translates this word (*komois*) as "orgies" in Romans 13:13.

All three of these words suggest to me a breakdown of the ego boundary. What is the ego boundary? According to M. Scott Peck, the ego boundary has formed in most of us around the time we hit puberty.[96] It is that psychological boundary that protects our psyche (our unique combination of mind, emotion, and will—our inner personality, if you will). According to Peck, it is this ego boundary that awakens us to our uniqueness— there is no one like me in the world, never has been, and never will be. This is good; it helps us "find our way" in the world.

However, with this awareness of our uniqueness goes a profound sense of loneliness. God tells us Adam was alone *before* the fall. We wonder, how could he be alone when he enjoyed God's love and fellowship every day as they walked in the garden? Answer? Uniqueness. There was no one else like Adam. He may have been made in the image of God, but he was not a divine being; he was

---

96   M. Scott Peck, *The Road Less Traveled* (New York: Simon & Schuster, 1978), 85-97.

a human being. Not merely one step removed from the apes, but a completely unique being. Alone.

So, according to Peck, we long for the sense of enjoying the imagined power we had when we were younger and at one with the universe, before our sense of uniqueness overwhelmed us. So we begin looking for someone to take away our loneliness. When we find the "right one," our ego boundaries open up and we merge, psychologically. This is what Peck calls cathexis. It is what songwriters and romance novelists call "falling in love." It is a euphoric, cloud-nine, free-fall experience. So powerful that once the drug wears off (eighteen months on the average, according to Peck), many people go on searching for "love" over and over and getting hurt over and over because—we are looking for love in all the wrong places.

The reason I go into all this is because the emotional aspect we call "falling in love" is like a drug, and this drug opens up our ego boundaries. People in love are just a tad crazy. But cathexis is better than decathexis. If you understand the first word, you can figure out the second—falling out of love. Unfortunately, in a society where there are usually multiple breakups before marriage and multiple breakups after marriage, most people discover that "breaking up is hard to do." Often when people "decathect," one ego boundary closes while the other doesn't. The one with his or her ego boundary still open is twisting in the wind, in pain and open to doing all kinds of things he or she wouldn't do if that ego boundary were closed.

Many times people break up involuntarily because of parents, geography, all sorts of things. When that happens, both ego boundaries are left open, and there is often a rebound effect in which the couple gets back together. This can happen many times. But while that ego boundary is open, the individual psyche is without protection. But here is the scary thing. We can voluntarily open that ego boundary. How? Drugs. That is one reason why they are so dangerous. In a controlled environment like a hospital when there is a lot of pain to deal with, okay. But at an orgy…to do it for fun? There's your trouble.

Without the protective ego boundary, we can merge with all sorts of things. Again, this is why sexual encounters with someone other than one's spouse are a danger to our human spirit. For one thing, the Holy Spirit is not controlling the person who has artificially opened up his ego boundary. God wants us to merge (cathexis) with our spouses and with him (John 14:20, 23; 15:4-5)—no one else. When we merge with a spouse and with him, we get life, peace, and a fellowship that cures loneliness. Drugs are catalysts to cathexis with the wrong people, and that compounds loneliness and pain.

4. **And the Like**

Notice Paul's list is not exhaustive. All of these works of the flesh have short-term gains. Many, if not all of them, have short-term losses as well. But all of them have long-term losses.

B. Long-Term Losses   21b

…of which I tell you beforehand, just as I also told you in time past, that those who practice such things will not inherit the kingdom of God.

This part of the verse has been the subject of theological debates for centuries. There are three popular approaches in Protestantism:

1. **Loss of Salvation.** This is an Arminian approach. The understanding is that a true Christian who practices these

works of the flesh will ultimately lose his justification salvation if he has not repented before his death. Thus, anyone who wrestles with an ongoing anger problem will not be in heaven. That leaves Moses out. Because of uncontrolled anger he killed an Egyptian when he was forty. Forty years later he broke some pretty important tablets. And forty years after that he got mad at a rock and started beating it. Because of this ongoing anger problem, Moses forfeited the Promised Land—the physical kingdom of Israel. Does that mean Moses also forfeited *the Promised Land* of heaven? No.

We know that is not the case, because he conferred with Jesus on the Mt. of Transfiguration (Matt. 17:3).

2. **Never Had Salvation.** This is a Calvinistic approach. Five Point Calvinism claims if you are not sanctified at the end of a normal life span, then you were never justified. Since a person has no choice in his justification, neither does he have a choice in his sanctification. It is guaranteed for the elect. So anyone practicing these works of the flesh is obviously not sanctified; therefore, he was never justified. As Reformed theologian Anthony Hoekema says, "How can we know that we are in the faith? We can know this only from our continuation in the life of faith, our perseverance, our standing firm to the end."[97] Or John Murray, who writes, "We may entertain the faith of our security in Christ only as we persevere in faith and holiness to the end."[98] Of course, by "the end" these writers mean the end of one's life. No final sanctification?

---

97   Anthony A. Hoekema, *Saved by Grace* (Grand Rapids, MI: William B. Eerdmans, 1989), 255.

98   John Murray, *Redemption Accomplished and Applied* (Grand Rapids, MI: William B. Eerdmans, 1955), 193.

Then no initial justification. Of course these Calvinists are not consistent with the notion men have no choice in their lives. They actively try to get people to agree with them or alter their behavior. And they threaten those with hell who won't behave (follow a list) based on this verse.

Both of these approaches have subtly thrown works back into the justification equation. They would equate the promise of heaven embedded in justification with "inherit the kingdom of God." Both groups *must* remain faithful with good works as the evidence of their justification or to maintain their justification. As soon as we put a "must" in front of works, we have moved into Neo-Galatianism. But there is a third approach, a dispensational approach.

3. **Loss of Rewards.** Dispensationalism is a self-contained system of theology. So is Five Point Calvinism. I know many good and godly people who try to combine the systems, but it cannot logically be done. The only way to do it is to redefine one or both of the systems to come up with some sort of hybrid system. The dispensationalist does not *have to* be good the rest of his life in order to maintain his justification or to prove he has it. There is no "have to." The dispensationalist has the option to live a *thank-you* life and a *want-to* life.

Only dispensationalism makes rewards the issue at the Judgment Seat of Christ. And only dispensationalism makes rewards the issue at the Great White Throne. This is because only dispensationalism has a millennium (a thousand-year reign of Jesus from Jerusalem in Israel) between the two judgment seats. Neither judgment seat is to determine one's destiny. Your eternal destiny determines which judgment seat you go to. Faith or no faith—that is the difference. Believers go to the Judgment

Seat of Christ. Unbelievers go to the Great White Throne. But once one appears at one of these judgment seats, his works are judged to determine his reward.

"Inheriting the kingdom of God" in this approach does not refer to *entering* the kingdom. Rather it refers to our reward in the kingdom. To fully develop this would require a theology book, not a commentary. Suffice it to reference just one verse, and this verse ought to be enough, actually. Colossians 3:24 says, "Knowing that from the Lord you will receive the **reward** of the **inheritance**; for you serve the Lord Christ." Notice that the inheritance for serving the Lord Christ is a reward. If believers live a defeated Christian life by practicing the works of the flesh, they lose this inheritance; that is, they lose their rewards (some or all) at the Judgment Seat of Christ. Moses did not lose going to heaven for disobedience; he lost his reward of possessing his inheritance.

You simply cannot have it both ways. You can't say justification salvation is a free gift and then turn around and say you **have to have** good works to keep that salvation or prove that you have it. To practice the works of the flesh is certainly a tragedy. It means never discovering the purpose for one's life. It means losing the intimacy we could have with Jesus for all eternity (a lost reward). It means losing countless other rewards that would make up the crowns that represent the fulfillment of our greatest longing, to be pleasing to our Creator. But it does not mean exclusion from the kingdom of God.

So there are definitely long-term losses. But let us not forget the short-term losses as well. An old man who lived alone had only one friend. It was a cute little Scottish terrier. For fear of losing his best and only friend, the old man usually kept the dog in the house. But on a nice day, the dog was so eager to get outside to freedom the old man would tie a rope to the dog's chain and then tether the dog to a tree in the front yard.

At first the dog was ecstatic at its newfound freedom. It would run and bark and jump in the air out of sheer happiness of being free. But it soon discovered that it wasn't free indeed. It could run no farther than the rope would allow. But so as to maximize its freedom, the dog would sometimes run in a circle around the tree. Alas, as the owner watched from his swing on the front porch, before too long, the dog was sitting by the tree, panting in frustration at having less freedom than it enjoyed in the house. Then the old man would unwind the rope, and the dog would begin the process all over again.

That's the way the sin nature works. It deceives us into thinking we are free to frolic in its lusts. We can run around all we want, but soon we find ourselves tethered so tight to our sin nature that we are left panting and desperate to be set free again.

So much for the works of the flesh. What about the fruit of the Spirit?

II. FRUIT OF THE SPIRIT   5:22-24

But the fruit of the Spirit is love, joy, peace, longsuffering, kindness, goodness, faithfulness, gentleness, self-control. Against such there is no law.

An analysis of the fruit is not germane to the primary focus of this book (Neo-Galatianism), so I do not intend to analyze each fruit here. However, the fruit are such an important part of the victorious Christian life, we will look at each one closely in the appendix. Here we will just make some general observations.

A. **The Holy Spirit produces the fruit, not the Christian.**

The Holy Spirit is pictured by John in his gospel as a River of Life (John 4:10, 14; 7:38-39). Paul uses the metaphor of a Tree of Life. An apple tree does not get up in the morning and do calisthenics to produce fruit. The apple tree simply allows the sap to flow, and apples are produced. The Christian yields to the Holy Spirit when he allows himself to be led by the Spirit (Gal. 5:16), and not only does he not fulfill the lusts of the flesh, but fruit is produced *by the Spirit*. The responsibility of the believer is to walk by the Spirit or, in John's terms, to abide in the vine (John 15:4).

B. **The fruit is internal, not external.**

We may see external evidence of this fruit, but it is definitely internal. Because it is produced by the Holy Spirit, and because a believer is immediately indwelt by the Holy Spirit the moment he believes in Christ for the first time, the fruit is instantly available as well. A change has taken place. **We categorically reject any caricature of any dispensational position (free grace or otherwise) whether explicit or implicit that we believe a person can be regenerated by the Holy Spirit without any change in his life.**

The moment a person receives the Holy Spirit (when he is regenerated) he is a new person (2 Cor. 5:17). A monumental change has taken place. The issue is not whether there has been a change. The issue is how observable the change might be. Men can see the fruit. Only God can see the root.

I had a friend from my pre-Christian days. He was very promiscuous. A Campus Crusade for Christ staff member led him to Christ. But he already had plans to be with a girl for the upcoming weekend. And he did. There was no observable change in his lifestyle. He continued in this manner for three more months. But inside there was something different. Several months after receiving Christ he was convicted that his promiscuity was wrong. He turned from that sin, got married, and has been faithful to his wife for over forty years. But for quite some time after receiving Christ, it would have been hard for another human being to see any change in his life. Calvinists will say, "But he turned." The point though is that the fruit was working inside him before anything was externally visible. That young man could have hardened himself to the Spirit and continued in promiscuity and experienced self-destruction and loss of inheritance. But his justification and indwelling by the Spirit took place prior to any change in behavior.

Galatians makes it clear that believers are free to choose. And we only have two options: the flesh or the Spirit. If we are honest, we all have a steady progression in our lives of "waking up" to sin of which we were not previously aware. We come to see one sin for what it is, become repulsed by it such that it really isn't an attractive option any longer, then along comes awareness of another aspect of our flesh, and we have new choices to make. This occurs because our flesh is always present on this side of our glorification salvation, when we receive a "new tent."

C. The fruit does not depend on our circumstances.

The late Howard Hendricks had a favorite response to any believer who told him he was doing okay under the circumstances. "How'd you get under those?" Hendricks would ask. The Christian does not have to be under the circumstances; he can be over the circumstances. We can have "joy in jail," as the letter to the Philippians proves. We can praise God in the "good times" and do the same in the "bad times." In fact, according to James, the "bad times" may be the "good times." It is a matter of perspective. Romans 12:2 does not tell us to be renewed by a renewing of our circumstances (a new spouse, a new job, a new car) but by a renewing of our mind. Our key to happiness is not the right circumstances but rather what we think (our mind) about our circumstances. The fruit of the Spirit is available to us no matter the circumstances.

D. **The fruit listed here may not all be needed at the same time, but all are available at any given time.**

I wonder whether it is possible to become a mature Christian in continuous isolation. It seems that our vertical relationship with God and our horizontal relationship with men are interrelated. We see this at the most fundamental level in Jesus's summary of the Ten Commandments into two: love God and love men. And God's love language is to keep his commandments (John 14:21). He commands us to love other people. Therefore, we cannot love God if we don't love his people (1 John 2:9-11).

Most of the fruit of the Spirit show up in community. We would not need patience (longsuffering), self-control, kindness, gentleness, and love if we lived alone. As we interact with other people, we may need to call on one or more of the fruit. All of them are available as needed.

Furthermore, we can grow in these areas. As we mature, we should become more loving, more peaceful, gentler, more patient, and so on. If a person's knowledge of the Bible increases without him also becoming a more loving person, a kinder person, and a person with more self-control, we may question whether he is ever learning and never coming to a knowledge of the truth.

E. **The fruit are a measure of the victorious Christian life.**

The victorious Christian life is not measured by how many people I lead to Christ, by how big my church or ministry gets, or by how much money I make. No, it is measured by how consistently I enjoy the fruit of the Spirit. The defeated Christian life is measured by the works of the flesh. The opposite of that is to be led by the Spirit so we don't fulfill the works of the flesh. Rather we "fulfill" the fruit of the Spirit.

As far as I know, only Christianity offers this kind of life. It is a way to have love, joy, peace, and so forth anywhere, anytime. Because it is internal, we can carry it with us. In my last pastorate I had a big, beautiful office where the elders or the staff often met, but I spent little time there. Instead, since I was in on the building of the church, I had a small room built off to the side of my office. A hidden room. That is where I prepared most of my messages. No windows, no distractions. I had some of the best times of my life with the Lord in that little room. The fruit travel with you.

F. **The fruit listed here are not an exhaustive list.**

The Majority Text lists goodness, righteousness, and truth as fruit of the Spirit in Ephesians 5:9. And Matthew 11:29 tells us that Jesus was meek (gentle) and humble (lowly). Humility is not listed in Galatians 5:22-23, but the act of following the lead of the Spirit is the essence of humility. Though all of us wrestle with pride in one form or another, the essence of pride is: "I will control my own destiny." This is a promise the flesh makes, but of course in actuality it brings slavery. We cannot be led by the flesh and also be led by the Spirit at any particular moment. We cannot get close to Jesus while following our own prideful way.

So here is dessert in the desert. A fruit cocktail. This same Spirit gave Daniel peace in the lions' den. He gave David strength against Goliath. And he gave Paul joy in jail. Lions, giants, prison bars—no problem when empowered by the Holy Spirit and enjoying his fruit.

Remember Rapunzel. If the witch represents the flesh that holds us as prisoners with its ugliness, then Prince Charming is Jesus. The fruit of Galatians 5 are the character qualities of Jesus. As we look into the mirror of who we really are in Jesus and release the Holy Spirit within to do his work, then these character qualities are developed in us (2 Cor. 3:18).

Like Rapunzel, we will have difficulty living the substitutionary life if we think we are still just our old, ugly flesh. In Galatians 5:24 Paul again reminds us of the reality of this transformed self God has given us upon the moment of our justification salvation: "And those who are Christ's have crucified the flesh with its passions and desires." This is the new man, the new creation in Christ—our true selves. The old man and its sin nature have been crucified. As Paul asked in Romans 6, "Why, having been freed from death, would you go back into it?" We live the substitutionary life by walking by the Spirit in accordance with the reality of our true identity in Christ.

CONCLUSION

More consistent victory comes as we *focus on the fruit* instead of the flesh. We are all familiar with Michelangelo's beautiful painting on the ceiling of the Sistine Chapel. But it wasn't his favorite work. Michelangelo preferred sculpture to paintings. And perhaps his sculpture of David (in Florence), or the *Pietà*, or his sculpture of Moses pops into your mind.

But most people don't realize that Michelangelo attempted forty-four statues in his life. He finished only fourteen. The thirty he did not finish are also on display in a museum in Italy. In one case there is a huge chunk of marble from which he sculpted only an elbow or the beginning of a wrist. Another shows a leg, the thigh, the knee, the calf, the foot—even the toes. The rest of the body is locked in the chunk of marble and the mind of the sculptor. It will never come out now. Still another reveals a head and shoulders, but the arm and hands are still frozen inside.

That is what happens when we resist the work of the Holy Spirit in our lives. We can quench him with our hardened hearts, we can grieve him with our sin, and we can go through life's museum on display as an unfinished work. Even worse, does any of us want to show up before Jesus and his angels (Matt. 16:27) as one of his unfinished works? We don't have to. We can walk by the Spirit and let him finish his work. "Are you so foolish? Having begun in the Spirit, are you now being made perfect by the flesh?" (Gal. 3:3). We conclude with the words of Lewis Sperry Chafer:

> It may be said...that a spiritual Christian is a...Christian in whom the unhindered Spirit is manifesting Christ by producing a true Christian character, which is the fruit of the Spirit.... It is a divine output of the life, rather than a mere cessation of things which are called "worldly." True spirituality does not consist in what one does not do; it is rather what one does. It is not suppression; it is expression. It is not holding in self; it is living out Christ.[99]

---

99 Lewis Sperry Chafer, *He That Is Spiritual* (Grand Rapids, MI: Dunham, 1966), 68.

15

BAND OF BROTHERS
Galatians 5:25-6:5

Stephen Ambrose came out with a book some years back that struck a chord with its readers and became a best seller—*Band of Brothers*. It was turned into a ten-part TV miniseries as well. It was a book about war, but not just another war book. It was really a book about human interdependence or what Ambrose calls camaraderie. The bonding that took place between the soldiers of E Company of the 101st Airborne, which parachuted into Normandy and fought its way to Hitler's Eagle's Nest, was simply unparalleled. The men got to where they could recognize each other's shadows, smells, and even breathing. The intimacy of their band of brothers was so intense, they never experienced anything like it again and spent the rest of their lives looking for it.

The men of Easy Company came from different backgrounds and different parts of the United States and different socioeconomic backgrounds. They came together in the summer of 1942 after the Europeans had been at war for three years, but by October 1944, "it was as good a rifle company as there was in the world."[100] All

---

100 Stephen E. Ambrose, *Band of Brothers* (New York: Simon & Schuster Paperbacks, 2001), 16.

but three out of the original 140 were unmarried. Most of them grew up as hunters and athletes. "They were special in their values. They put a premium on physical well-being, hierarchical authority, and being part of an elite unit. They were idealists, eager to merge themselves into a group fighting for a cause, actively seeking an outfit with which they could identify, join, be a part of, relate to as a family."[101]

And family they became. They were linked by their chanting, their singing in unison, cadence counts, and by the misery of their endless exercises. They learned to act as a unit. Within days of their formation, Easy Company "could make a one-quarter or one-half turn, or an about-face, as if one." They could set off at double-time, or on a full run, or drop to the ground to do push-ups. They shouted "Yes, Sir!" or "No, Sir!" in unison.

> The result of these shared experiences was closeness unknown to all outsiders. Comrades are closer than friends, closer than brothers. Their relationship is different from that of lovers. Their trust in, and knowledge of, each other is total. They got to know each other's life stories, what they did before they came into the Army, where and why they volunteered, what they liked to eat and drink, what their capabilities were. On a night march they would hear a cough and know who it was; on a night maneuver they would see someone sneaking through the woods and know who it was from his silhouette.[102]

Ambrose agrees with philosopher J. Glenn Gray, who wrote, "Organization for a common and concrete goal in peacetime organizations does not evoke anything like the degree of comradeship commonly known in war.... At its height, this sense of comradeship is an ecstasy. Men are true comrades only when each is ready to give

---

101 Ibid.

102 Ibid., 21.

up his life for the other, without reflection and without thought of personal loss."[103]

And this sense of comradeship, which began during their training but was steeled during combat, was never forgotten. Private Don Malarkey of Oregon observed forty-nine years after entering Easy Company, "So this was the beginning of the most momentous experience of my life, as a member of E company. There is not a day that has passed since that I do not thank Adolf Hitler for allowing me to be associated with the most talented and inspiring group of men that I have ever known."[104] But it was also never recaptured. It couldn't be. Not unless they went back to war. It was war with its life-and-death struggle that created the need for intense interdependence.

As we read the book of Acts, we get the impression that the early Christians understood this kind of intense intimacy and, because of the spiritual dimension, perhaps an even greater intimacy. Early on they sold their possessions and gave the proceeds for the common good. They were meeting daily from house to house for worship and encouragement. And when persecution began, they were at war. All kinds of bands of brothers and sisters developed. We call them churches. But I have a feeling these early churches were quite a bit different from what we have in our minds today when we think about church. I am not referring just to the obvious contrast in church buildings. I am thinking more about the lack of bonding, the lack of interdependence, and the lack of willingness to sacrifice for one's brother or sister in today's modern churches.

We can never return to those early days of the church. But isn't there something we can do to recapture that team spirit they had? Isn't there something we can do to become a band of brothers? We can, and we should. That's what Paul's lesson is all about in Galatians 5:25-6:5.

---

103 Ibid., 22.

104 Ibid.

GALATIANS
"The Gospel of Grace"

We are still learning about sanctification by faith. The key word is *freedom*—freedom from a life of legalism, freedom to choose to follow the Spirit and live a substitutionary life. We have illustrated the facts of freedom, indicted the foes of freedom (the legalists) and the follies of freedom (using freedom for the flesh), and now we are illustrating the fruits of freedom: loving men (5:25-6:5) and loving God (6:6-10). Paul's big idea on loving men is that we should be a band of brothers.

The idea of a marching band is not really foreign to the text; although, he doesn't have music in mind. Paul is thinking about war. He says, **"If we live in the Spirit, let us also walk in the Spirit."** The problem with this translation is that it completely misses the fact that the word translated "walk" is a different word from the one used in 5:16. There it was the usual Greek word for "walk"—*peripateō*. Here Paul uses *stoicheō*, which is the Greek word for "march." Paul envisions an army and probably has the Roman phalanx in mind, the marching formation that became the juggernaut of the Roman army. It was formed in such a way that someone always had your back, and when it came to war tactics of the day, it was unstoppable. Paul envisions such a formation, only this is the Christian army where someone always has your back. The call is to become a soldier in this army. But this is not a draft call. We are free, but he encourages us to use our freedom to serve. Volunteer. Join the "band of brothers." Become part of a community of people who are committed to serving the King by serving each other. And here is how to serve: stifle a competitive spirit (5:26) and stimulate a community spirit (6:1-6:5).

I. STIFLE A COMPETITIVE SPIRIT   5:26

Let us not become conceited, provoking one another, envying one another.

One of the early strains of Greek philosophy that crept into Christianity through Augustine (d. AD 430) was ascetic (denial of the flesh) mysticism. Marriage was discouraged. Denial of the flesh was encouraged. Through solitary contemplation and denial of the flesh, one could hope to have an ecstatic experience of closeness to God. This was Christian ascetic mysticism.

Monastic orders developed—entire communes of men who took vows of chastity and poverty in an effort to heighten their spirituality and find sublime truth. When this solitary approach to God coupled with the triumph of reason during the Enlightenment, the result was a rugged individualism, even in Christianity. A sense of community was lost. The interdependence of believers was viewed as weakness. "Lone Ranger" Christianity and the privacy of the believer filled the atmosphere of the church. As Anne Ortland put it in her excellent book *Up with Worship*:

Every congregation has a choice to be one of two things. You can choose to be a bag of marbles, single units that don't affect each other except in collision. On Sunday morning you can chose to go to church or to sleep in: who really cares whether there are 192 or 193 marbles in a bag?

Or you can choose to be a bag of grapes. The juices begin to mingle, and there is no way to extricate yourselves if you tried. Each is part of all. Part of the fragrance. Part of the "stuff."[105]

But rugged individualism has no place in God's "band of brothers." The band of brothers were rugged individuals, for sure. But they were also a unit. If you want to blow your own horn, you will forever be a soloist without a band to back you up. In God's church there is only one Superstar, and it is not the pastor or the worship leader. Even modern business is turning away from the superstar model of management. Many of the top CEOs of Fortune 500 companies are "sleepers"; that is, they grew up within the ranks of the company without fanfare but over time proved themselves to be great team builders with the ability to promote esprit rapport and productivity.

In his book *The Fifth Discipline*, Peter Senge uses the Boston Celtics, when Bill Russell was at the helm, as an example of how the whole can be greater than the sum of the parts, but only when the parts are properly lined up and point the same direction.[106] That takes great teamwork, and Bill Russell was a great team leader. Subsequent NBA championship teams made up of great individual stars have had to learn this lesson in order to win it all (the Celtics with Ray Allen, Paul Pierce, and Kevin Garnett or the Heat with Chris Bosh, Dwyane Wade, and LeBron James).

But the flesh can so easily get in our way, especially among the gifted and talented. The word for "conceited" here is *kenodoxoi* = *keno* + *doxoi* = empty + glory. So it refers to someone who is out for an empty glory, which is a glory apart from God. I used to belong to a ministerial association, but I stopped going because of

---

105 Anne Ortland, *Up with Worship* (Ventura, CA: Regal, 1982), 102.

106 Peter M. Senge, *The Fifth Discipline* (New York: Doubleday/ Currency, 1990), 233-34.

the competitive spirit among the ministers. Is this something new? Don't think so. Over and over Jesus tried to demonstrate and teach his disciples that the greatest among them was the servant of all. But even during the Last Supper their competitive spirit was still there. Luke 22:24 says that even during the meal they were arguing over "which of them should be considered the greatest." They were **"provoking one another, envying one another."** They were striving for glory not by serving one another but by pushing down one another. There is no place for that in a marching band of brothers.

Romans 2 commands us to seek glory by doing good. John 17 makes it clear Jesus sought glory, and Philippians 2 tells us to have the same mind as Jesus. But the Bible wants us to gain glory (recognition) from God, not man. The same Romans 2 passage contrasts seeking glory from God with "self-seeking." Our greatest reward is the pleasure of God. And arguably our greatest self-inflicted harm comes when we are self-seeking. If the fruit of the Spirit is love and all its benefits, the fruit of the flesh is self-seeking and the division it brings.

Competition destroys community. I don't think God minds if we compete; he asks us to do so in spiritual warfare. We are competing against the flesh and the world in order to win his approval. But the kind of competition that brings worldly glory often involves the destruction of others, and that must make God very sad.

God recorded the Upper Room account to teach servanthood, not one-upmanship. I enjoyed reading Rick Reilly before he left *Sports Illustrated* to do his own thing. He always had the last article on the last page. His pen could be complimentary or caustic as the mood hit him. One week it turned on an athlete without mercy. The article began, "On the official Ten Most Selfish, Greedy, Spoiled to the Spleen, Multimillionaire Athletes You'd Most Like to See Thrown to a Dieting Lion list, you'd have to rank Latrell Sprewell one through at least eight."[107]

---

107 Rick Reilly, "Getting by on $14.6 Mil," *Sports Illustrated*, November 15, 2004, www.si.com/vault/2004/11/15/8191994/getting-by-on-146-mil.

Latrell was playing at the time for the Minnesota Timberwolves as a guard. His playing mate, who later went to the Celtics to win a championship, was the MVP of the league, Kevin Garnett. The Timberwolves needed Sprewell's talents to win it all, but he was unhappy. He was due to make $14.6 million in the upcoming season, but he was disgruntled because a contract extension had not been worked out to his satisfaction. He was thirty-six years old, an age when most NBA guards can't cover the territory anymore. But the Timberwolves were willing to give him a three-year extension for $21 million. Sprewell was disgusted and pouting, right in front of reporters no less. One of them said, "Why don't you just help the T-Wolves win the NBA title this season and then see what happens?" His response? "Why would I want to help them win a title? They're not doing anything for me. I'm at risk. I have a lot of risk here. I got my family to feed. Anything could happen." Reilly's retort?

> Whose family is this guy feeding, Brigham Young's?... He could feed not only his family, but 8.3 million people for one day. Or a village of 400 for nearly 57 years.... Spree can't relate. Spree doesn't have time to. Spree is busy tending to his huge yacht. Spree is busy driving his fleet of cars, including a custom-designed Lamborghini Diablo, a Rolls-Royce Phantom, and a $300,000 Maybach, the one with a champagne cooler in the armrest.[108]

Selfishness, greed, individualism. How do you think Sprewell's attitude affected his teammates when they went out on the court with him? Needless to say, the T-Wolves never won that championship. How could they win with rugged individuals like Latrell Sprewell bringing the ball up the court?

Yes, God wants us to stifle a worldly competitive spirit and, by contrast, to stimulate a team-oriented community spirit.

---

108 Ibid.

II. STIMULATE A COMMUNITY SPIRIT   6:1-5

Paul suggests three ways we can stimulate a community spirit, a band of brothers: correcting your brother (6:1), carrying your brother's load (6:2), and carrying your own load (6:3-5).

A. Correcting Your Brother (6:1)

> Brethren, if a man is overtaken in any trespass, you who are spiritual restore such a one in a spirit of gentleness, considering yourself lest you also be tempted.

We have a military unit in mind or, if you will, a marching band of brothers. One member of the unit or band steps out of line. Others could trip over him; the entire formation could be ruined. Out of love he should be brought back in line. Unfortunately, it has been said with more truth than error that the Christian army is the only army in the world that shoots its wounded.

As I sit here, I am thinking of three men who are not currently in ministry, unjustly so. That took about three seconds of thinking. I wonder how long a list I could make if I thought for an hour. One of these men had multiple gifts, the kinds that win you awards at graduation. He took a job as the number two man in an evangelical church. I had known and followed this young man since he was a youth. He had great potential, but he also had a problem—pornography.

Not wanting to be a hypocrite or a defeated Christian in ministry, during his second year of seminary he sought out an accountability group. With their support he was pornography-free during his last three years of school. Then after settling into his new ministry, the church was upgrading their computer system. He requested a filter for the new system. When asked why, he told them of his weakness. With no evidence at all of any misbehavior, they asked him to leave, and he was gone in three months. He asked me to fly up to his out-of-state home to console his wife and support him. I was glad to do so, but that young man never went back into the ministry. He was too shattered by getting shot by "friendlies."

Galatians 6:1 is about restoration. In the illustration above, our brother hadn't even done anything wrong. In fact, he should have been commended for his honesty. In contrast, in Galatians 6:1, we have a brother who is caught red-handed (*prolambanō* carries the idea of being detected, caught by surprise) in some trespass. The particular trespass is not specified, so it could cover a wide range of issues. So he's caught. So now let's shoot him. Not at all. He is to be restored. What does that mean and how do we do it?

1. **Who?** Who does the restoring? It says "you" who are "spiritual." It is very important to recognize the plural in this instruction. The "you" in this verse is plural in the Greek and emphatic (*humeis*). The emphatic use of *humeis* underscores an important principle of restoration: *do not go alone*. The place for going alone is in Matthew 18:15 when someone has sinned against *you*. Then you first go alone to the offending person. That is not the situation here. If you go alone, you will most likely find a reactive, defensive, angry person who will throw it in your face. That is much harder to do with a group or at least two, preferably three. It identifies these confronters as "spiritual." That is probably a reference to the church leadership. In other words, if you are not an elder in your church and you find out someone in your circle is involved in gross moral sin, it is not your responsibility to confront the sinner since you have no spiritual authority over him. That is the responsibility of the church leaders. This works best if one or more of those who go have a close relationship with the offender. Children receive discipline best when they know their parents love them. That is also true of church discipline.

2. **What?** What are they supposed to do? The text says to "restore" him. The word used here is very instructive (*katartizō*). It is used in setting bones, of restoring the bone to its former usefulness. That should be the goal

of this process. Let's get this soldier out of the infirmary and back on the front lines. The only one who wins if he is never restored to usefulness is the devil himself. Must he be restored to the same position he had before his fall? Not necessarily. But restore him to usefulness on the front lines. Sometimes the restoration is done too quickly. Some of these broken bones can take years to heal. Oftentimes it has something to do with the reformation of the ego boundary referenced earlier. If that ego boundary has not reformed, the individual in view can quickly and easily fall into the same trap as before. It takes, on average, two years for a broken ego boundary to reform.

3. **How?** Meekly (*prautēs*—a fruit of the Spirit in Gal. 5:23) or gently. Approaching someone who is wounded or has an open sore must be done sensitively and gently. You don't use a screwdriver to cut off skin cancer. Trying to do so would reap a strong reaction.

4. **Why?** Anyone can step out of line when tempted. Anyone can trip—even you. In fact, 1 Corinthians 10:12 suggests that spiritual pride is a precursor for falling—"Let him who thinks he stands take heed lest he fall."

So, helping to pick up our brother when he falls, and I mean falls into serious sin, is an act of love. And you have to love enough to caringly confront even when there is personal risk. I can never forget the words of Martin Niemöller, a Lutheran pastor who survived a Nazi concentration camp:

In Germany they came for the Communists, and I didn't speak up because I wasn't a Communist. Then they came for the Jews, and I didn't speak up because I wasn't a Jew. Then they came for the trade unionists, and I didn't speak up because I wasn't a trade unionist. Then they came for the Catholics, and

I didn't speak up because I am a Protestant. Then they came for me, and by that time there was no one left to speak up.[109]

Knowing we are there for each other promotes a community spirit. So does carrying our brother's load.

B. Carrying Your Brother's Load (6:2)

Bear one another's burdens, and so fulfill the law of Christ.

The word for "burdens" is really two Greek words: *ta barē* = things too heavy for one person to carry. There are a lot of things like that, aren't there? Is your wife an alcoholic and you are hiding it from the rest of the family? Is your child a homosexual and you are too ashamed to let anyone know? Has your husband walked out ard left you alone? Have you just been fired and you don't have a network to help you get a job? Has one of your children just gotten out of jail? Is your daughter pregnant and unmarried but you are going to hide it from the church by sending her out of state to have the baby? Are you on the verge of a breakdown with no one to talk to? Have you become a drug addict but your parents don't know? All these are burdens too heavy to carry alone.

Someone will surely say, "But these things are too private to share." Really? William Holden was a movie star of yesteryear (*Bridge on the River Kwai, Love Is a Many-Splendored Thing*). When he died, the report read:

William Holden was a private man, and he died a very private death. Alone in his apartment in Santa Monica, Calif., he bled to death from a gash in his forehead caused by a drunken fall against his bedside table. It was four or five days later that his body was found. He was 63.[110]

---

109 "Martin Niemöller," Wikiquote, accessed August 14, 2014, en.wiki quote.org/wiki/Martin_Niemöller.

110 David Ansen, "Golden Boy of the Movies," *Newsweek*, November 30, 1981, 106.

When I read that, I thought, *Four or five days later? You've got to be kidding me. He was so isolated from people that no friend knew he was missing for almost a week?* The end of the article gives us a clue: "Holden guarded his privacy with increasing vigilance." Do we Christians not do the same? The priesthood of the believer is not intended to be kept private. You might not die from a drunken fall like Holden did, but isolationism can throw you into a spiritual depression Paul calls death (Rom. 8:6) just the same. All forms of death are matters of separation. The first physical implementation of death on Adam and Eve was exile from the garden and spiritual separation from God. When we put ourselves in exile, we are choosing a form of death.

When we bear one another's burdens, Paul says we "fulfill" the law of Christ. That word "fulfill" doesn't quite give us the full picture. The word used here is *anaplēroō = ana + plēroō* = up to the top + fill = completely fulfill—to the brim. The "law of Christ" most likely refers to John 13:34-35 where Christ gave his disciples a new commandment to love each other as he had loved them. Wow. So Paul is saying that bearing burdens too heavy for one person to handle is completely fulfilling Christ's law of love.

To open up takes trust. It takes feeling safe. You have to sense that if you share these deeply private burdens you won't get burned. A man in our church got a DWI. I knew him well enough to ask, "Why don't you just drink at home? Why go to a bar and risk hurting yourself or someone else?" I'll never forget his reply: "I don't go to the bar to drink; drinking is the price I pay for unconditional love. I can't seem to find that in church." Sometimes it is easier to find this kind of safe house in a bar rather than a church. Bruce Larson comments:

> The neighborhood bar is possibly the best counterfeit there is to the fellowship Christ wants to give His church. It's an imitation, dispensing liquor instead of grace, escape rather than reality, but it is a permissive, accepting and inclusive fellowship. It is unshockable. It is democratic. You can tell people secrets and they usually don't tell others or even want

to. The bar flourishes not because most people are alcoholics, but because God has put into the human heart the desire to know and be known, to love and be loved, and so many seek a counterfeit at the price of a few beers.

With all my heart I believe that Christ wants His church to be...a fellowship where people can come in and say, "I'm sunk!" "I'm beat!" "I've had it!"[111]

It can happen. Some years ago I spoke at a men's retreat for a large church in Austin. They had a couple of hundred men. Like most retreats there was some singing, and then I was on—Friday evening, Saturday morning (twice), Saturday evening. But then something happened I had not seen at a retreat before. Sharing time began. Men would come up to share a burden with the understanding that two or more would immediately come to pray with him and for him. But those same two or more were also committing to a year of accountability to meet with this brother and bear his burden for that year. Awesome. Men shared as I had never seen men share before. I met six men who had divorced their wives but had formed a "Get 'Em Back" club devoted to winning their wives back (none of the six wives had remarried). A year went by, and I got a call from the same church. Their speaker had suddenly taken ill. Could I come on short notice to speak? I agreed on one condition—that I could bring some of my staff with me to witness this kind of retreat (to God's glory we were able to replicate what was going on in Austin; although, it took about three years to get the men to really open up). I saw the guys with the "Get 'Em Back" club. Over the year three of them had been able to remarry their former wives. These men were bearing one another's burdens.

In order to stimulate a community spirit we need to be willing to correct our brother and to carry our brother's load. But we also need to carry our own load.

---

111 Bruce Larson and Keith Miller, *The Edge of Adventure* (Waco, TX: Word Books, 1974), 156.

C. Carry Your Own Load (6:3-5)

> For if anyone thinks himself to be something, when he is nothing, he deceives himself. But let each one examine his own work, and then he will have rejoicing in himself alone, and not in another. For each one shall bear his own load.

When Paul tells us to carry our brother's burden, he uses the words *ta barē*, a load too heavy for one person to carry. But when he tells us to carry our own burden, he uses the word *phortion*, which literally referred to that which you could carry in a backpack—a reasonable load. He is talking about a band of brothers. If I am supposed to be playing the violin in a quartet and don't do my job, the music won't sound right. Each person is there for a reason. Each must do his part. In another passage (1 Cor. 12), Paul compares the church to a body. Each part of the body is important. Rigor mortis sets in to the degree there are parts of the body not functioning. A dead church most likely is one with only a few moving parts.

I'm not a bumper-sticker kind of guy. My wife is a bumper-sticker kind of gal. She has bumper stickers for all sorts of things, most of them political. When election time gets near, she slips out at five in the morning to put bumper stickers on *my* car. Isn't that a bit intrusive? **My car.** Well, during one of the presidential elections I must have heard ten times about early voting, not waiting in line, don't forget. Frankly, it wears me out. But she was headed to Minnesota with seventy other Texas women to drum up votes for their presidential choice. She had voted early; I had not. So she's calling me long distance to tell me not to forget. While she was gone, I read an article about how my vote in Texas really wouldn't count— the electoral thing and all that. So I knew my vote wouldn't count. But I knew my vote would count, maybe not in the final outcome, but it would at election central (my house). So I went over at three o'clock on Tuesday to vote. No line. In and out. But as I left, they gave me a sticker. I started to toss it, but I looked and it said, "I Voted." *Man*, I thought, *here's proof.* So I marched over to my car and slapped on that bumper sticker faster than a mosquito can suck blood. First bumper sticker I ever put on a car. Don't tell me I don't know how to build a rock-solid marriage.

But what if I didn't vote…and you didn't vote…and no one voted? The saying goes, "Bad people are elected by good people who don't vote." Could we say something similar about the church: "Bad churches are made up of good people who do nothing"? We can build a community spirit by correcting our brother, carrying our brother's load, and carrying our own load.

It has been said that one can acquire everything in solitude… except character. You can live for decades all by yourself. You will survive. Hermits have done it. But you won't spiritually survive. To build Christian character you've got to be in community. It is in community that you see mistakes; it's in community that you learn forgiveness; it's in community that you practice mercy; only in community can you fulfill the law of Christ. In community we learn patience, kindness, and love—all these Christian virtues, none of which can be learned in isolation.

Not that I don't enjoy solitude and a little isolation. Right now I have sequestered myself in northeastern Oregon, in a cabin, alone. This is where I write. Yesterday I hiked up Bear Creek a few miles. As I neared the top, I had to stop to enjoy the view over a gorge with a rippling river at the bottom. I looked around at the gigantic pine trees that stood at attention like thousands of Green Berets ready to guard their turf. I sat on a rock and closed my eyes for a moment. A cloud passed, and the sunshine opened my eyes. I imagined God smiling down and his love, like the sunshine, covering the mountainside like a warm blanket. I watched the grass bend over as though the gentle breeze were God's fingers stroking the mountain's hair as she put her head on his majestic shoulder to rest. And then a doe hopped up to stare at me like a sentry guarding the peaceful solitude of a lost world. Yes, I like a little solitude. And sometimes I fantasize about retiring in just such a place. But then I am reminded that God's will involves people. Voluntary isolation for a prolonged period of time does not build Christian character.

There is another problem with isolation. Have you ever noticed that lions like loners? Yes, animals of prey single out the loner and wait for a moment of weakness to attack. It is dangerous to be alone for too long. In the Jewish synagogues both ancient and contemporary, at the end of a reading from the book of Moses, the Torah, the congregation will shout out in unison: "*Hazeq, hazeq, ve-nithazeq,*" which means "Be strong, be strong, and let us strengthen one another." It's a cheer, a cheer for community.

In the summer of 2002, I went to Germany to write—alone. The aloneness is heightened in a country where the language is not your native tongue. As I was leaving, my daughter asked me if I was taking any music. I said I hadn't thought of it. So she just grabbed a bunch of her CDs and said, "Take these." I didn't listen to them for about six weeks, but then I found myself starving for a little English, so I looked at what she had given me. Her tastes and mine don't exactly coincide (surprise, surprise). She had one by Garth Brooks. Even though I grew up in Nashville, the Grand Ole Opry was not where I hung out. But wanting to hear some English, I put Garth in the CD player. I found out that Brooks knew something about community. It wasn't because he had "friends in low places," but it was because he understood the danger of loneliness. Here are the lyrics to a song he called "Wolves":

> January's always bitter
> But Lord this one beats all
> The wind ain't quit for weeks now
> And the drifts are ten feet tall
> I been all night drivin' heifers
> Closer in to lower ground
> Then I spent the mornin' thinkin'
> 'Bout the ones the wolves pulled down
> Charlie Barton and his family
> Stopped today to say goodbye
> He said the bank was takin' over
> The last few years were just too dry
> And I promised that I'd visit

When they found a place in town
Then I spent a long time thinkin'
'Bout the ones the wolves pull down
Lord please shine a light of hope
On those of us who fall behind
And when we stumble in the snow
Could you help us up while there's still time
Well I don't mean to be complainin' Lord
You've always seen me through
And I know you got your reasons
For each and every thing you do
But tonight outside my window
There's a lonesome mournful sound
And I just can't keep from thinkin'
'Bout the ones the wolves pull down
Oh Lord keep me from bein'
The one the wolves pull down.[112]

A band of brothers is protection against the wolves. Insulation overcomes isolation. As I read that book by Ambrose, I wondered why more churches or even small groups never find that kind of intimacy. After all, we are brothers and sisters in a way men of war are not. We have the bond of the Holy Spirit to bind us in a way the world will never know. But, as a general rule, this kind of bonding does not take place. I have often wondered why. **Could it be that we don't know we are at war?** Paul himself calls us to arms. He says we are in a battle for control of the entire universe. But how many of us are aware that a war is going on around us? And how many of us have volunteered for his army, regardless of the cost? Soldiers at war. That's where we find bands of brothers.

---

112 Garth Brooks, "Wolves," accessed August 14, 2014, www.azlyrics. com/lyrics/garthbrooks/wolves.html.

16

FOR THE LOVE OF GOD
Galatians 6:6-10

What is the most outrageous thing you would do for $10,000 cash? That was the question recently posed by Chicago radio station WKOX. They got responses from more than six thousand full-tilt crazies. The eventual winner was Jay Gwaltney of Zionsville, Indiana, who consumed an eleven-foot birch sapling—leaves, roots, bark, and all.[113]

For the event Gwaltney donned a tux and dined at a table set elegantly with china, sterling, candles, and a rose vase. Armed with pruning sheers, the Indian State University sophomore began chomping from the top of the tree and worked his way, branch by branch, to the roots. His only condiment: French dressing for the massive birch-leaf salad. The culinary feat took eighteen hours over

---

113 Diane Swanson, *Burp!: The Most Interesting Book You'll Ever Read About Eating*, Barnes & Noble, www.barnesandnoble.com/w/burp-the-most-interesting-book-youlll-ever-read-about-eating-diane-swanson/1114143181?ean=9781550745993.

a period of three days. When it was all over, Gwaltney complained of an upset stomach. Evidently the bark was worse than his bite (sorry).

Yes, there are many extremes we might go to in order to get a large sum of discretionary money. After all, with enough money, we can pay cash for a house, a luxury car, even an airplane, or, like Johnny Depp and Marlon Brando, our own island. But can we buy happiness? Seems like everyone says no, but the Bible says yes. That's right, the Bible says there is a direct link between money and happiness. Let's see how in Galatians 6:6-10.

To the mind of a Protestant, one of the strangest connections in the Bible is the connection between money and eternal life. We believe that eternal life is the gift of God through Jesus Christ (John 3:16; Eph. 2:9-10) to those who believe in Christ alone. But Galatians 6 tells us we can reap eternal life by giving money. And 1 Timothy 6:6-12 claims we can lay hold of eternal life if we flee the love of money and pursue godliness and fight the good fight of faith.

How can eternal life be both a gift we receive by faith and something we can lay hold of when we fight the good fight of faith? Again, the answer is in Galatians 6:6-10. We want to look at the principle of sharing (6:6), the principle of reaping (6:7-8), and the principle of waiting (6:9-10).

I. THE PRINCIPLE OF SHARING 6:6

Let him who is taught the word share in all good things with him who teaches.

This may be my favorite verse in the Bible. Not yours? Well, perhaps it is because you are not a pastor. I used to keep this displayed in my church office for all to see who dared to enter. It just says you ought to support the pastor with material things. Of course, I am kidding about this being my favorite verse and displaying this verse in my office. But I am not kidding about the following.

I don't watch much TV other than for sports or old movies, but on one particular Sunday I was trying to relax after preaching three morning sermons in four hours, so I channel surfed. There are a lot of church services on at that time, and I landed on one. It was a well-known pastor in one of our large metropolitan cities. He had declared this particular Sunday to be Pastor Appreciation Day. Of course, one of the best ways to appreciate your pastor is with Galatians 6:6—give him some money. So he called for the congregation to respond on the spot. The first one down the aisle was a wealthy professional football player (all-pro) with a check for $100,000. Another famous football player was in the congregation, and he wasn't to be outdone, so he also forked up $100,000. When it was all over, the pastor had truly been appreciated—over a million dollars had been given for his personal account.

I could hardly contain my excitement. I announced to my wife that the very next Sunday would be Pastor Appreciation Day in our church. And I announced it to our congregation. I didn't ask them to come down front because I eschew ostentation, but I allowed they could put their designated checks in the offering boxes in the back. Alas, the deacons did not find a single check designated for me. Now, I truly did make that announcement, but my congregation knew me well enough to know I wasn't being serious (not sure it would have mattered). My church paid me very generously without any extra appeals. They were more than fulfilling Galatians 6:6.

Of course, this verse can be abused and it is. But proper support of pastors and teachers is right and good. Some groups teach that it is more noble and good for the teachers and preachers to support themselves. That is an option, but it is not necessarily a better option. Material giving to the church and other ministries is a necessity for spiritual health. Our root problem is selfishness. Giving tears away at our root problem. We shouldn't say we have given our bodies as living sacrifices (Rom. 12:1) if we are not giving sacrificially of our money. That would be self-deception. The smaller (money) comes before the larger (our bodies).

According to Ronald Blue and Company (a Christian financial

services company), people who do not go to church or claim any religious faith give 1.7 percent of their adjusted gross income. The average evangelical gives 2.5 percent. My last eighteen years of pastoring were with the same church. It was an affluent church. We never passed a plate, but we never missed our budget. I can never remember making a financial appeal. All I had to do once a year was get up and say thank you. But looking back, I believe I did the people of that church a disservice.

As a pastor, I never wanted to know what my congregants were giving. I was afraid it might influence my attitudes toward them, for good or bad. But one day our finance manager told me that about a third of our attendees never gave anything. Now obviously we didn't need their money to do the work of the ministry. But by not teaching more about biblical giving, I had done those people a disservice. And I wonder about the two-thirds. I wonder how many of them were giving according to the evangelical average. Am I writing these words to get more money? Hardly. I am no longer a pastor. I am writing them to help believers be happier.

What can bring greater happiness than to be close to God? David wrote, "In Your presence is fullness of joy; at Your right hand are pleasures forevermore" (Ps. 16:11). First John is a book about getting close to God, and it promises sustained joy to those who are intimate with him. In Galatians, Paul is teaching us our money can be used to bring us closer to God or to drive a wedge between us. Jesus simply said we cannot love God and money (mammon) at the same time.

One day a certain miserly man who was plainly miserable visited a rabbi to find out why he was so unhappy. The rabbi took the wealthy man by the hand and led him to a window. "Look out there," he said. The rich man looked into the street. "What do you see?" asked the rabbi. "I see men, women, and children," answered the rich man. Again the rabbi took him by the hand and this time led him to a mirror and asked, "Now what do you see?" "I see myself," the old man replied.

Then the rabbi said, "Behold, in the window there is glass and in the mirror there is glass. But the glass of the mirror is covered with a little silver, and no sooner is the silver added than you cease to see others, but you see only yourself." So it is when money gets between God and us. Just a little silver can change our focus. Perhaps that is also why Jesus said riches can be so deceitful (Matt. 13:22).

But money can also be a great tool to help us get closer to God. That takes us from the principle of sharing to the principle of reaping.

II. THE PRINCIPLE OF REAPING   6:7-8

> Do not be deceived, God is not mocked; for whatever a man sows, that he will also reap. For he who sows to his flesh will of the flesh reap corruption, but he who sows to the Spirit will of the Spirit reap everlasting life.

The word for "mocked" (*muktērizoō*) means to "ridicule" or "outwit" (BDAG/MM). Paul says we cannot outwit God when it comes to the physical or spiritual laws of the universe. We cannot jump off buildings and fly. Nor can we serve God with our time and talents, but rob him of our tithes and offerings and fool him into thinking our hearts are with him. Jesus set forth the law: "Where man's treasure is, there his heart is also" (Matt. 6:21).

Here Paul applies the physical law of reaping to the spiritual life. Same principle. Only here it is more the idea of "where" instead of "what." If you sow in the physical world, you will reap in the physical world. If you sow in the spiritual world, you will reap in the spiritual world. As Robert Louis Stevenson wrote, "Sooner or later each of us sits down to a banquet of consequences."

But the physical world will perish, while the spiritual world will last. Nevertheless, there is a **crossover** principle. *We can sow physical things that will reap spiritual things.* We can sow in the physical world and reap in the spiritual world. When we give money to God's work, our material things can reap spiritual benefits. In this case the spiritual benefit is "eternal life." This does not refer to length of existence. All people will exist forever. It refers to our *quality* of existence. And we don't wait until we die to get this eternal life. We get our first installment when we first trust Christ as our Savior. It's a free gift.

But our experience in quality of life becomes tangible as we exercise the substitutionary life. Eternal life could be translated "age-long fulfillment." When we gain the free gift of eternal life, we get a promise of life with God for eternity and the presence of the Holy Spirit; that is irrevocable. But whether we experience this gift through the substitutionary life is a matter of our choice. And if we make a good choice to walk by faith, we gain the reward of experiencing the current reality of the gift. Thus, our quality of life can get better as we sow material things into the spiritual world. And the effects will live on forever. This, then, is the connection between our money and our happiness. Money can make us miserable or money can make us happy. It all depends on where we do our sowing.

Now one branch of Neo-Galatians have taken advantage of giving to turn it into legalism. They teach "Give to get." It is very subtle. "You can't out-give God," they claim. That is true. The misleading part is to leave the impression that God will give "in kind" or "as we demand." In other words, legalism says that if I tithe, God will bless me in the way I want, like making my business financially profitable. So I give money to God to get money from God. I "give" as if God were a slot machine. That is legalism pure and simple.

The mistake is believing my obedience will determine physical blessings as I demand. God can, and often does, give us physical blessings. But most certainly we do not control what God does. God will decide what is best for us, and what blessing we need, thank you very much. And if you get sucked into a ruse that treats God as a slot machine, you may wind up very disillusioned indeed. Blessings *are* guaranteed both in this world and the next (assuming our motive is right—1 Cor. 13:3), but while the blessings may include physical blessings, we can be sure there will always be spiritual blessings. One thing is for sure: it is *giving* money that brings happiness, not making money.

In 1928, a group of the world's most successful financiers met at the Edgewater Beach Hotel in Chicago. The following were present: the president of Bethlehem Steel, the greatest wheat speculator, the president of the New York Stock Exchange, a member of the president's cabinet, the greatest "bear" on Wall Street, the president of the Bank of International Settlements, and the head of the world's greatest monopoly. Collectively, these tycoons controlled more wealth than there was in the US Treasury, and for years newspapers and magazines had been printing their success stories and encouraging the youth of the nation to follow their examples. Twenty-five years later, this is what had happened to these men.

- The president of Bethlehem Steel, Charles M. Schwab, lived on borrowed money the last five years of his life and died broke.

- The greatest wheat speculator, Arthur Cutten, died abroad, insolvent.

- The president of the New York Stock Exchange, Richard Whitney, served a term in Sing Sing Prison.

- The member of the president's cabinet, Albert Fall, was pardoned from prison so he could die at home.

- The greatest "bear" on Wall Street, Jesse Livermore, committed suicide.

- The president of the Bank of International Settlements, Leon Fraser, committed suicide.

- The head of the world's greatest monopoly, Ivar Kreuger, committed suicide.

All of these men had learned how to make money, but apparently none of them had learned how to live. "As you sow, so shall you also reap."

We have looked at the principle of sowing and the principle of reaping. Now, what about the principle of waiting?

III. THE PRINCIPLE OF WAITING   6:9-10

> And let us not grow weary while doing good, for in due season we shall reap if we do not lose heart. Therefore, as we have opportunity, let us do good to all, especially to those who are of the household of faith.

A farmer came to the city. He hadn't seen elevators before. In the reception area of his hotel he watched an elevator open, and an older, overweight woman entered. As soon as the doors shut, the doors to an elevator next to the first elevator opened, and a gorgeous young woman walked out. The farmer's eyes bulged, and he turned to his teenage son and said, "Billy Bob, you go out there and fetch your ma out of the pickup. I'm gonna run her through these things myself."

It's hard to be patient. We all would like to see instant results. But when sowing material things into the spiritual world, we won't always see immediate results. Most of them we probably won't see until we are living in that spiritual world. But one immediate result we can see is joy and happiness in our own lives (eternal life). "God loves a cheerful giver" (2 Cor. 9:7), and "It is more blessed [happier] to give than to receive" (Acts 20:35).

So Paul tells us not to grow weary while doing good. Marching is not easy. Remember Galatians 5:25 where we were told to march in step (*stoicheo*, the word translated "walk" means "to march in step")? This sentiment is still in Paul's mind. I get tired just thinking about marching. I went to a military prep school in Chattanooga, Tennessee. When we were disciplined, we got to march around the football field. Greater the offense, greater the number of laps. As you might imagine, I got more than my share of marching; although according to his autobiography, Ted Turner beat me out for most marching around the football field at this same school.[114]

The marching here is in the context of giving our money.

---

114 Ted Turner, *Call Me Ted* (New York: Grand Central Publishing, 2008), 13-14.

Unfortunately, when we give our money, we often expect to see God's blessing in the physical world. If we are not careful, we will wake up in the world of legalism (Neo-Galatianism). The "health and wealth" gospel of so many TV ministries is an example of this kind of legalism. Remember, the legalist thinks his obedience is going to guarantee physical blessings in this life: perfect spouse, perfect kids, perfect job, perfect health, perfect church, and so on. But God never promised us all these things. In fact, James 1:2 and 1:12 tell us God actually gives us trials from time to time to make us happier. Sooner or later the legalist will grow weary; he will lose heart; then he will drop out of line (marching). Why? Because his obedience is not yielding the results he believes he is owed.

John F. Walvoord was the president of the seminary where I got my degrees. He became a committed Christian at a Bible study on Galatians while still a teenager. Later, he and his wife had four children. Two of them were so mentally incompetent they lived in homes. One of his sons was something of a renegade up into his thirties before he turned back to the Lord. The apple of their eyes was their fourth child, a son. This son was bright like his parents. He did well enough to get into medical school. Then, while driving off to med school, he was hit by a car and killed. You can believe we all kept a sharp eye on Dr. Walvoord as he was dealing with his grief. We could tell the tragedy had affected him (and who wouldn't be?), but he never stopped marching. His obedience was not tied to physical blessings in this world.

Spiritual blessings in this world? Absolutely. That's what we mean by happiness here and now as a result of the joy of giving. It's the walking-by-faith part of the eternal life package, that quality of living the world will never know. Am I saying unbelievers can't experience the happiness of giving? No, of course not. I am sure Warren Buffett and Bill Gates derive great satisfaction from giving away their billions. But they cannot reap eternal life (that quality of spiritual life that consists mainly in the fruit of the Spirit), which comes from marching by the Holy Spirit. After all, it's his fruit. He is the source. We must have him to have his fruit.

Paul indicates we will not always have an opportunity to do this kind of sowing. "Opportunity" probably means "while we are still able or still have time," not "when I get the time." The night comes when no man can work. This is our opportunity. We will have no other time to do our sowing than in this life.

And where should we give our money? Paul says to do good to all men (believers and unbelievers), but especially to those who are part of the "household of faith." That could mean the church or all those who are part of God's house. It would seem that God encourages us to be generous to all sorts of needs, but it makes sense to start with the church. In due season we will reap, even if we don't see all the ripple effects in this life.

Philippians 1:6 is one of the most quoted verses to try to prove that one who is justified will inevitably be sanctified. After all, it says God will keep on completing the work he began in us until the day of Christ. But wait a minute; the Philippians have been dead a long time. And Christ hasn't come yet. Does that mean God is still working on the Philippians in the afterlife to sanctify them? If so, that would be pretty good support for a Protestant purgatory. A little closer look at the words involved in Philippians 1:3-12 reveals that this letter is a thank-you letter for money the Philippians sent to Paul. It would take a commentary on that book to fully support that statement, but humor me for a moment. If the work begun by God in the Philippians was their financial support to Paul, then God is saying their giving will have ripple effects until Christ comes. That is exactly where Paul goes in the conclusion to Philippians. In his introduction to the letter he speaks of his gratitude for the Philippians' gift, but in his conclusion to the letter he speaks of his attitude toward the Philippians' gift. Philippians 4:10-16 explicitly states that the Philippian church gave money as partners in Paul's gospel ministry, the good work that God began. And Paul says he is not writing this letter to get more money out of them. He has learned to be content whether he has too much or too little. Rather, he is seeking fruit for their account in heaven. And as they give sacrificially, Paul is confident that God will supply all their needs according to his riches in glory in Christ Jesus (Phil. 4:19).

Did you get that? Our giving will have ripple effects for eternity. Think of it. You couldn't even read the letter to the Philippians if they had not given Paul that financial support. Talk about ripple effects. Their act of generosity is recorded for all time in God's Word, which will never pass away. In fact, almost any act of kindness can have ripple effects in eternity.

Edward Kimble was a junior high Sunday school teacher. He made it a point to tell each boy about Christ. One of the boys had language with such poor grammar that all the other boys used to laugh at him. But Kimble wanted to witness to each boy. So he sought out this young man at his place of work, a shoe shop where he was a clerk. Kimble said:

> When I was almost there I wondered if I should do this during working hours. I thought my mission might embarrass the boy, and when I left the other clerks might make fun of him and ask if I were trying to make a good boy out of him. While I was wondering all this, I walked right by the store. When I realized I had walked past it, I decided to make a dash for it and have it all over as quickly as possible. So I ran in, talked to the boy about Christ, and to my amazement, the boy trusted Christ right there in the store. His name was Dwight L. Moody.[115]

While Moody was preaching in London, a young man named F. B. Meyer felt his heart moved by the good news and trusted Christ. He also became an evangelist and came to the States to do evangelism

---

115 "Strategies for Evangelism," accessed August 15, 2014, www.google. com/url?sa=t&rct=j&q=&esrc=s&source=web&cd=3&ved= 0CC4QFjAC&url=http%3A%2F%2Fwww.smallgroups.net%2F Downloads%2FSG-Download-Process.php%3Ffile%3DKimble- to-Billy-Graham.pdf&ei=py2zU4rxKcmlyASZkIEQ&usg=AFQj CNGpBoI4-hTqsjHcEId1uvQNqM3W5Q&bvm=bv.70138588,d. aWw.

in New England. This led to the conversion of J. Wilbur Chapman, who also became an evangelist. He hired Billy Sunday, a former professional baseball player, to do evangelistic work for him. Sunday went down to Charlotte, North Carolina, where he held an evangelistic rally. The response was tremendous. The people of Charlotte wrote back to Chapman asking for Sunday again, but he was booked up. So Chapman sent Mordecai Ham to Charlotte. The first night of the meeting, Ham preached his heart out, but only one teenager came forward—a tall, gangly guy named Billy Graham.

Could humble Sunday school teacher Edward Kimble ever imagine the spiritual avalanche that would result from the single gospel echo he sent into the shoe store? The time is short. There will come a time when we cannot sow any longer. Stephen Grellet wrote in 1885, "I expect to pass through the world but once. Any good I can do or any kindness I can show to any human being, let me not defer it, for I shall not pass this way again."[116]

CONCLUSION

Let me share with you what I believe are the four spiritual laws of finances:

1. **Give by Faith.** Proverbs 3:9 says, "Honor the Lord with your possessions, and with the firstfruits of all your increase." When we give the firstfruits, we are giving by faith. After all, we don't know the future. So to give off the top is to tell the Lord that our gifts are an expression of our faith in him to meet all our future needs. If we give by sight, we are saying, "Lord, I'm not sure we will have enough to make it to the next paycheck, but we'll *see.* If we make it, we will give to you from the leftovers." Surprising how often we don't have anything left over when we give by sight rather

---

116 "Stephen Grellet," Wikiquote, accessed August 15, 2014, http:// en.wikiquote.org/wiki/Stephen_Grellet.

than by faith (see Mal. 3:7-12 where the "devourer" is an insect sent by God to eat up the crops of those who did not bring him the whole tithe, the firstfruits).

2. **Borrow by Sight.** Proverbs 22:7 reads, "The rich rules over the poor, and the borrower is servant to the lender." If you cannot *see* where the money is available to pay off a loan in time of emergency, better not borrow lest you become a slave to that loan or lender. If you have liquid assets to pay off a loan, no problem. Or if you have enough equity in a piece of property that you could pay off a mortgage against it in a "fire sale," no problem. But if you don't, watch out. Even in business this can be a problem. The banking crisis of 2008 was caused by creative leveraging through credit default swaps and fraudulent triple-A ratings of B-mortgage packages. On a personal level, I had two friends in real estate in the eighties in the same city. One leveraged to the hilt and made tens of millions. The other made it a point not to borrow more than he had cash to pay off. He did well, but made only a tenth of the money the other fellow made. When the S&L crisis of the late eighties and early nineties hit, the first guy lost everything. He lived in a mansion but was mowing his own grass. The second guy just kept on trucking. He couldn't lose his properties because he did not owe anything.

3. **Save by Faith.** Proverbs 6:6-12 tells us to learn from the ant. No one has to tell the ant to provide for a cold winter during the summer. Save some from the harvest for a time when there is no reaping. By faith we are to save for a future we don't know will come. James 4:13-14 teaches us not to get consumed by overconfidence in a future we don't know will be there. But planning for a future when we will not be able to work or harvest is wise. Just don't let your saving turn into hoarding like the rich man in Luke 12:15-21. He was rich on earth but poor in heaven.

4. **Spend by Sight.** If you can't see it, don't spend it. I'll never forget the day when my first son came home from college with a wallet full of credit cards. "Where did you get those, son?" In the mail. The credit card companies knew college kids couldn't resist credit cards. I knew more than one college kid who had to drop out because of gambling debts run up through credit cards. If you can't see it, don't spend it.

Yes, there is a connection between our money and happiness. For when our money becomes seed that we sow for eternal purposes, it turns into showers of blessings that bring us joy and peace and happiness, a greater quality of life than hoarding a million or a billion could ever do.

John G. Wendel and his sisters were some of the most miserly people of all time.[117] Although they had received a huge inheritance from their parents, they spent very little of it and did all they could do to keep their wealth for themselves. John was able to persuade five of his six sisters not to marry, and all of them lived in the same house in New York City for fifty years. When the last sister died in 1931, her estate was valued at more than a hundred million depression dollars. Her only dress was one that she had made herself, and she had worn this same dress for twenty-five years. Does that sound like much quality of life?

But we have to be careful of Neo-Galatianism in our giving as well, don't we? Having traveled for ministry in most of the continents, I sometimes hear stories about "health and wealth" preachers who prey on the poor people in third world countries. One of these guys flew into an African country known for its hunger and poverty. People poured into the public arena to listen to this man's promises of health and wealth. At least once an hour the death bell would toll for another

---

117 Richard Barry, "The Fate of the Wendel Millions," *New York Times*, February 28, 1915, http://query.nytimes.com/gst/abstract.html?res=9E01E5D61E3EE733A0575BC2A9649C946496D6CF.

person who had just died from AIDS. But the "good news" kept coming: "Give and you will be blessed with good health and unimagined riches. Remember, you can never out-give God." And the hopeful came. They brought what little they had, trusting that God would multiply it a hundredfold. But alas, the healing evangelist was not happy with the yield after two days. So he uprooted, loaded up his jet, and he flew away. It was supposed to be a five-day crusade, but apparently this country was too poor for the evangelist to waste his time.

What a sad perversion of a true principle: sow after the Spirit, and after the Spirit you will reap eternal life. The true promise is that *material giving will reap spiritual living*. Of course, God could bless a person with health and wealth if he so chose. I watched a documentary recently called *Nicky's Family*. It was about an English stockbroker named Nicholas Winton.[118] In 1939, he and a friend were to go skiing in the Alps when his friend suggested they spend some time in Czechoslovakia to see what was happening to the Jews. War had not yet broken out, so they went.

The Nazis had occupied Czechoslovakia. The Jewish families were being rounded up and put in refugee camps. Nicky Winton could see what was about to happen. Families lined up to urge him to get their children out. He was able to get about seven hundred young children out before war broke out. He raised funds, he found foster homes in England, he got the passports—Nicky Winton spearheaded the mission. After the children were placed in homes, he never heard what happened to them. On their part, they never knew who had saved them from certain death. All their parents were killed in the death camps.

Nicky never saw himself as a hero. He kept a scrapbook in the attic with the names of the children and their pictures, but he never even told his wife, Grete, whom he married after the war, what he had done. She discovered the scrapbook after it had been collecting dust for decades. The BBC got ahold of the story and arranged for 254 of

---

118 "Nicholas Winton," Wikipedia, accessed August 15, 2014, en.wiki pedia.org/wiki/Nicholas_Winton.

the surviving children to meet Nicky Winton fifty years after their rescue. Queen Elizabeth knighted Nicky. Then on his one hundredth birthday, a huge gathering of all the people who had been inspired by his story to help others in dire need gathered to honor him. One young Slovakian couple had gone to Cambodia and rescued over five thousand children from disease and death on the streets. The ripples of this man's good deeds multiplied to effect hundreds of thousands. And guess what? God chose to bless this man with good health. The documentary was made in 2011, and Nicky at one hundred years old was fully functional and bright as a lightbulb.

But this is not always the case. My former youth pastor at the church I pastored for about twenty years loved kids more than anyone I have ever met. Beyond his own three children and the hundreds of kids at the church, Adam Lacy and his wife, Kelly, chose to be foster parents to scores of children. They even adopted a couple of these foster children. Good deeds galore.

But when Adam had trouble getting rid of a cold, he went to the hospital for help. There he picked up a staff infection. It went to his heart. For over a year he has been at death's door with an ejection ratio of just 20 percent (amount of blood his heart can process—normal is around 50 percent). Finally, after months on the transplant list, the Houston surgeons worked from 1:30 last night (April 21, 2014) until 9:00 this morning to replace his heart. As I write this, he is in critical condition while his family and friends pray for no infection and no rejection. Health and wealth? Even if the surgery is 100 percent successful, Adam has about fifteen years left. He is forty-five.

Anger at God? Legalism? Not Adam. He doesn't think God owes him anything, and he is confident that he will see God's blessing someday, though it may not be in this life. Is he all smiles? No, Adam has wrestled with depression. He is a bit like the deer caught in the headlights. But reactive depression to loss is normal grieving, and grieving in this way is how we heal. And all during this past year, when Adam was not in the hospital getting treatments and learning how to carry a bag around 24-7 to keep his damaged heart beating, he has been working with kids at the church. A Neo-Galatianist? Not Adam Lacy.

17

DIVINE BOASTING
Galatians 6:11-15

Boasting can be tiresome to listen to, and some people will go to great lengths to silence a boaster. A sightseeing bus was making the rounds through Washington, D. C. and the driver was pointing out spots of interest. As they passed the Pentagon building, he mentioned that it cost taxpayers millions of dollars and that it took a year and a half to build. While everyone was looking at it, a little old woman piped up: "In Peoria we could have built the same building for less, and it would have been completed even sooner than that!" The next sight on the tour was the Justice Department building. Once again the bus driver said that it cost so many millions to build and took almost two years to complete. The woman repeated: "In Peoria we would have done it for less money and it would have been finished much sooner." The tour finally came to the Washington Monument, and the driver just passed slowly by without saying a word. The old woman was curious. "Hey," she shouted to the driver, "what's that tall white building back there?" The driver looked out the window, waited a minute, and then said, "Search me, lady. It wasn't there yesterday."

Yes, boasting is tiresome because invariably a person's boasting in some way draws attention back to himself. We like to boast about our kids, our accomplishments, our education, our acquaintances, our roots, and so on. Most of these things can be traced back to what Paul calls the flesh. From the time a little boy can flex his muscles or a little girl can look into the mirror, we are tempted to boast "in the flesh," meaning to boast about our gifts or accomplishments in the arena of this physical world.

Apparently, one of the effects of the fall of man and our sinful condition is an overwhelming sense of insecurity and insignificance. This sense of insecurity and insignificance manifests itself in different ways, but one way is boasting. As a general rule, the greater the boasting, the greater the sense of insecurity or insignificance or both. James 4:16 says, "All such boasting is evil." The context in James is to use material things and accomplishments to offset our sense of insecurity and insignificance. But oddly enough, the Bible does not condemn all boasting. There is something we might call "divine boasting," which can legitimately offset our deep feelings of insecurity and insignificance. We find one form of it in Galatians 6:11-15. As we begin these verses, we are also going into Paul's conclusion to his letter. Here is our outline:

GALATIANS
"The Gospel of Grace"

In this conclusion Paul goes to the heart of the gospel: the cross. Over the years I have had the privilege of preaching in many African-American congregations. These congregations are much more participatory than Anglo congregations. They interact with me as I am preaching. And as my time is running out, I begin to hear statements like "Take it to the cross." Apparently, their tradition is to bring each sermon to the foot of the cross no matter where they have been on the journey. It all ends at Golgotha. That is what Paul is doing here. In his conclusion he comes to the cross. We will see that boasting in the flesh is empty vanity (6:11-13), but boasting in the cross is eternally significant (6:14-15).

I. BOASTING IN THE FLESH   6:11-13

> See with what large letters I have written to you with my own hand! As many as desire to make a good showing in the flesh, these would compel you to be circumcised, only that they may not suffer persecution for the cross of Christ. For not even those who are circumcised keep the law, but they desire to have you circumcised that they may boast in your flesh.

Paul mentions "large letters." He claims to have written this conclusion himself, as opposed to using a secretary, which he did for the rest of the letter. His reasons for writing this himself were: (1) to authenticate the letter; and (2) to emphasize this section of the letter—it would be like putting what you wanted to say in bold-face type or italics in a book. Now Paul is coming to the heart of the matter. We remember how he began the letter—with boiling hot ink. Anyone, including an angel or Paul himself, who preaches a different gospel than the one they received is accursed. Now at the end, Paul writes with 24-point font. He's trying to be as emphatic as he can be.

The apostle is concerned about those who "desire to make a good showing in the flesh." The words "good showing" translate a compound verb in Greek: *eu + prosōpēsai* = good + to make a face =

248

to make a good face = to look good. Their focus was on the externals, the flesh, instead of the internals, the spirit and the fruit of the Spirit. And it certainly was not on the cross.

When I was a boy, we could do what we called "midnight bowling." Starting at midnight, we could pay two dollars and bowl all night. We could get in over twenty games before our thumbs gave out and were sore for a few days. Not being a very good bowler, I bought a couple of books to learn how to bowl. They talked about spot bowling. The idea was never to look at the pins on the first ball. Pick one of the diamonds about six feet down the lane as a spot and bowl your ball over that spot. You determined the spot you wanted according to whether you threw a curve, a hook, or a straight ball. The idea was to hit the spot and the pins would take care of themselves. But if you looked at the ten pins, you would have trouble being consistent.

These law lovers were focusing on the Ten Commandments and missing the spot. The spot in this case is the cross. Focus on the cross, and the commandments tend to take care of themselves. David Brainerd was a missionary to the Indians in the Hudson River area of New York. He did not speak their languages, so he took along an interpreter who had a weakness for alcohol. Many of Brainerd's sermons to the Indians came through the slurred speech of this drunken interpreter. But they believed. According to Brainerd, "I never got away from Jesus and him crucified. The Indians were so gripped by this message of the cross that I had no need to give them instructions on morality."

But some would like to avoid the persecution associated with the cross. Again, rarely are legalists persecuted. The flesh loves legalism; it hates grace. And the cross is the fountainhead of grace. In order to put on a good show, many churches avoid any mention of the cross or its associates: sin, condemnation, hell, judgment, and justice. Oh, they like to talk about the positive outflow of the cross—forgiveness, love, mercy, compassion—but not the negative.

No, the cross is not popular today. The concepts of sin and judgment and condemnation don't tickle the ears of listeners.

Fortunately, the cross does speak of love and mercy and forgiveness. But you can't have one without the other. Only sinners need a Savior. Only the condemned need mercy. Only prisoners need to be set free.

Samuel Coleridge once wrote: "Truth of all others the most awful and interesting are too often considered as so true that they lose all power of truth and lie bedridden on the dormitory of the soul side by side with the most despised and exploded errors."[119] Translated, he is saying that truth, when it becomes so familiar, when we have heard it so many, many times, often lies bed-ridden in the dormitory of our soul side by side with the most despised and exploded of errors or heresies. It is possible to hear a truth over and over again until it loses, for the hearer at least, its potency and power. So it is with the cross.

As I type these words, I have just returned from a hike in the gorgeous Wallowa territory of northeastern Oregon. John Denver's song that says "You fill up my senses" could apply to what God does to anyone sharing this part of planet earth. As my wife says, "It's one big greenhouse." But locals tell me that Oregon and Washington have the lowest percentage of churchgoers in the lower forty-eight. This story from Eugene, Oregon, might illustrate that very fact.

A sand and ore company decided to erect a great cross. The people took pride and found joy in the cross until the day came that a group of people decided the cross was violating the principle of separation between the church and the state. A Unitarian minister in Eugene persuaded his congregation to sue the city because this principle of separation of church and state had been violated. It went to court, and in the local court, the Unitarians won. But it went to the state supreme court, and the Unitarians lost. The cross was to remain standing. But here is what is interesting. The reason stated for allowing the cross to remain was: "A higher court ruled the cross

---

119 Samuel Coleridge, *The American Quarterly Register,* Google Books, books.google.com/books?id=j_5JAAAAMAAJ, 212.

could stay because it was simply a symbol universally accepted and now has no religious significance and therefore does not violate the principle of separation between church and state." In other words, because the cross no longer means anything, you can keep it. But without the cross and Christ's work upon it, we have no good news to share. As Paul told the Corinthians, "For I determined not to know anything among you except Jesus Christ and Him crucified" (1 Cor. 2:2).

The people chasing Paul around didn't even keep the law they were loading on the Gentiles, the God-fearers who had begun attending their synagogues. They were like the Pharisees who put a yoke on the people they taught that they, the teachers, were not able to bear. Jesus got to the heart of the law in the Sermon on the Mount by showing that it reached inside. Holiness was not external, but internal. It started with the heart. But because these Pharisees could not uphold their own standard, they shifted their attention to externals: circumcision, praying aloud while standing in the streets, tossing their gifts (coins) into a metal trumpet at the temple so people could hear the money sliding down the trumpet. They were whitewashed tombs—clean on the outside but full of dead men's bones. Hypocrites. That's what Paul says about these religious leaders trying to circumcise the Gentiles. They just wanted the show. They wanted to brag about how many converts they had.

Do we have this today? Of course we do. Religious leaders don't boast about circumcisions anymore, but they boast about baptisms, church membership, budgets, the size of their facilities—it's all about the megachurch. But is *big* really beautiful in God's eyes? Maybe... maybe not. In this passage Paul warns us about the fallacy of looking good to get more members, or the big show. It does not make the big church wrong. The first church was a megachurch with over ten thousand coming on a regular basis (see Acts 2-4). Persecution ended that. The church went small. So God doesn't seem to grade by size, but he does by doctrine. How do you pick your church?

Now Paul turns to the kind of boasting that is not evil—boasting in the cross.

II. BOASTING IN THE CROSS   6:14-15

But God forbid that I should boast except in the cross of our Lord Jesus Christ, by whom the world has been crucified to me, and I to the world. For in Christ Jesus neither circumcision nor uncircumcision avails anything, but a new creation.

When Paul writes, "God forbid," he is using the strongest negative possible in the Greek language—*mē genoito*. It was a horrifying thought to Paul that he would fall prey to the temptation to boast in the flesh. He gives us his brag rag in Philippians 3:4-6, adds all his accomplishments in the flesh, and concludes that it is just so much manure. In our world it would be like saying I was a Heisman Trophy winner, a Rhodes scholar, and made my first million on the Internet when I was sixteen, but these things of the flesh will pass away with the flesh. As he said earlier in Galatians 6:8, if he sows to the flesh, he will reap corruption.

But Paul is more than willing to boast in the cross of our Lord Jesus Christ. Do we have the urge to boast? Then let us boast in the cross of Jesus. When we boast in the cross of Christ, we become the aroma of God, a perfume to some and a stench to others: "For we are to God the fragrance of Christ among those who are being saved and among those who are perishing. To the one we are the aroma of death leading to death, and to the other the aroma of life leading to life" (2 Cor. 2:15-16). The late John Stott wrote about this kind of boasting:

> There is not an exact equivalent in the English language for *kauchaomai*. It means to boast in, glory in, trust in, rejoice in, revel in, live for. The object of our boast or glory fills our horizons, engrosses our attention, and absorbs our time and energy. In a word, our glory is our obsession.[120]

What a magnificent obsession! In the cross I find my security, eternally so, for with his finished work on the cross, nothing can

---

120 John R. W. Stott, *The Cross of Christ* (Downers Grove, IL: InterVarsity, 1985), 349.

separate me from the love of God in Christ Jesus. In the cross I find my significance, for not only does his death for me say that I mean something, but it also gives me a transcendent cause to live for, a cause with an eternal impact. Nothing is more significant than that which lasts forever—a cup of water in his name, the widow's mites. Eternal security; eternal significance—this is what my soul cries out for. This is what sin robbed Adam and Eve of in the garden. The cross not only redeems, it also restores our very reason for living. A magnificent obsession.

Note the subtle shift in the middle of verse 14. The first half was about the cross of Christ, but the second half is about the cross of Paul. It is the call to discipleship, a shift from the price Chrsit paid to the price a disciple might have to pay. Christ paid the price for my sins on his cross; I pay the price for the privilege of marching with him by my cross. "If anyone desires to come after Me, let him deny himself, and take up his cross, and follow Me" (Matt. 16:24). The cross before me; the world behind me.

Samuel Zwemer, a missionary to the Muslims, wrote:

> If the cross of Christ is anything to the mind, it is surely everything, the most profound reality and the sublimest mystery. One comes to realize that literally all the wealth and the glory of the gospel center here. The cross is the pivot as well as the center of NT thought.... We rediscover the apostolic emphasis on the cross when we read it with the Muslims. We find that although the offence of the cross remains, its magnetic power is irresistible.[121]

Yes, there is an offense associated with the cross as well as a magnetic power that draws people. That is Paul's message—the power of the cross.

Paul ends his conclusion by reminding his readers that the beauty of Christianity is that it is not about a set of rules. Neither circumcision

---

121 Samuel Zwemer, quoted in Stott, *The Cross of Christ*, 41.

nor uncircumcision means anything when one is "in Christ." Earlier he told us that in Christ there is neither Jew nor Greek, slave nor free, male nor female (Gal. 3:28). He could have added to his list—neither circumcision nor uncircumcision. The Christian life is about being a new creation, a new creature, a new person. And what's different? Nothing on the outside. We don't look any different when we become believers in Jesus. No, but we are different. There is a change on the inside. The entire Godhead comes to dwell inside of us, in our human spirit. God takes up permanent residence, and we will never be the same. And change begins from the inside out.

While teaching at the Jordan Evangelical Theological Seminary, I enjoyed hearing testimonies of the various students. Jordanians were not allowed to study there, so all of my students were from Iraq, the Sudan, Israel, Egypt, and other Middle Eastern countries surrounding Jordan. There was one exception. He was a Jordanian who came to the seminary under the guise of being the bookkeeper for the school. He kept their books, but he took classes on the side. I asked him how God had worked in his life. He told me a fascinating story.

Everything had become dark in the life of Omar. Everything depressed him. To symbolize his internal darkness he painted his bedroom black and his windows black. His father said he could not sit at the family table until he repainted his room. One day he met and soon fell in love with a Jordanian Christian. Muslims are not allowed to marry Christians in Jordan. If a woman were to do it, it could lead to an honor killing in which her father would be honor bound to kill his daughter. But this was a man. Omar decided to visit the church of the woman he loved. It was communion Sunday. As the blood and body of Christ were discussed, he was repulsed. He thought they were teaching cannibalism. He couldn't wait to get out of the service. He thought they were all crazy. But when he stepped outside, the strangest thing happened—the world wasn't dark anymore. He could see color in the grass, the flowers, and the sky. He saw a fellow Muslim walking on the other side of the street and had compassion for him—a completely new experience for him. Although the cross repulsed him, it also drew him back. He kept going to the church until he trusted Christ as his Savior. And now he had given his entire life and was risking his life to share these wonderful truths with others like him that they too might be delivered from darkness.

William Holman Hunt painted in the Holy Land from 1870-73. He was determined to "do battle with the frivolous art of the day" with its superficial treatment of trite themes. So while on the roof of a home in Jerusalem he painted a picture of Jesus, which was imaginary in its history but accurate in its theology. The picture lets us look inside the carpenter shop of Joseph when Jesus was a young apprentice. He is stripped to the waist and standing beside a wooden trestle on which he has laid his saw. He lifts his eyes toward heaven, and the look on his face is one of either agony or ecstasy or both. He also stretches, raising both arms above his head. As he does so, the evening sunlight streaming through the open door casts a dark shadow in the form of a cross on the wall behind him, where his tool rack looks like a horizontal bar on which his hands have been crucified. The tools themselves remind us of the fateful hammer and nails.

In the left foreground a woman kneels among the wood chippings, her hand resting on the chest in which the remains of the gifts from the magi are kept. We cannot see her face because she has averted it. But we know that she is Mary. She looks startled (or so it seems) at her son's cross-like shadow on the wall. The painting stands in the Manchester City Art Gallery and is called *The Shadow of Death*. Historical fiction, but theological truth. Jesus was born to die.

I cannot think of any better words that summarize Paul's thoughts on "divine boasting" than these:

When I survey the wondrous cross
On which the Prince of glory died,
My richest gain I count but loss,
And pour contempt on all my pride.
Forbid it Lord that I should boast

Save in the cross of Christ my God;
All the vain things that charm me most,
I sacrifice them to his blood.[122]

God forbid that I should boast in anything other than the cross of the Lord Jesus Christ.

---

122 Isaac Watts, "When I Survey the Wondrous Cross," accessed August 16, 2014, www.cyberhymnal.org/htm/w/h/e/whenisur.htm.

18

GRACE ON LINE
Galatians 6:16-18

S omeone has well said, "Until we find something worth dying for, we haven't found anything worth living for." Have you found something worth dying for? Jay Richardson, a former youth pastor on the staff of our church, was organizing a scuba diving trip and asked me along. As it turned out, everyone else had to cancel, so when it came time to go, it was just Jay and me, but off we went. It was a whole week of diving, and with our dive watches we could spend about four hours a day underwater. The destination was Bonaire, a very small island about fifty miles north of South America.

After we had been diving for four days, Jay asked me if I'd like to do a night dive. I had never done one, but it sounded fun, so sure, let's do it. Bonaire is only about eight miles long and four miles wide. The northern half of the island has no lights, and that is where we were headed. Turns out it was also an overcast night, so without electricity and starlight, it was really dark. We parked our truck at the top of a bluff and got out.

"Are you nervous?" Jay asked. "No, not really," I said. We put our gear on in silence. Then he asked again, "Are you sure you're not nervous?" By then I knew that Jay was the one who was nervous. He wasn't afraid of the actual diving; he was afraid I'd go off and leave him underwater. In scuba diving one of the cardinal rules is that you never leave your buddy. And when you are diving in darkness, you can put that rule in bold print. So I just said, "Don't worry, Jay, I'm not going to leave you." He had good reason to be nervous because in a couple of our day dives I had drifted about twenty feet away from him. So I reassured him, and we finished getting our gear on, then plodded down about twenty steps to the beach.

The beach itself was about thirty yards from the cliff to the ocean. The locals put buoys at the point where the wall begins. Many of these Caribbean islands are sticking up from the ocean floor like long fingers. Once you reach the wall underwater, you are hanging over an abyss that goes down for two miles. It's fun to dive the wall, but only very experienced divers go down more than a hundred feet. Well, Jay was a little ahead of me and reached the buoy first (it was about thirty yards from shore). When I got there, he signaled that he would go down first. So I was coming down about thirty feet on top of Jay. When I got there, I heard him talking underwater. This was a first. Then he grabbed my arm that held the light and pointed to the right. Suddenly, I looked square in the eye of the largest turtle you could imagine—much larger than any of the turtles you see people riding in TV documentaries. It looked like a living Volkswagen. It was perched on a large piece of coral trying to sleep. We had obviously interrupted its siesta.

Well, I had seen people ride these things on land, so I thought it would be fun to try it. I wasn't going to sit on it, but I thought I would grab it from behind and let it pull me for a few yards. So I swam around to get behind the turtle. Jay was still talking underwater. I had no idea what he was saying, but I could imagine. So I grabbed the giant turtle, and it took off. You can't imagine how fast something that big can swim. I let go almost immediately. It was accelerating too fast to hold on. We followed the turtle as far as our lights would shine, watching it zigzag through the water like a much smaller fish.

From there we went to the wall and dove for about thirty minutes.

As we did so, we drifted about a hundred yards horizontally along the wall. It was time to go back up, so we worked our way back to where we had started. You have to picture this. Remember, the buoy is thirty yards from shore. The water at the buoy is about thirty feet deep. So the sandy bottom extends from the top of the wall to the shore, a nice, smooth, sandy bottom. But when we came up the wall, I saw a sight I will never, ever forget. There must have been two hundred lobsters marching to shore. Of course, they were not in rank and file, but since they were all headed to the shore, to feed I presume, it looked like an army marching to shore. This is something you would never see in day diving.

You can't believe how big some of these lobsters were. They aren't Maine lobsters with the big pincers. They have long, pointed tines—two of them, coming out of their foreheads, so to speak. They use those for defense. Well, this was as irresistible as the turtle. I had to touch one of the tails, not with my hands, but just sort of poke at it with a foot-long stick. So I found a stick. Jay knew what I was going to do, so he began talking underwater again. I picked out what looked like a ten pounder, a monster. Its tines were three feet long. I poked at the tail, and zap—its right tine flicked backward to try to poke me. I backed off until it began moving again and then touched its tail again. Zap—it tried to get me with its left tine. Finally, I poked it a third time, and now its whole body did a one-eighty and it was moving its tines around like a kung fu fighter as though saying, "Okay, you want some of this? Give it your best shot."

So, I had a decision to make. Did I really want to die fighting a large lobster in the Caribbean? After much prayer and careful consideration, I did not think this was a cause worth dying for. Do you have a cause worth dying for? Oh, you might die for your wife and kids and maybe your country. What else? Is there anything else? Paul had something he was ready to die for. His message of grace was worth dying for, living for, and fighting for. When it comes to the true gospel of grace, Paul would rather fight than switch. Would you?

The top reasons why people choose a church still amaze me. What a church believes doctrinally is tenth on the list of why people

259

choose a church. If the main things people want (convenient location, wonderful facilities, an outstanding nursery, great music, an on-fire youth group, a not-too-radical preacher, and a friendly congregation) can be found, most folks will find a way to squeeze themselves into the doctrinal mold of most any church. After all, the church scholars cannot come up with a consensus on doctrine, so as long as the basics are there, why bother? Who cares whether the church preaches free grace or costly grace, just so it's grace? Well, one person who cared was Paul. For him, a proper understanding of grace was the difference between both heaven and hell in eternity and heaven and hell on earth.

It should not surprise us to find that Paul winds up his letter with grace (6:18). That is the core of his gospel. That is what he is willing to fight for, to die for. So, in these closing verses of Galatians, we will look at marching for grace, the marks of grace, and the message of grace.

I. MARCHING FOR GRACE   6:16
And as many as walk according to this rule, peace and mercy be upon them, and upon the Israel of God.

The reason we mention "marching" is because the word used for "walk" is not the normal word (*peripateō*) used for "walking" in the Greek NT. It is used only five times in the NT, four times by Paul and once by Luke. We saw it earlier in Galatians in 5:25 where it talks about the victorious Christian life: "If we live by the Spirit, let us also walk by the Spirit." The word really speaks of marching. The implication is that one marching by the Spirit will not get out of line. It is so easy to get "off line" when it comes to our understanding of grace. Paul wants us to stay "on line."

The word for "rule" here is *kanon*, which is used in Philippians 3:16 in the Majority Text to refer to the lane marker around the Olympic track. We speak of the canon of Scripture when we refer to the books regarded as inspired and to be included in the Bible—the canon of Scripture. Certain rules or standards had to be met for a book to be included in the canon. The runner at the Olympics had to stay in his lane or be disqualified. So it is with the gospel. There are certain standards, certain measures. In context, the rule looks back to the contrast between the flesh and the cross, between self-effort and Christ-effort. It's the contrast between law and grace.

Paul is saying that his teachings about the gospel in Galatians have set the standard, the rule, the lane, the line. Don't cross the line. But when we couple this word with the previous word about marching, we are once again picturing an army that is marching in line. No one is out of step. And the canon, or line, or measure to keep this marching army moving together in cadence is grace. Yes, grace is the standard found in every section of Galatians. To be pulled out of rank and file in this army is to be pulled away from grace. Paul probably has the Roman phalanx in mind, a marching formation that the Roman army used to conquer the world. If enough Christians will march in line with grace, our phalanx can bust through the forces of Neo-Galatianism.[123]

So, to review once again, what is grace? By definition, grace is an undeserved favor. But certain law lovers were saying that keeping of the Mosaic Law and circumcision were required either for justification or sanctification. No, Paul cries, we are justified by grace and we will be sanctified by grace. That's good news (the gospel).

---

123 Interpreting "the Israel of God" has proved problematic for exegetes. Those who hold to Replacement Theology see the phrase as evidence that the Church replaced Israel in God's plan for the ages. However, Romans was written after Galatians, and the extended passage dealing with physical Israel (Rom. 9-11) would argue against Replacement Theology. Probably best to take it as Longenecker does: "that they [the Galatian converts] are truly children of Abraham together with all Jews who believe, and so properly can be called 'the Israel of God' together with all Jews who believe" (Richard Longenecker, *Word Biblical Commentary*, vol. 41 [Dallas: Word Books, 1990], Logos on Gal 6:16).

But it requires faith to believe this good news because something inside of us tells us we only get what we deserve. The devil and our worldly way of thinking make us believe we must do something in our own strength in order to win God's blessing in this life or the next. That is legalism. I was watching a local television broadcast of one of our popular local preachers. Here are eleven tests he suggested to help you determine whether you are one of God's children:

1. Have you enjoyed fellowship with Christ and the Father?

2. Are you sensitive to sin?

3. Do you keep God's commandments?

4. Do you reject this evil world?

5. Do you eagerly await Christ's return?

6. Do you see a pattern of decreasing sin in your life?

7. Do you love other Christians?

8. Do you experience answered prayer?

9. Do you experience the ministry of the Holy Spirit?

10. Do you discern between spiritual truth and error?

11. Have you suffered rejection because of your faith?

Now any thinking person looking over this list should be plagued with doubts about his faith. Almost every question has an open-ended answer. Do I keep God's commandments? Well, not perfectly. How perfectly do I have to keep them? The big ones and the little ones? This kind of introspection is exactly what has led me to write this book. This list is Neo-Galatianism. This introspection is Neo-Galatianism. But it doesn't make the people who slip into it bad people. Peter was not a bad person, but he slipped into Proto-Galatianism, we might say, the original problem Paul was fighting. That's why Paul opposed him face-to-face. If an apostle can slip into it, anyone can, and everyone should be on the lookout for this subtlest of errors.

One less-than-subtle sign of Neo-Galatianism is a hatred of grace. Its opponents get venomous. I have a picture in my files of a group of Russian Orthodox priests dressed in their black garb. They are walking single file, about twelve of them. From the picture you might think they are marching to church. Well, they are, but not their church. My home church started a bunch of house churches in the former Soviet State of Georgia. These priests are marching to one of these house churches to pound on the windows during the church meeting. You see, grace is a threat to their legalism. Legalism means control. It is a way to quantify their relationship to God. So they were going to pound on the windows as their way of expressing their disapproval of the grace message. That's the same kind of hatred of the grace message Paul got from the religious leaders of his day, and not very far away from this Georgian church. Legalists hated the message, so they tried to kill the messenger. And that leads us to the marks of grace.

II. MARKS OF GRACE 6:17

From now on let no one trouble me, for I bear in my body the marks of the Lord Jesus.

From time to time we hear reports of "stigmata." These are usually Roman Catholics who claim a special intimacy with Christ such that they have been chosen by God to display the very marks of the cross on their own bodies. These are usually the nail prints of the cross in their hands and feet. Proof will be blood that flows from these nail holes. We have no way of verifying these stories. To my knowledge the only one who legitimately wrote about the *stigmata* was Paul himself. He mentions them in this verse. The word for "marks" is *stigmata*. But he was not referring to nail holes. Rather, he was pointing to the scars on his back and perhaps elsewhere due to the stoning and beatings he had taken on behalf of the gospel.

In a subtle way, Paul is probably comparing himself to his attackers. It was unlikely they had suffered for their message of legalism as he had suffered for the message of grace. Legalists usually don't suffer for their message. The flesh loves their message. It appeals to our built-in sense that we only get what we deserve. The flesh jumps at the opportunity to win God's blessings. But it recoils at the concept of grace. Literally, he was probably contrasting his *stigmata* with theirs. Their only mark was circumcision. His additional marks came from his beatings. He says circumcision (even his own) is irrelevant (v. 15) to those who are in Christ. But the *stigmata* he bears are significant because they mean he belongs wholly and solely to Jesus. He is a fully devoted follower of Jesus Christ, that is, a disciple.

What would you die for? It was January of 2001 when I decided to up the ante in my fight for grace. By that I mean the Lord led me to start Grace School of Theology, which is a seminary. As the neo-Reformed movement in America turned into a tsunami, it seemed to me we needed an accredited school to train ministers both at home and abroad to offer a viable alternative. Two months after making the decision to start the school, the *stigmata* began. I don't want to suggest that what I have endured is any comparison to what Paul went through, but it has been significant. It began with a broken hip. After skiing for thirty years without incident, I hit a patch of ice and broke a hip. The operation did not go well. In fact, the surgeon performed it twice the same night because he messed up the first time. It was not successful. After three years the hip had died and had to be replaced. Coincidence? Maybe.

A year later while I was in Germany for a sabbatical to do some writing, a disgruntled employee I had had to let go because he had embezzled money from the school began a slander campaign of egregious proportions. I wasn't around to defend myself, but it all started coming out when I got back. The elders did church discipline and put the brother out of the church, but much damage had been done. Several families left the church. I learned from that experience that once poison has been spread into the circulatory system of a church body, it is very hard to reverse the flow. There was no truth to anything he said, and seven years later he came back to seek forgiveness. Of course, I forgave him, but I was tempted to ask if he believed in restitution, like how about writing a letter to all the people he infected to tell them everything he said was untrue. But I didn't.

I thought it was a big step for him to seek forgiveness. Besides, the damage had already been done.

A year later my oldest child, my firstborn son, was walking across the street to his car when a drunk woman hit him with her truck and killed him. He was a seminary student looking to go to the mission field when it happened, February 23, 2003. Another coincidence? Maybe. I won't go on. Enough to say that about once a year some pretty significant attack comes along to leave another scar. But I am still alive and vertical. And with the beloved apostle, I would like to say when I am no longer vertical that I fought the good fight because I found something worth fighting for, something worth dying for, something worth living for. Have you?

According to the Book of Martyrs about a thousand Christians are killed every day for their faith in this sin-sick world. It is a great irony that we can pay no price in order to receive God's grace, but we may be called on to pay a great price not to compromise God's grace. The suffering does not have to be martyrdom or even physical. It could be verbal, social, family, church—any number of things. But mark it down; if you choose to carry the banner of grace, there will be a price.

So, Paul calls us to grace "on line." We are soldiers in a battle, marching forward, rank and file, according to God's grace. And because it is a battle, there will be *stigmata*. To march into war with this army could cost you your life (Luke 14:22ff.). Is the message worth it?

III. MESSAGE OF GRACE   6:18

Brethren, the grace of our Lord Jesus Christ be with your spirit. Amen.

Paul ends each of his letters with a mention of grace. Do you think maybe he was trying to tell us something important? So did Peter. Do you think Peter got the grace message after the confrontation from Paul? So does the Bible (Rev. 22:21). Are you starting to see something stick out? The writer to the Hebrews says, "Do not be carried about with various and strange doctrines. For it is good that the heart be established by grace, not with foods which have not profited those who have been occupied with them" (13:9). Once again, he tells his readers to test any church or Christian group by this doctrine of grace. It should be the first thing on the list. In fact, in this day and age you can do it online. Before ever visiting to see if you like the facilities, the nursery, or the preacher, check out what they believe. Most churches have a website and a doctrinal statement on that website. The heart will never be established (*bebaioō* = confirm, establish, strengthen) by Neo-Galatianism, which invariably breeds doubt and fear.

Yet, despite the instruction and warnings found in this letter to the Galatians, by AD 100 we cannot find a trace of grace teaching in Christian literature. How soon the church had slipped away from grace! The last word of pure grace we have is the last verse of Revelation. From then until today the literature is full of: "Grace to you…if…"

My wife came in from the car one day and said, "Dave, I was listening to a Christian program called *Grace to You*. I think it should be called *Grace to You…If…* They attached all sorts of conditions for a person to be a beneficiary of God's grace." Astute. Augustine taught "grace to you…if…" So did Luther, Calvin, Arminius, and Wesley. They all said, "Grace to you…if you remain faithful until the end of your life" (see Matt. 24:13). On this both the Calvinists and the Arminians are in full agreement. The only difference is this. The Calvinists say if you are not faithful until the end of your life, you never had salvation. The end result is that you are not one of the elect. Likewise, the Arminians say you must be faithful until the end of your life or you will lose your salvation. The end result is that you are not one of the elect. We cannot stress enough that in either system a person cannot know if he or she has eternal life until death. Thus, there is no assurance, no strengthening of the heart, no peace in this life. Remember, Paul always says "grace and peace" in that order. There is no peace until we understand grace.

And we don't understand grace until we understand that it is free. Free grace. Isn't that a redundancy? I get that question all the time. If by definition grace is an undeserved favor, then why attach the word *free*; it's already free, right? Good question. However, apparently the Holy Spirit knew that every group that names the name of Christ would also claim to believe in grace. The Roman Catholic Church has more to say about grace than the Protestants do. So the Holy Spirit decided to make the doctrine clearer by describing it as free. He does that in a number of passages—Romans 5:15ff.; Ephesians 3:7; Revelation 21:6; and Ephesians 2:8-9. In each of these passages the word for "free gift" (*dōrean*), or a form of it, is used. The word means "something given with no strings attached." And since it was the Holy Spirit who put this word next to the word "grace" (*charis*), he must have understood that the flesh would try to attach things to God's grace either to get it or to prove you have it. God's grace is absolutely free. There is no such thing in God's Book called "Grace to You…If…" That's Neo-Galatianism.

Do you remember that giant lobster? He was marching well. He wanted to stay in line. But I kept poking at him. I slipped up behind him and tried to get him going the wrong direction. So he turned around and was ready to fight. Now no one, even a lobster, really wants to fight. But his life source (food on shore) was threatened. So he was ready to fight. There are some things worth fighting for. Those are the things worth living for. Those are the things worth dying for. Grace is our life source. That's what Galatians is all about.

William Holman Hunt painted many pictures of Jesus while he was in Jerusalem. One of his favorites was taken from Revelation 3:20. "Behold, I stand at the door and knock." It shows Jesus standing outside a home and knocking at the door. He obviously would like to come in. But when one looks closely, he observes that there is no handle on the door. Jesus will not open the door. He is waiting for us to open the door. Grace is there. Jesus is coming to you. He offers himself to you and for you. But Jesus will not kick the door in. He is not going to force himself upon you. He knocks, but each person must respond. All you have to do is open the door.

APPENDIX
Galatians 5:22-23

The following is a study of the fruit of the Spirit. Though not germane to the thrust of this book on Neo-Galatianism, we offer it for those who may want to study the fruit for their own edification or to teach others. The fruit of the Spirit would make a nice Sunday school, preaching, or small group series.

LOVE—HEAVEN'S CONCERN
Galatians 5:22

axwell Maltz wrote a couple of books about plastic surgery that were technical. Then he wrote one about his observations regarding his patients.[124] He said many of them were burn victims, traffic accident victims, people with birth defects, and so on, but he said most of his patients did not need plastic surgery. But that was his business, so he usually did what they asked him to do. In following up with these patients, he discovered that most of them were not any happier after their surgery than before, even though he had improved their appearance significantly. He found that each person had an inner image as well as an outer image. He could help their outer image, but there was not a whole lot he could do about their inner image, which was usually rather negative in the way these people thought about themselves.

Christianity helps us understand the inner negative image in that we think much of it is a product of our sin nature that is constantly trying to pull us down by focusing on our failures over and over and over. As such, this inner image can have a major influence on our

---

124 Maxwell Maltz, *Psycho-Cybernetics* (New York: Simon & Schuster, 1969), vi-xv.

lives. We tend to live down to or up to our self-image. The good news is that once we become Christians, God the Father sends the Holy Spirit and his Son to live in us. One of the reasons they are there is to enhance the image of God already stamped upon us at creation. This image of God (the *imago Dei*) may be somewhat recessed or tarnished, but part of the Spirit's work is to work on our character qualities until our inner image begins to reflect the image of Jesus himself. Like a well-worn coin that's been around the block a time or two, it will need some polishing for us to see the image stamped on the coin clearly.

The goal of the Christian life is **not** to get us to heaven when we die. That is certainly a wonderful promise and it takes away the sting of death, but if that were the goal, then once we have received Christ, God might as well take us home. The ultimate goal according to Romans 8:29; 2 Corinthians 3:18; and Philippians 3:10 is to be conformed to the image of Jesus Christ. Receiving Christ as one's personal Savior is the starting point of the Christian life. If we were running the hundred-meter dash at the Olympics, we would get into the starting blocks if we wanted to run the race. But it would look pretty funny to hear the gun go off and not leave the blocks. Someone in the stands might cruelly yell out, "What's the matter with you? Are you deaf?" The purpose of getting into the starting blocks is to run the race. If you were on the Olympic team, someone spent a lot of money to get you to Beijing or London. If you told them, "Oh, I didn't want to run a race. I just wanted to go to the Olympics and watch," your sponsor would probably have been none too happy with you.

The Father, our heavenly sponsor, paid quite a price to get us into the starting blocks. How disappointing for him if we choose to simply watch everyone else run the race set before us. Of course, that race is not to beat out any other Christian. It is more like we are playing football against the devil and his demons. They are trying to tackle us before we can reach the goal line, which is Christ-likeness. And the really cool thing we have learned in Galatians is that we cannot win that race as long as we depend on our own strength or abilities to get us to the goal line. In fact, we will most likely trip and fall so many times we won't be able to finish the race.

The flesh simply isn't able to produce spiritual things. Not in its nature, you might say, since the flesh is the sin nature. No, we must release the Spirit within us, and he will produce the fruit of Christlikeness. The fruit of the Spirit here in Galatians is not an exhaustive list, as we have already noted. But as suggested, a focus on this fruit would be a good study. Each would describe what our Savior is like, so if we want to become like him, why not focus on the fruit? The first of these is love. Let's focus on love—heaven's concern—as we get a definition of Christ's love, a description of his love, and finally a look at the development of this kind of love.

I. DEFINITION OF CHRIST'S LOVE

The following chart is a bit of an oversimplification, and there are exceptions (Matt. 6:24; 2 Pet. 2:15; Luke 16:13—where the word used for loving money is *agapē*; and Matt. 5:46; Luke 7:5; 11:43; John 3:19—where unbelievers exercise *agapē*), but it is generally true.

EROS	PHIL	AGAP
BODY	SOUL	SPIRIT
SEXUAL	EMOTIONAL	SPIRITUAL
SELFISH	EMOTIONAL	SELFLESS
GETTING	GETTING & GIVING	GIVING

From this chart we can see that each part of the person (body, soul, and spirit) has a type of love associated with it. I say the chart is an oversimplification because it identifies *eros* as selfish. Well, that sounds sinful and negative. But God gave *eros* as one of his gifts. In and of itself, *eros* is not evil. God created it. That means it is good. But often what God creates Satan can corrupt. In its corrupted form, *eros* is evil and the source of all sorts of evil. Augustine thought it was the actual source of sin and that sin was passed down through the human race by *eros*.

I was having lunch some years ago with Haddon Robinson, one of my former professors. He said that he believes a mistake made in many churches by preachers is to put these three types of love on a totem pole with *agapē* at the top. In this totem-pole approach each form of love is better than the one below. That makes *eros* the lowest form of love, something to be suppressed. But Robinson said whenever something that God made is suppressed, it will sometimes pop out later on in an unhealthy way. In what was called the Victorian Era (1839-1901) *eros* was suppressed. It popped out in an unhealthy way decades later with Alfred Kinsey's misrepresentations and through one of his friends named Hugh Hefner.

Philē is also a gift from God. The older women are actually told by God to teach the younger women how to have *philē* for their husbands (Titus 2:4). A wife is never commanded to have *agapē* for her husband in Scripture, but she is to learn how to have *philē*. During the '40s and '50s in our country feelings were suppressed. Real men don't cry, for example. Real men don't tell their wives or children they love them. That is too emotional. But wait a minute. God made feelings and has feelings. Remember the shortest verse in the Bible in the English language? "Jesus wept," after his friend Lazarus died. The Jews watching him weep said, "See how He loved him!" That's the verb *phileō*, not *agapaō*. But when feelings are suppressed, they pop out in unhealthy ways—children with father wounds, women stuck on Harlequin novels, and so on. More and more women divorcing their husbands.

But *philē* has a reciprocity in view. It involves giving and getting. Here is a gal who has broken up with her fiancé but soon after finds herself writing a letter to him: "Dear Jimmy, no words could express the great unhappiness I have felt since breaking our engagement. Please say you will take me back. No one could ever take your place in my heart. Please forgive me. I love you, I love you, I love you. Yours forever, Marie.... PS: Congratulations on winning the State Lottery." That's *philē*.

When I was in grammar school, we had boyfriends and girlfriends. But if we wanted girls to be our girlfriends, we often didn't have the courage to ask them directly. We used intermediaries. So, I'd write a note that said, "Janice, I will like you if you will like me." But I wouldn't hand the note to Janice. I would give it to my friend Paul to give to Janice. Then I would wait for a return note. Janice would give a note back to Paul to give to me. The future of my whole love life hung on the contents of this return note. Unfortunately, it might say, "Dave, I don't like you. Janice." Well, such rejection necessitated a return note to her return note. My return note to Janice would say, "Then I don't like you, either." Reciprocity: I'll like you if you will like me. If you don't like me, then I for sure don't like you. Getting and giving—that's *philē*.

But rather than putting these three types of love on a totem pole, Robinson suggests they should be on a level plane. Each one was intended by God to be good and available for use when needed. Of course, the biblical emphasis is not on *eros* or *philē* but on *agapē* because this kind of love is the word for his love. It is sourced in him. It is a fruit of the Holy Spirit, which is why we are studying it. Thus, we will use the following as a working definition of the love of Christ: ***it is a selfless attitude that seeks God's will in the person loved.*** From this definition we can see that disciplining a child, though not pleasurable for the parent or the child, is an act of love (see Heb. 12:5-11 for the difference between the goal of an unbelieving parent as opposed to a spiritual parent).

If we were to use just one English word to distinguish this type of love, we might use the word *selflessness*. The description of *agapē* found in 1 Corinthians 13:4-7 works pretty well when we translate *agapē* as "selflessness": "*Selflessness* suffers long and is kind; *selflessness* does not envy; *selflessness* does not parade itself, is not puffed up; does not behave rudely, does not seek its own, is not provoked, thinks no evil; does not rejoice in iniquity, but rejoices in the truth; bears all things believes all things, hopes all things, endures all things."

With this definition of Christ's love, let's move in for a description of it.

275

II. DESCRIPTION OF CHRIST'S LOVE

Somewhere around 1973 I realized the goal of the Christian life is not to go to heaven when I die or to see how big a splash I can make in the ocean. Rather, God will focus more on what we become than on what we accomplish. This is hard for our flesh to accept. We tend to measure our significance in terms of doing rather than in terms of being. Not God. He will be looking for Christ-likeness. How much did you become like my Son? Of course, we cannot become like Jesus if we don't do some of the things Jesus did. We can't just sit in a monastery and become like Jesus. Yes, being leads to doing. And the best way to become like Jesus is to think about Jesus. We become what we think about. "As a man thinks in his heart, so is he" (Prov. 23:7).

So, as we study the fruit of the Spirit, we are thinking about character qualities exemplified by Jesus. I used to take a different fruit each month, look it up in the concordance, and find as many significant verses concerning this fruit as I could find. Then that month I would study two or three of those verses. For love I found fifteen significant verses. Space limits us, so we will pick just a few of these verses to paint a picture of Christ's love.

A. It Is Unconditional

1. Romans 5:8—"While we were still sinners, Christ died for us."

   Chuck Swindoll tells the story of a Vietnam soldier who was discharged to go home.[125] He arrived in Los Angeles and called home. He was from a well-to-do family in the New England area. His mother answered the phone and was thrilled to hear her son was coming home—couldn't wait for him to get there. Then her son said, "Mom, I have

---

125 Chuck Swindoll, "Romans 5:1-10" (sermon series on Romans, First Evangelical Free Church, Fullerton, CA, 1974).

a friend with me who doesn't have anywhere to go. Can I bring him home with me?" "Well, sure, son. Any friend of yours is a friend of ours. Bring him home for as long as you like." "Okay, Mom, that's great. But I need to warn you. He's pretty beat up. He is missing an eye and part of his face." No problem, son. Bring him here for a couple of weeks. "Well, Mom. It's even worse. He doesn't have legs and must navigate with a wheelchair. He's my best friend, and I really want him to live with us." "Well, son, I don't know...." Click. The line went dead.

A couple of days later the phone rang again. It was the LAPD calling. They identified the Vietnam soldier's mother and asked if so-and-so was her son. She said, "Yes." Then the policeman said, "Well, you will need to come to identify his body. He took his own life, poor guy. He just has one leg and one eye."

Christ's love for us is unconditional. He loved us while we were messed up by sin and ugly as sin.

2. Matthew 5:43-47—"Love your enemies.... For if you love those who love you, what reward have you?"

Louis Zamperini was known for setting records. A champion runner, he ran before Hitler in the 1936 Olympics. In WWII he set a record for survival afloat a rubber raft in the Pacific before he was picked up by the Japanese—forty-seven days. In his POW camp he probably set a record for survival under torture, though no one could prove it. His tormentor, Watanabe (known as the Bird), was aware of Zamperini's Olympic notoriety, so he made it his goal to break Louie's will through inhumane torture. Although he tortured most of his prisoners and killed scores of them, he singled out Zamperini for special treatment. It was as though Louie personified American strength and freedom. The Bird wanted to destroy him, slowly. With no limits to his sadism, according to Laura Hillenbrand, the Bird seemed to derive sexual pleasure from inflicting pain.

During one rampage of torture, Zamperini was hit in the head 220 times. Only the indomitable will of an Olympic runner kept him alive. He finally resolved to kill his tormentor, but the war ended before he could do it. The Bird disappeared. Most thought he was dead. When Zamperini learned that his enemy was still alive fifty years after the war, he resolved to go to Japan (in his seventies) to kill him. Only expunging the Bird from the planet would drive away the hatred that had dogged him for decades and destroyed much of his life.

Zamperini finally got to Japan in 1998, but he was not there to kill the Bird. He was there to carry the Olympic torch. But he also wanted an audience with his old enemy. CBS contacted Watanabe and let him know that Zamperini wanted to meet. It was not to be. Here is the letter Louie had prepared for the Bird:

To Matsuhiro [sic] Watanabe,

As a result of my prisoner of war experience under your unwarranted and unreasonable punishment, my post-war life became a nightmare. It was not so much due to the pain and suffering as it was the tension of stress and humiliation that caused me to hate with a vengeance.

Under your discipline, my rights, not only as a prisoner of war but also as a human being, were stripped from me. It was a struggle to maintain enough dignity and hope to live until the war's end.

The post-war nightmares caused my life to crumble,

but thanks to a confrontation with God through the evangelist Billy Graham, I committed my life to Christ. Love replaced the hate I had for you. Christ said, "Forgive your enemies and pray for them."

As you probably know, I returned to Japan in 1952 [*sic*] and was graciously allowed to address all the Japanese war criminals at Sugamo Prison.... I asked then about you, and was told that you probably had committed Hara Kiri, which I was sad to hear. At that moment, like the others, I also forgive you and now would hope that you would also become a Christian.

Louis Zamperini

This story is recorded by Laura Hillenbrand in her book *Unbroken* about Zamperini's life.[126] After decades of trying to drink his demons away, Zamperini found peace in Christ. But he also found a love so great that he could not keep it in, so he became a minister to young people telling them about the kind of love you don't have to earn and you can never lose.

B. It Is Unlimited

1. Quantity—"Greater love has no one than this, than to lay down one's life for his friends" (John 15:13).

2. Quality—"Love one another; *as* I have loved you" (John13:34).

I went through the pre-med program at Rice and thought upon graduation and marriage that I would go to seminary for a couple of years and then medical school. My brother-in-law was in Vanderbilt Medical School while I was in seminary. Knowing my interest in medical missions, while I was home (Nashville) during a Christmas

---

126 Laura Hillenbrand, *Unbroken* (New York: Random, 2010), 287-398.

break, he invited me to a Christian Medical Society meeting to hear a medical missionary speak. I will never forget his talk.

This medical missionary explained that after his third year in medical school, he had to do an externship during the summer (find some other doctor[s] to work with for a summer). He heard of a need in Africa, had never been out of the States, and thought that would be good experience. As he went to Africa, he had no interest in missions at all. His whole life was planned out before him here in America. He would become the typical affluent, well-respected doctor, have a couple of kids, and retire after a good life. When he got to Africa, he was somewhat aloof. The African people had no special place in his heart. In fact, the whole experience kind of repulsed him.

Then one day it happened. There were some lepers in the mission hospital. As he was passing the bed of an old woman suffering from leprosy, he heard a rasping sound. He realized she might be suffocating. He looked at her and could easily see she was in the third stage of leprosy—fingers deformed and shortened, nose and ear cartilage eaten away. She was near death anyway and would probably die of asphyxiation if he just kept walking. But something inexplicable took over him. He bent down, plugged what was left of her nostrils with his fingers, put his mouth over her mouth, and began breathing for her. He saved her life. And, he said, he found his life.

Jesus said, "Whoever desires to save his life will lose it, but whoever loses his life for My sake will find it" (Matt. 16:25). That is selflessness—unlimited in both quantity and quality. Jesus himself came to us to heal us from the leprosy of sin, and he put his life on the line to do it.

C. It Is Unreserved

1. No Fear—"Perfect love casts out fear" (1 John 4:18b).

   What do we fear? The passage says that fear keeps our love from being complete, a finished product, mature, perfect (all of these meanings can fit *teleia*—"perfect"). May I suggest—the fear of rejection? Our desire to be liked and accepted by people is so strong that the fear of rejection keeps us from reaching out as we might if this fear did not exist.

Strangely enough, this shows up in a very real way in many marriages. It has been said that a man's greatest fear is the fear of rejection by a woman. That may be why after a guy finds the one he would like to spend his life with, he might do five "trial closes" before actually popping the question: "Will you marry me?" He wants to be sure she is going to say yes before he asks her. Getting a no would be too much of a blow to his ego. And even after marriage, a series of rejections will build up walls, walls that are very difficult to penetrate. But perfect love casts out fear.

2. No Restraint—"Fear involves restraint" (1 John 4:18c).

The NKJV translates 1 John 4:18c as "Fear involves torment." The ESV and the NASB and the NIV have "punishment" instead of "torment." Fear has "punishment." They probably translate the word *kolasin* as "punishment" because it occurs only one other time in the NT (Matt. 25:46), where it certainly does mean "punishment." However, the papyri have been helpful here, as I see it. The word was used in Egypt during the time of Christ in reference to stunting the growth of a tree by pruning. Thus, the dictionary that is an authority on these papyri suggests "deprivation"[127] in this context. The word was used for pruning, for cutting off. It was to keep something from developing to its completion or fullness. Thus, I would suggest the word "restraint." Fear holds us back. It keeps love from being fully developed.

---

127 James Hope Moulton and George Milligan, "κόλασις," *The Vocabulary of the Greek Testament* (London: Hodder and Stoughton, 1963), 352.

That meaning makes perfect sense to me, especially in light of the following verse (1 John 4:19): "We love Him because He first loved us." Jesus's love was perfect. Perfect love casts out the fear of rejection. Thus, Jesus had no restraint. He was rejected pretty much everywhere he went, but he kept on loving, kept on reaching out, right up to Golgotha. Thus, as it says in John 13:1, he loved us *eis to telos*, all the way. Because his love was perfect, he had no fear to "restrain" him from reaching out. Our rejection could hurt him and it did, but it could not destroy him. He was secure in his Father's love.

When the walls get thick in a marriage to the point that couples can't reach out anymore for fear of rejection, someone has to overcome this fear of rejection and bust through the walls. And usually that will have to be the more secure and the more mature of the two. Knowing that one is secure in Christ's love can help here. With his love behind you, you can reach out, knowing the other person can deeply hurt you, but he or she cannot destroy you.

I was preaching this truth one Sunday morning, and after the service, one of the husbands came up to me. He said, "Dave, that was really convicting. You really had me…until you said the more mature person in the relationship needs to initiate. Well, that person is clearly my wife. I'll just wait until she reaches out. Until then, I'm going back to my cave." I couldn't tell if he was kidding with me or serious.

Even though I have preached for over forty years, I am somewhat reserved. Not very outgoing. Give me a choice between a room full of people and a room full of books, I'll head for the books every time. I love people, but I have an inner fear of rejection, and books don't reject me. So it helps me in dealing with other people to think about those who are naturally outgoing. One such person who has helped me in this has been a former missionary to Haiti, Walt Baker. Walt has never met a stranger. It really doesn't matter who it is, but if a person gets within a four-foot radius of Walt, he is going to smile, lift up his hand, and say, "Hi, I'm Walt." His smile is disarming, and his "Hi, I'm Walt" is engaging. He can open up a conversation with most anyone.

So I have found it helpful for me to think of Walt when I am around a bunch of strangers. I see him in my mind, then I say, "Hi,

I'm Dave." It helps. As we grow in love, we have less and less fear and, therefore, less and less restraint. But that leads to the question of how to grow in love. If love is "selflessness" and we are basically selfish creatures by nature, how can we become more selfless? It must be possible, for Paul prayed that the love of his Philippian converts would abound more and more (Phil. 1:9). So, after getting a definition and description of Christ's love, let's see how it is developed.

III. DEVELOPMENT OF CHRIST'S LOVE

A. Do What He Did

"The Son of Man did not come to be served, but to serve" (Matt. 20:28). Our natural tendency is to want to be served. While the disciples were sitting and arguing over which one of them was the greatest, Jesus was preparing to wash their feet. He wanted to give them an object lesson on service (John 13:1-17). This same passage is introduced by speaking of his love for them (John 13:1).

Do we come to church to give or to get? Why do you come to church? To soak it up? Howard Hendricks used to call this the "Sit, Soak, and Sour Syndrome." We sit in church, soak it up, and then begin to sour if we don't do something about what we are hearing. He says that's why most of the problems in churches are not started by the new Christians but rather by those who have been Christians for twenty years.

Jesus said, concerning serving others, "If you know these things, blessed are you if you do them" (John 13:17). If we sit, soak, and serve, then we smile; but if we sit, soak, and don't serve, then we sour. Paul encourages us to present our bodies a living sacrifice, which he calls our "reasonable service" (Rom. 12:1).

B. Go Where He Went

Loving as Jesus loved involves going. That doesn't mean we must go to a foreign land, but it does mean going somewhere. He, of course, left us the supreme example in that he left the creature comforts of his home in heaven, where he was rather rich, to humble himself to become a poor servant to a people in a foreign land, people, in fact, far inferior to himself (Phil. 2:5-11). Paul holds this up as the supreme example of selflessness. "Let this mind be in you which was also in Christ Jesus" (v. 5). The word "mind" in both noun and verb form (*phroneō*) is found ten times in Philippians. It speaks of an attitude, an attitude of love or selflessness. The by-product of that attitude is joy. When I am selfish, it leads to an aftertaste of emptiness or even depression. When the Spirit enables me to go against my natural bent (selfishness), I experience joy (the second fruit of the Spirit).

C. See What He Saw

1. Jesus saw himself in every person. One reason I think he could love everyone the same is that he saw the image of God in every person. God has created every person in his image. Every person is of equal value. If only one person needed to be saved, Jesus would have come to earth to die for that person. He loved the leper, and he loved the lame; he loved the healthy, and he loved the helpless; he loved the rich, and he loved the poor. He loved them all the same.

    My brother-in-law, Charles Younger, an orthopedic surgeon in Midland, Texas, has a unique ability to make every person he meets feel important. Even though he is a successful surgeon with a lot of education and a lot of important friends (he grew up across the street from George Bush), he treats everyone like he or she is an important person. Why? I think it is because he believes each person is an important person. But no one person is more important than anyone else. This is the way Jesus was, and it helps us develop love for other people when we see them as Jesus sees them.

    I don't know if this is fact or fiction, but it is said that Michelangelo sculpted his greatest work from a piece of marble rejected by another sculptor. When that sculptor came along and watched Michelangelo begin his work, he asked, "Why on earth do you want to work on that piece of marble? It is a hunk of junk." The great artist replied, "In this piece of marble I see an angel trapped, and I want to bring him out." Well, it turned out to be David instead of an angel, but Jesus is doing the same thing. He sees the divine in us and wants to bring that out.

2. He saw tomorrow's kingdom as more important than today's (Matt. 16:22-27). The devil took Jesus up on a high hill and promised him all the kingdoms of the world if he would just forego Operation Crucifixion and bow down to him. But Jesus could see the coming kingdom where he would reign on earth for a thousand years. The coming kingdom was more real to him than the present world. Like Abraham, he looked for a city not built with hands. The city that is coming already is. That's what Jesus saw. That's what Moses saw (Heb. 11:27). And their vision of the reality of the coming kingdom caused them to make choices around that world. "Seek ye first the kingdom of God" (Matt. 6:33 KJV).

CONCLUSION

We will become what we think about. If we want to become like Jesus, we must think about Jesus. And one good way to do that is to think about his character qualities, one by one. Love is one of those qualities. And the good news is that we don't have to produce this fruit with our own strength. It is a fruit of the Holy Spirit. When we allow the Spirit to flow through us by walking with him, he produces the fruit; we only bear the fruit.

If we focus on our failures and the evil within us (the flesh), our condition will only get worse. But when we look to the author and finisher of our faith, Jesus, we become more like Jesus: Doing what he did; going where he did; seeing what he saw. And over the years, progressively, the Holy Spirit within us will develop his love within us.

I find it interesting to read about the spies who were sent into the land to check it out. They had some instructions. They were to see what the people were like, but they were also to see what the soil was like. They were to bring back some fruit—figs, grapes, and pomegranates. So, that's what they did. But when they got back, what did they talk about? The giants in the land. "We're like grasshoppers next to them." They certainly did not focus on the fruit. They focused on their fears, their inadequacies, and their flesh. By doing so, they missed the opportunity of a lifetime.

Lewis Sperry Chafer said we Christians who have been buried with Christ, raised with Christ, and sit at the right hand of the Father in Christ, should come back to earth and bring some of that heavenly fruit with us, fruit that Chafer calls the "fragrance of heaven." Love is heaven's concern; joy is heaven's song; peace is heaven's contentment; longsuffering is heaven's patience; kindness is heaven's benevolence; goodness is heaven's uprightness; faithfulness is heaven's tenacity; gentleness is heaven's disposition; and self-control is heaven's constraint.

What we want to do is to stop focusing on the flesh and start focusing on the fruit.

JOY—HEAVEN'S SONG
Galatians 5:22

According to Robert Wayne Pelton's book *Laughable Laws and Courtroom Capers*,[128] there is a community in Idaho that requires its citizens always to appear to be happy when seen in public places. Rexburg, Idaho retains an old ordinance prohibiting local citizens from walking down the street while "looking gloomy." Think of that—a law to look happy. Legislated joy. But can the law ever produce genuine joy? Doubtful. It is a fruit of the Spirit, we learn from Galatians 5:22. Previously we said that Lewis Sperry Chafer has suggested that these fruits are the fragrance of heaven. So if love is heaven's concern, then, suggests Chafer, joy is heaven's song. Could be. Remember the words of Jesus to the faithful servant in Matthew 25:21—"Enter into the joy of your Lord." We get a glimpse of this joy right now because the joy of the Lord is our strength (Neh. 8:10). But can this joy be sustained in the good times and the bad?

Larry Crabb wrote these words in an article on the occasion of his friend's retreat into sin:

> We're trying very hard in Christian circles to convince ourselves that even without the prospect of heaven, the

---

128 Robert Wayne Pelton, *Laughable Laws and Courtroom Capers* (New York: Walker and Co., 1993).

Christian life is worth living. It is not. Unless, like me, you've been blessed with a spouse you genuinely like, kids who delight your heart, a job or ministry that provides both meaning and income, and decent health. Then keeping your nose clean makes sense as long as the blessings keep coming. Why give up the enjoyment of what you have? Christian living then is pragmatically smart.

But mess with the blessings, let just enough go wrong to reduce the pleasure you feel in them to a lesser intensity than the pleasure that comes from bagging Christian standards and doing whatever makes you feel alive, and doing wrong will seem justified, necessary, legitimate, reasonable. The wrong way will seem right.[129]

Anyone can be happy and joyous when things are going his way. This is especially true for the Christian because he can enjoy a wonderful life here and now as well as have the blessing of eternal security in the future. But what happens when our temporal security is threatened through a reversal in finances or bad news about our health or, perhaps the hardest, sad news about one of our children? Do we still have the joy? Is this still the "abundant" life?

Some Christians take a nosedive into depression when circumstances roll over them like an unexpected tsunami. Others go under the waves only to pop up again as though protected by a life jacket of joy around their waists. Are these joyous Christians merely self-deluded, or have they found a genuine source of joy that can be sustained no matter which way the wind blows? Here are three sources of joy that all qualify as the kind of joy listed in Galatians 5:22 as a fruit of the Spirit.

---

129 Larry Crabb, "On the Occasion of a Friend's Retreat into Sin," accessed August 18, 2014, http://chrismiller.cedarville.org/content/crabb.pdf.

I. JOY OF SALVATION

David speaks of this joy when he says, "Restore to me the joy of Your salvation, and uphold me by Your generous Spirit" (Ps. 51:12). This joy is a fruit of the Spirit we receive immediately at the point of our justification. But the joy can be lost through known sin. David lost it in his dealings with Bathsheba. Now he confesses that he might be forgiven and his joy be restored. This is the principle of fellowship. Our deep joy comes from being close to our Savior. We find this closeness through:

A. His Word

1. Jeremiah 15:16a—"Your words were found, and I ate them, and Your word was to me the joy and rejoicing of my heart."

2. Isaiah 55:11-12—"So shall My word be that goes forth from My mouth; it shall not return to Me void.... For you shall go out with joy."

Recently a couple of friends took me to lunch to talk about some of the "bad" things that have happened to my family in recent years. They wanted to make sure I wasn't going under the water, and I appreciated their love and concern. But I said, "I am so blessed. In his Word I have a retreat center, a place to which I escape daily, sometimes several times a day. There I find peace, rest, and joy." Do you have such a retreat center?

B. Our Worship

1. **Our Singing**—"Let all the peoples praise You. Oh, let the nations be glad and sing for joy!" (Ps. 67:3-4).

2. **Our Shouting**—"Oh come, let us sing to the Lord! Let us shout joyfully to the Rock of our salvation" (Ps. 95:1).

3. **Our Sharing**—"Our fellowship is with the Father and with His Son Jesus Christ. And these things we write to you that your joy may be full" (1 John 1:3-4).

People like to talk about the vibrancy of the first-century church. And I am sure it would have been a thrill to worship with those early Christians. But, you know, if I just look at the Scriptures, the OT worship appears to have more joy than the NT worship. I am sure I am wrong about that, but in the *Jewish Encyclopedia* Kaufmann Kohler makes the claim that no language has as many words for joy and rejoicing as does Hebrew. In the OT, thirteen roots found in twenty-seven different words are primarily used for some form of joy or joyful participation in worship. In contrast to the ritualistic forms of worship found in so many other Eastern religions, Israelite worship was essentially a joyous proclamation and celebration. The good Israelite looked at the act of thanking God as the supreme joy of his life.

Now that I no longer pastor the same church every Sunday, I enjoy visiting and preaching in some of the churches pastored by students at Grace School of Theology. It is fun seeing the different approaches to worship. Some are quite reserved, while in others there is never a dull moment. One thing seems pretty clear in both the OT and NT— worship was a time for great thanksgiving and joy (Eph. 5:18-21).

As sports fans go, I am pretty laid back. It usually takes something special for me to shout while watching something on TV. But one Super Bowl I was really getting after it. My ten-year-old daughter was in the same room with me. After one of my animated expressions (all clean), she excused herself from the room. I didn't think much of it since I was immersed in the Super Bowl. But when I shouted again, a little voice came from the staircase but behind a wall: "You're not supposed to worship football, Dad." Whoaaa. Where did that come from? Christie would not sit in the same room as this idolatry was practiced, but she would sit around the corner out of sight and let me know when I had committed another idolatrous act.

We really can't hide from our kids what we love, can we? Do we love our sporting events more than God? I really don't think so, but it would be hard to convince a visitor to most of our church auditoriums during worship of that fact. I was leading a tour of Israel a few years ago. When I first began leading tours about twenty years ago, I remember hearing of roughly twenty Messianic congregations in Israel (Jewish-Christian churches). Now there are over a hundred. So I thought I would take one of my tour groups to one of their services. My high school daughter was sitting next to me on about the sixth row of an auditorium that held about four hundred when the dancing began. The Jewish Christians start a line and begin to dance. This is not line dancing country western fans do. The line just keeps getting longer until it goes all the way around the auditorium. Anyone who wanted to dance for the Lord could join. I looked at Laura and said, "Let's go." She covered her face and said, "Oh, Dad, please," which was her way of begging me not to embarrass her. But I did. Only time I have ever danced in church. It was great. Sometimes a little physical involvement opens the closet to joy.

Bruce Larson tells about a conference at a particular Presbyterian church in Omaha in his book *Luke*.[130] The people were given helium-filled balloons and told to release them at some point in the service when they felt like expressing the joy in their hearts. Since these were Presbyterians, they weren't free to say, "Hallelujah, praise the Lord." All through the service balloons ascended, but when the service was over, one-third of the balloons were unreleased. Want to add a little joy to your life? Why not let your balloon go?

II. JOY OF SERVICE

There is a certain joy that comes from serving God, even though the task may be difficult and the road long. Simply being faithful and enduring will yield the fruit of joy. And much of enduring is a matter, once again, of focus.

---

130 Bruce Larson, *Luke: The Communicator's Commentary*, ed. Lloyd J. Ogilvie (Nashville: W. Publishing Group, 1983), 43.

A. Focus on the Race   Heb. 12:1c-2

Let us run with endurance the race that is set before us, looking unto Jesus, the author and finisher of our faith, who for the joy that was set before Him endured the cross, despising the shame, and has sat down at the right hand of the throne of God.

Though I certainly could not support his theology (did he have any?), I agree with these words from George Bernard Shaw:

This is the true joy in life, the being used for a purpose recognized by yourself as a mighty one: the being thoroughly worn out before you are thrown on the scrap heap, and being a force of nature instead of a feverish selfish little clod of ailments and grievances, complaining that the world will not devote itself to making you happy.[131]

Many years ago I saw a man reading the Book of Mormon in the local library. I asked him if he were looking for truth. He said yes. He was a graduate of Annapolis Naval Academy, flew about thirty missions in Vietnam, and was a Delta pilot when I met him. He came to Christ, and I spent about two years discipling him. We spent time in Scripture, prayer, and sports. He loved tennis. One day when he was about thirty-five, he said he wanted to train for a marathon. When the day of the race came, he asked if I would run the last half with him to help make sure he finished. He hit the wall at about twenty miles. I had to turn him around three times to get him going in the right direction. He was running an eight-mile loop around White Rock Lake in Dallas, and it was easy to get disoriented when there were no more electrolytes left in his body.

It was obvious that Dick was in great pain as he endured to the finish. But I must say the joy I saw on his face at the finish line was greater than any joy I had witnessed in him prior to that point. The

---

131 "Quotes about George Bernard Shaw," Goodreads, accessed August 18, 2014, www.goodreads.com/quotes/tag/george-bernard-shaw.

euphoria must have been somewhat addicting because he continued running marathons for many years.

The Christian life is a race...longer than a marathon. There is pain; there is temptation to quit, perhaps even disorientation at times. But the joy of finishing the race is incomparable.

B. Focus on the Reward   Matt. 25:21

Well done, good and faithful servant.... Enter into the joy of your Lord.

Part of the joy of the Christian life is living for a transcendent cause. By transcendent we mean a higher purpose and goal for living than the routine, humdrum cycle of life. There is more to it than having 2.3 kids, a sufficient 401(k), and having a nest in the West where you can rest with the best.

Jesus gives us that transcendent cause when he says, "Seek first the kingdom of God and His righteousness, and all these things [the necessities of life] shall be added to you" (Matt. 6:33). When one is using his or her talents (spiritual gifts and opportunities) for his kingdom and his glory, the trials of life become just bumps in the road or, even better, the means by which we glorify him. It doesn't mean these bumps don't hurt. Some of them are incredibly painful. But they are bumps, not roadblocks.

The "joy of the Lord" coming to the faithful servant is part of the reward of living for him. Rather than focusing on the starting blocks (when we became believers), we have a race to run and a goal line in front of us. And when we reach the goal line, there is a reward, part of which is joy.

III. JOY OF SUFFERING

Christianity offers a plausible reason for suffering and a way to enjoy life in the midst of suffering. There is even the suggestion that some of life's greatest joy can come in the midst of outright persecution (Matt. 5:12). But there are two broad categories of suffering: deserved and undeserved. Can Christianity bring joy in both categories?

A. In Deserved Suffering   James 1:2

My brethren, count it all joy when you fall into various trials.

The word translated "various" is the one from which we get *polka-dotted.* It paints a picture of trials of all different colors, shapes, sizes, and shades. It does not limit our trials to just those we do not deserve. For many of us (myself included), most of our trials we bring on ourselves are due to our foolishness or our sinfulness. If the only trials I could count as joy were the undeserved, I would still spend most of my life moping over my mistakes. But our God is so great, so sovereign that he can take the free choices of a sinful human that are wrong and still work them together for his glory and the good of that person. In this we can rejoice.

B. In Undeserved Suffering   1 Peter 4:12-13

Beloved, do not think it strange concerning the fiery trial which is to try you, as though some strange thing happened to you; but rejoice to the extent that you partake of Christ's sufferings, that when His glory is revealed, you may also be glad with exceeding joy.

I went to a debate some time back between two men who believe in evolution and two who believe in intelligent design as the best explanation for our universe and life on earth as we know it. During one of the rebuttals, the only PhD in the group, a professor from the University of London, spoke of two alternatives—evolutionary chance as the explanation for life or divine design. Though he grew up, by his own admission, believing in divine design, he could not explain the many deformed human beings in the world. To his thinking these divine "accidents" were proof that a loving, all-powerful God could not exist. He, therefore, rejected God and grasped evolutionary chance as the best explanation for life as we see it.

This professor did not understand the biblical explanation for suffering. Of course, it cannot be found in this world. The explanation lies in the next. The book of 1 Peter was written to help explain this mystery—suffering before glory (1 Pet. 1:10-12). And this is where I find joy in the midst of underserved suffering. It is precisely because I do believe God loves me, and God has the power to control my personal history within some self-imposed limitations, and God knows all the details of my life—from all this I can find joy because it tells me there is a plan; there is a rest of the story; there is another world where the sufferings of this present time are not worthy to be compared to the glory that shall be revealed in us, the grown-up, mature sons of God.

CONCLUSION

So the fruit of joy is a wonderful gift to us from God. We can find joy in our salvation, in our serving, and in our suffering. The joy of the Lord is our strength. Strange, isn't it, but as we choose to endure the race, we are looking for a strength to run we have not. But as we yield our lives daily to the Holy Spirit, he gives us his fruit. One of these fruits is joy. And this joy becomes the very strength by which we run. I picture marathoners along their routes. Periodically their electrolytes run low. That is when they reach over for some liquid like Gatorade to replenish their electrolytes. As we run this race, we too have the need to replenish our spiritual electrolytes periodically. And the Holy Spirit gives us a bottle of joy to do just that.

As I have mentioned, my daughter and her husband adopted two children from Russia when the kids were just babies. Now the kids are ten years old, and we have been able to watch them grow up. One evening when they were still quite small, Betty and I went over to babysit and give Scott and Christie a night out. While we were sitting in the backyard, my grandson, Drew, got off my lap, picked up a small basketball, waddled over to a toy basket about three free high, and dunked—jammed. Betty and I cheered and clapped. He turned with a big smile, laughed, and clapped. He liked that. So he kept doing it.

Soon his sister saw the attention Drew was getting. So she began to dunk. We cheered and clapped for her too, though not quite as much, because it was easier for her. Not to be outdone, she found a very light but very big ball, about thirty inches in diameter, and started trying to dunk that ball. Of course, the baby basket, being only twelve inches across, would not accept the big ball. But Betty and I laughed and laughed as Grace kept trying to dunk the giant ball. So did she. There was joy everywhere.

I think it is the same for us as God's children. When we dunk for Jesus, there is clapping and cheering in heaven, and we get a kick out of it too. And the most fun is when we are so encouraged by making a few easy buckets that we pick up the impossible-for-us-to-dunk ball. That's when heaven really goes wild. And so do we.

PEACE—HEAVEN'S CONTENTMENT

Galatians 5:22

You have heard it said that love makes the world go round, but I say unto you, "That's not true." I can't explain all the world's wars with love. So I would suggest that testosterone makes the world go round. I can explain the majority of the wars with testosterone. How many millions and millions of lives have been snuffed out because some egomaniac wanted to be the alpha male of the world? How we long for a Messiah who will say, "Peace on earth, goodwill toward men."

But it has been so long since a war has occurred on our soil that we think, *War, oh yeah, that's Iraq, Afghanistan, Africa. But not in my house.* Oh yeah? Someone in my church recently was in tears over the neighborhood war where they live, among Christians, no less. Or on the golf course. Someone recently shared the weirdest story with me about a guy right here in Houston, Texas, who pulled a gun on another person on the golf course. Why? Because of an argument that erupted because a man on the tee hit into the foursome on the fairway before they had had a chance to hit their second shots—a major breach of golf etiquette. One member of the foursome who was hit into began yelling at the man on the tee. So the man on the tee jumped in his golf cart, drove down to the man who was yelling at him, and shared a piece of his mind he probably couldn't afford to lose. Words were exchanged. The man from the tee yelled, "I'm just going to blow you away." No one could have predicted it, but this man went back to his golf cart, unzipped his bag, and pulled out a gun. Another member of the foursome, who had been a professional athlete, picked the guy who was holding the gun up off the ground, thereby helping him understand that there would be no shooting on the golf course today. You can't explain that one with love. Testosterone? Yes.

Wars are everywhere—at work, at home, wherever you find human beings. Why? Because there is war in our hearts (James 4:1-2). And there will not be peace on earth until there is peace in the hearts of men. Of course, we believe the Messiah will bring that peace. But until he comes, he offers his children a glimpse of that peace through the fruit of the Holy Spirit. We have looked at love and joy. Now we want to take a look at peace, or what Lewis Sperry Chafer calls "Heaven's Contentment." Is there a way to enjoy peace on earth before the Messiah comes? Of course. We find peace is connected to our faith, our focus, our farming, and our future.

I. CONNECTED TO OUR FAITH

A. At Justification   Rom. 5:1-2a

Therefore, having been justified by faith, we have peace with God through our Lord Jesus Christ, through whom also we have access by faith.

The first time we ever experience heaven's contentment (peace) is the moment we trust Christ as our personal Savior. That is when the enmity in our hearts toward God is taken away. H. G. Wells, the famous science fiction author of *War of the Worlds*, *Time Machine*, and *The Invisible Man*, wrote, "I cannot adjust my life to secure any fruitful peace. Here I am at sixty-five still seeking for peace...dignified peace...is just a hopeless dream."[132]

Dante of Dante's *Inferno* decided he couldn't find peace in Italy so he would walk all the way to Paris and study at the Sorbonne, the University of Paris. As he was walking along, it was getting late, and he hadn't found a place to spend the night. So he knocked on the door of Santa Croce Monastery. An old monk opened the front door and growled, "What do you want?" Dante responded with just one word: "Peace." Do you have that peace?

Romans 5:1 tells us how to have heaven's contentment. It comes through our Lord Jesus Christ. In Romans 5:10 it says we are not only sinners but also enemies of God before Christ comes personally into our lives to take away the enmity. Heaven's contentment begins with receiving heaven's offer of peace through the Prince of Peace.

B. During Sanctification   Phil. 4:6-7

> Be anxious for nothing, but in everything by prayer and supplication, with thanksgiving, let your requests be made known to God; and the peace of God, which surpasses all understanding, will guard your hearts and minds through Christ Jesus.

These beautiful verses have two words that are often left out when people recite them from memory. I have heard them left out so many times, I believe the devil snatches them out of our memories. They are the key, at least in my thinking, to having peace. The words? "With thanksgiving." When I go to God with my concern(s) and can only be happy if my prayers are answered according to my preferred future, then I will not have peace. But when I can thank God if things go this way or that way or another way I might not have anticipated, then I will have the peace that passes all understanding.

---

132 H. G. Wells, quoted in "Calm in the Storm," accessed August 18, 2014, issuu.com/vcbc/docs/2010_10_03calminthestorm.

Martin Rinkart was a Jewish-Christian pastor in Germany back in 1636 during the Thirty Years War. The superintendent of the region where Rinkart was a pastor left him with two other pastors to shepherd the Christians in that region. There was a lot of disease and warfare. One-third of his little city died, including the other two pastors. In one year Rinkart buried over five thousand people, including his own wife. But in the midst of all that, Rinkart sat down and penned these words:

Now thank we all our God
With heart and hands and voices;
Who wondrous things hath done,
In Whom this world rejoices.
Who, from our mother's arms,
Hath led us on our way;
With countless gifts of love,
And still is ours today.[133]

A beautiful hymn. But what is the key to the hymn, to the man who could write it in the midst of a world of famine, disease, and death—a man who buried fifty people in one day? It's in the first line, isn't it? "Now thank we all our God." He was able to thank God in the midst of all these tragic deaths? Can you thank God for the tragedies in your life? Can Betty and I thank God for the death of our firstborn son, killed by a drunk driver? If not, we are out of God's will for our lives, for it says in 1 Thessalonians 5:18, "In everything give thanks; for this is the will of God in Christ Jesus for you" ("will" in this verse is *thelēma*, which means God's desire for us, not some predetermined plan). Only when we are able to give thanks in the bad times as well as the good times can we enjoy peace, heaven's contentment.

Some will say, "That's craziness." Well, I don't think the Bible teaches craziness. I just finished reading *From Tyndale to Madison*,

---

133 Martin Rinkart, "Now Thank We All Our God," accessed August 18, 2014, cyberhymnal.org/htm/n/o/nowthank.htm.

a book about how we got our English Bible and all those killed along the way by Henry VIII, Bloody Mary, and Elizabeth I. Sometimes the wood used to burn these people just for wanting a Bible in their own language was green and burned slowly. One such man watched his legs burn off, but then the fire went out. He yelled for his executioners to light the fire again so he could die. They lit it again, and this time his right arm burned off, the fire went out, and he was still alive. They lit the fire again—it took forty-five minutes for him to die, all the while watching his fleshly body burn in the flames and smolder in the embers.[134] But he died in peace. Why? Is this craziness?

The answer is yes. Yes, it is craziness to find peace and thanksgiving in such demonic conditions perpetrated by Christians, unless there is something that makes it all right in another world. Of course, that is what we believe. That is what we preach. I once led a tour of Israel and was flying to Tel Aviv on El Al, the Israeli airline. I was seated next to the window on my left and my wife on my right. To the right of my wife sat a Jewish man. Betty got him talking about Judaism. He said he had given up his faith—his whole family had been wiped out by the Holocaust. How could a personal God allow such a thing? If we Jews are the chosen people, then God, if he exists, must be a monster. Betty patiently listened and then shared her own testimony. The guy responded, "Religion is the opium of the people," quoting Karl Marx. For whatever reason, Betty had never heard that before and it left her momentarily stumped. She didn't know what to say. Then she turned to him with her magnificent smile and said, "Yes, and it is wonderful!"

That threw the guy. He finally opened up to her, and before we landed, they were both in tears. Yes, our faith is not a drug, but it most definitely can help us deal with pain in this life. Just believing there is something else, another world where wrong will be made right, helps

---

134 Michael Farris, *From Tyndale to Madison* (Nashville: B&H, 2007), 59.

us with our pain. And our peace is in direct proportion to our faith. But there is something else that brings peace. It is connected to our faith, but it is also connected to our focus.

II. CONNECTED TO OUR FOCUS

A. Our Mind-Set   Isa. 26:3

You will keep him in perfect peace, whose mind is stayed on You, because he trusts in You.

In the Hebrew "perfect peace" is *shalom shalom*: peace × peace = peace² or peace on top of peace. The word *shalom* has all sorts of meanings. "Complete" is one. So "complete peace," "perfect peace." This implies there are different levels of peace, but complete, perfect peace comes from a focus on God.

The word "stayed" is *samuk*, which means "to rest one's weight upon." We can figure this one out. It is to take our burdens, our cares, and our concerns to his broad shoulders. At the cross he took the burden of our sins away. And now he will be there to help us carry the load in this life. Casting all our cares upon him because he cares for us. It is the OT equivalent of Matthew 11:28-30:

Come to Me, all you who labor and are heavy laden, and I will give you rest. Take My yoke upon you and learn from Me, for I am gentle and lowly in heart, and you will find rest for your souls. For My yoke is easy and My burden is light.

Remember, Peter did not begin to sink when he stepped out of the boat; it was when he stopped looking at Jesus. Norman Vincent Peale writes about his visit to Breendonk, Belgium.[135] This is the prison where the Nazis put the Belgian Christians whom they caught

---

135 Norman Vincent Peale, cited at Terry Risser, *Daily Living*, blog, accessed August 19, 2014, http://terryrisser.blogspot.com/2014/04/april-1-rest-when-youre-stressed.html.

hiding Jews. As Peale looked at the dark, dank little cells and some of the torture equipment, he blurted out to his guide, "How could they possibly endure this?" The guide said many of them did not. In fact, his own father had died in that prison. But he took Peale into another room and said, "This is how they did it." He pointed to an etching on the wall. Barely perceptible was the outline of a face. The guide said to help himself focus on Jesus, one of the prisoners scratched out this face on the wall and imagined it was Jesus's face. Well, it was so dark in there that you couldn't see the face. But when a prisoner really got down, he would slip into this dark room and just run his fingers around the face of Jesus, over and over again. It gave them a measure of peace.

Closely related to our mind-set is our preoccupation. Both of them describe slightly different aspects of our focus. We have seen our mind-set. What about our preoccupation?

B. Our Preoccupation   Rom. 8:6
For to be carnally minded is death, but to be spiritually minded is life and peace.

If we fill our minds with things of the flesh, we will experience death even though we live. The word "death" in Romans 6-8 often means the depression and despair that comes from repeated defeat at the hands of the sin nature, just as a Christian can be dead even though he is alive (see 1 Tim. 5:6). But if we fill our minds with things of the Spirit, we will find life and peace.

An art contest was held and a prize offered for the best picture of peace. Think of peace. What would you paint? Well, the judges came in and narrowed the paintings down to two. Then the artists were called in. They pulled the cover off the first picture to reveal a beautiful mountain lake surrounded by pine trees and aspen trees, clouds creeping in for a peek, the setting sun reflected on the calm waters. Everyone thought, well that's it. That's peace. It's perfect.

Then they pulled the cover off the second painting, and the audience gasped—not because the picture reflected a tranquil pastoral setting, but because it was the picture of a storm. You could see the angry clouds belching thunder, see the lightning slicing up the sky, feel the sharp wind whipping across the scene. And the scene? This was not a lake, but a waterfall roaring as it crashed to the bottom. The audience recoiled. What is this? Was there a misunderstanding? And why did the judges choose this picture? Then they were invited to look a little closer. Right next to the waterfall was a protruding branch begging to be snapped off. And in the crook of the branch was a bird's nest. And in that nest was a mother bird protecting her eggs from the storm, and she was asleep. That's peace. Anyone can have peace when the weather in his or her life is calm. But can you have peace when you are in a storm? You can if your focus is right. You can if your focus is on the Master of the storm.

Peace is connected to our faith and our focus; it is also connected to our farming.

III. CONNECTED TO OUR FARMING   James 3:18

Now the fruit of righteousness is sown in peace by those who make peace.

Farming is a stretch, but it comes from the word "sown." As much as is possible, we should live at peace with all men. We will reap what we sow. If we sow peace, we reap peace. We should purpose to be peacemakers. It is a sign of Christian maturity. James 3:13 asks for the sign of a wise man. A characteristic repeated in James 3:13-18, and the only one repeated, is that of a peacemaker.

The last gladiator to die in the Roman Coliseum was a man named Telemachus. He really wasn't a gladiator at all. He was a monk living in France. But he wanted to visit Rome. When he got there, it looked like a modern traffic jam. He asked what was going on and was told it was Coliseum Day when the gladiators fought. He had never seen anything like this. So he wandered in and saw two gladiators facing off, ready to fight until one was dead for the honor of Rome. As they drew their swords and began to fight, Telemachus jumped over the wall and ran between the two gladiators and shouted, "In the name of Jesus Christ, forbear."

The gladiators were so shocked, they didn't know what to do. The crowd began shouting for one of them to kill the little monk. One of them used the back of his sword to knock Telemachus down. But he popped up, ran between the gladiators, and shouted, "In the name of Jesus Christ, forbear." Now the crowd was really agitated. They began chanting, "Kill him, kill him." So, one of the gladiators shoved his sword through the stomach of Telemachus. He lay there on the Coliseum sand while his blood poured out. There were no cheers, just a deathly silence. Finally, a man got up and walked out. Then another and another until the Coliseum was empty. No gladiator ever fought again in the Roman Coliseum. Telemachus had sown peace. And he did reap peace, but it came at the cost of his life.

The famous prayer of St. Francis of Assisi? "Lord, make me an instrument of your peace." Peace is connected to our faith, our focus, our farming, and finally, our future.

IV. CONNECTED TO OUR FUTURE   Jer. 29:11

For I know the thoughts that I think toward you, says the Lord, thoughts of peace and not of evil, to give you a future and a hope.

We love to quote this verse. It is such a good one. But rarely do I meet anyone who knows its context. To get that we need to read the verse before it. "For thus says the Lord: After seventy years are completed at Babylon, I will visit you and perform My good word toward you, and cause you to return to this place." The people of Israel had dug a deep hole for themselves because of their idolatry, their sinfulness. God could stand it no more, so he let Nebuchadnezzar deport them to Babylon.

We have to remember that when they went to Babylon, they did not know how long their captivity would be. They just knew that God was some kind of angry with them. For all they knew, they would never come back to Israel. Many of them thought God would not fulfill his promises to Abraham. Others thought God would just completely destroy them.

But God came to them through Jeremiah, the weeping prophet. We need to realize that Jeremiah was not deported. He was prophesying in Jerusalem. It was not until the Jews had been in captivity for over a generation that the word of the Lord through Jeremiah came to them. And Jeremiah 29:10-11 says, "No, Israel, I have not given up on you. I have disciplined you because of your sin, but I still have good thoughts about your future. You still have hope."

Sometimes we dig such a deep hole with our sin that we find ourselves in Babylon. We think God is through with us. It's all over. There is no more place for us in his kingdom program. But God comes along and says, "Stop thinking that way. If you are alive, I can still use you." God has a future for us in spite of our mistakes. And that future includes peace. Just knowing that our all-powerful, all-knowing, all-loving God has such a plan gives us hope.

CONCLUSION

"Let the peace of God rule in your hearts...and be thankful" (Col. 3:15). Since peace is a fruit of the Spirit, we can quench him and also his fruit. We don't have to let the peace of God rule in our hearts. We can stifle God's intended blessing for us. And notice again the connection between peace and thanksgiving. "And be thankful." Read the words of Joni Eareckson Tada about Thanksgiving at her house.

> I don't know how it is with your family, but with mine, especially on Thanksgiving when so many relatives are gathered, everybody is talking and laughing at the same time. Then after dinner, Dad speaks a word of thanks, and each one of us—sometimes as many as twenty-five—around the big oak dining table does, too.

> Thanksgiving 1967 came. I was in the hospital hooked up to intravenous tubes and to a catheter. I was strapped to a

smelling canvas Stryker frame that was both confining and claustrophobic. The darkness in my heart was as dreary as the hospital walls that surrounded me. In my bitterness, in my anger and resentment, and in my suffering, I felt as if it were impossible to thank God. I thought I could never thank God again.

Another year passed, and my heart had time to mellow. Thanksgiving 1968 came. My spirit had begun to soften and my ears were open and once again I was thankful. No more fox hunts for me, but I was home from the hospital with my family. After dinner, in our usual tradition, Dad stood up, and through his tears he said he was so thankful that I was home. When it was my turn, I looked down at my plate and then up at the faces of my family. I said, "I'm thankful that I'm sitting up in a wheelchair now. I'm thankful that I don't have any more bedsores and that I don't have to go through any more operations. I'm thankful that I'm home for good. I'm thankful that I found a corset that fits me right so I can sit up comfortably and breathe OK. I'm thankful for my family. Most of all, I'm thankful for God and all his blessings." And you know what? On Thanksgiving, 1968, it didn't matter that I couldn't go on a fox hunt or that my fingers couldn't braid the mane and tail of my thoroughbred. It didn't matter that I had no strength to polish a saddle or drive my car out to the farm. It didn't matter that I couldn't help my family prepare dinner or set the table. What mattered was that I was alive and that I was beginning to smile and feel. Thanksgiving 1968 was far more wonderful and meaningful to me than any other Thanksgiving I had ever had before.[136]

---

136 Joni Eareckson Tada, quoted in Sheila Crowe, "Winning over Worry," Sermon Central, accessed August 19, 2014, www.sermon central.com/sermons/winning-over-worry-sheila-crowe-sermon-on-worry-137715.asp?Page=4.

She found the peace that passes understanding. And I would say,

Sail the ship of your mind into the safe harbor of God's infinite wisdom; Drop the anchor of your soul into the calm, clear waters of his sovereign plan; Release the rudder of your uncertain future into the hands of his spirit; Look to the compass of his revealed will to guide you to peaceful shores.[137]

But perhaps the hymn writer put it best:

Like a river glorious is God's perfect peace
Over all victorious in its bright increase;
Perfect yet it floweth,
Fuller ever' day;
Perfect yet it groweth,
Deeper all the way.
Stayed upon Jehovah,
Hearts are fully blest;
Finding as he promised,
Perfect peace and rest.

---

137 Mine.

PATIENCE—HEAVEN'S ANGER MANAGEMENT
Galatians 5:22

nger may seem to be the best medicine, but more often than not, it turns into a deadly poison. Anger is one of man's most destructive emotions. Scripture says, "An angry man stirs up strife, and a furious man abounds in transgression" (Prov. 29:22). It was Frederick Buechner who wrote:

> Of the seven deadly sins anger is possibly the most fun. To lick your wounds, to smack your lips over grievances long past, to roll over your tongue the prospect of bitter confrontations still to come, to savor to the last toothsome morsel both the pain you are given and the pain you are giving back—in many ways it is a feast fit for a king. The chief drawback is that what you are wolfing down is yourself. The skeleton at the feast is you.[138]

That is his way of saying that the person who comes in last in the race toward anger is the person who comes in first. The person who

---

138 Frederick Buechner, "Anger," Sermon Illustrations, accessed August 19, 2014, www.sermonillustrations.com/a-z/a/anger.htm.

wins the race is the bigger loser. Anger, openly displayed, deliberately hidden from others, or unconsciously expressed, is at the root of many psychological, interpersonal, physical, and spiritual problems. Along with hostility, anger has been called "the chief saboteur of the mind" and "the leading cause of misery, depression, inefficiency, sickness, accidents, loss of work time and financial loss in industry…no matter what the problem—marital conflict, alcoholism, a wife's frigidity, a child's defiance, nervous or physical disease—elimination of hostility is a key factor in its solution."[139]

Peter Stearns, in his book *Anger: The Struggle for Emotional Control in America's History*, argues that the entire course of world history has been shaped by anger and the struggle for emotional control.[140] Christian psychologist Neil Clark Warren calls anger "our most baffling emotion" and concludes that "anger management is a shockingly underdeveloped skill in our society."[141]

You are probably thinking, *I didn't know anger was a fruit of the Spirit*. Well, you are right. It is not. Anger is a work of the flesh. We have covered the first three fruits of the Spirit: love, joy, and peace. Now we are ready for the fourth: patience. And we ask, "What does anger have to do with patience?" "Patience" is the best one-word English translation of the fruit of the Spirit known in Greek as *makrothumia*. It is a compound work in Greek: *makro* (long) + *thumia* (anger). You might think of the *thumia* as a stick of dynamite and the *makro* as a long fuse. But it is usually translated in the Greek OT (the LXX) as "slow to anger." That is really our best

---

139 Milton Layden, *Escaping the Hostility Trap*, quoted in "What Is Anger?," New Beginnings Christian Counseling, accessed August 19, 2014, http://christianmarriagecounselling.org/what-is-anger/.

140 Carol Zisowitz Stearns and Peter N. Stearns, *Anger: The Struggle for Emotional Control in America's History* (Chicago: University of Chicago Press, 1986).

141 Neil Clark Warren, quoted in Irene Prospere, *Jesus, the Ultimate Counselor* (Bloomington, IN: Xlibris, 2007), 52.

English phrase for this fruit of the Spirit. Hence, *makrothumia* = patience = being slow to anger. This is another way of saying that patience = anger management.

What we want to look at are the causes, consequences, and control of anger.

I. CAUSES OF ANGER

The following are suggested causes for anger:

A. **Hurt Feelings**—"And the Lord respected Abel and his offering, but He did not respect Cain and his offering, and Cain was very angry" (Gen. 4:4-5). Cain's anger led to murder. What was his problem? Lack of respect and acceptance of his work. He got hurt. We can be hurt by lots of things: being rejected, ignored, put down, demeaned, devalued—all sorts of things. Quite often when I get angry, I can slow down and determine the cause of this anger was from being hurt. Husbands and wives go through this all the time. So next time you are angry at your spouse, ask yourself if she or he did something to hurt you.

One husband said every time he tried to give a constructive criticism in his marriage, his wife would snap at him. So he tried the old sandwich approach: compliment, criticize, compliment. But the result was always the same. So they traced things back in her life and found that when she was a little girl, her father would make fun of her when she was practicing the piano. "Can't you do any better than that?" She was just five. But she was so wounded from this that as she grew up, any criticism from a man threw her into anaphylactic shock. Hurt feelings erupted in anger.

B. **Blocked Goal**—"When the donkey saw the Angel of the Lord, she lay down under Balaam; so Balaam's anger was aroused, and he struck the donkey with his staff" (Num. 22:27). Here is the earliest recorded case of "road rage." Next time you get mad on the road while driving, ask yourself whether other drivers are blocking your goal.

C. **Violation of Rights**

1. **Others'**—"So David's anger was greatly aroused against the man, and he said to Nathan: 'As the Lord lives, the man who has done this shall surely die!'" (2 Sam. 12:5). Of course, this is Nathan's indirect way of convicting David of his sins with Bathsheba and her husband, Uriah the Hittite. The man with many sheep violated the rights of the man with one sheep. David takes up the offense. There is a place for anger when the rights of others are being violated. What about the rights of the unborn? That ought to make us angry. But when we get angry over rights, it is usually our own rights we think are being violated.

2. **Ours**—"Saul was very angry, and the saying displeased him; and he said, 'They have ascribed to David ten thousands, and to me they have ascribed only thousands'" (1 Sam. 18:8). Saul was the rightful top dog. He thought the adulation of the crowds belonged to him. He became mad and tried to kill David.

D. **Our Sinful Nature**—"Where do wars and fights come from among you? Do they not come from your desires for pleasure that war in your members? You lust and do not have. You murder and covet and cannot obtain. You fight and war" (James 4:1-2).

A group of doctors from Coral Gables, Florida compared the efficiency of the heart's pumping action in eighteen men with coronary artery disease to nine healthy controls. Each of the study participants underwent a physical stress test (riding an exercise bicycle) and three mental stress tests (doing math problems in their heads, recalling a recent incident that had made them very angry, and giving a short speech to defend themselves against a hypothetical charge of shoplifting). Using sophisticated equipment, the doctors watched the hearts in action during these tests.

For all the subjects, anger reduced the amount of blood that the heart pumped to body tissues more than the other tests, but this was especially true for those who had heart disease. Why anger is so much more potent than fear or mental stress is anybody's guess, but until we see more research on the subject, it couldn't hurt to learn how to be slow to anger. That is what we call patience.

II. CONSEQUENCES OF ANGER

A. **Strife**—"A hot-tempered man stirs up dissension, but a patient man calms a quarrel" (Prov. 15:18 NIV).

B. **Foolishness**—"A patient man has great understanding, but a quick-tempered man displays folly" (Prov. 14:29 NIV). "Do not hasten in your spirit to be angry, for anger rests in the bosom of fools" (Eccl. 7:9).

C. **More Sin**—"An angry man stirs up dissension, and a hot-tempered one commits many sins" (Prov. 29:22 NIV).

D. **Broken Ego Boundary**—"Like a city whose walls are broken down is a man who lacks self-control" (Prov. 25:28 NIV).

E. **Depression**—"Cain was very angry *and his countenance fell*" (Gen. 4:5). One of the leading causes of depression is repressed anger.

F. **Divine Judgment**—"But I say to you that whoever is angry with his brother without a cause shall be in danger of the judgment" (Matt. 5:22).

Obviously, anger can be very destructive. In the spring of 1894, the Baltimore Orioles came to Boston to play a routine baseball game. But what happened that day was anything but routine. The Orioles' John McGraw got into a fight with the Boston third baseman. Within minutes all the players for both teams had joined in the brawl. The warfare quickly spread to the grandstands. Among the fans the conflict went from bad to worse. Someone set fire to the stands and the entire ballpark burned to the ground. Not only that, but the fire spread to 107 other buildings as well. All because two men got angry.

I saw the result of locked horns in Crested Butte, Colorado. A couple of bull elk were fighting over their territory, no doubt, when they locked horns. Unable to untangle their horns, they starved to death. But they really died because of uncontrolled anger. We need to learn how to control our anger.

III. CONTROL OF ANGER

A. **Recognize**—the anger. That's the first step. You have to know it is there. They say we either express anger, suppress anger, or repress anger. If you express it, you certainly know it's there. If you suppress anger, you know it's there, but you are hiding it. If you repress anger, you don't even know it's there. I remember when our first child hit first grade, the school gave a psychological test to the parents. I guess they were looking for early warning signals that one of their sweet, little first graders might be a future psychopath. Well, it was time to go over the test, so the school shrink asked her first question of me. She asked, "What do you do with your anger?" I replied, "I don't get angry." She said, "Well, this test says you do." In an angry voice I said, "Well, it's a dumb test." (No, no, no, I didn't really say that.) What I said was, looking at Betty, my wife, "Do I get angry?" She said, "No, I've never seen him angry." Fast-forward a few years. I tore my ACL (anterior cruciate ligament) and was laid up for ten days in the hospital. I found myself getting angry pretty much every day. This continued after I left the hospital. That's when I realized I do get angry, and always have. It's just that I used to run and exercise so much I dissipated my anger with sports. That's when I first got in touch with my anger. Since then I have realized I get angry at my wife, my kids, my dogs, my cats—pretty much anyone or anything I face in life. The Bible recognizes this possibility (Eph. 4:26). That anger shows up is not sinful. The question is, what will we do with our anger?

B. **Take**—every thought captive with the goal of obeying Christ (2 Cor. 10:5). The battle is in the mind.

C. **Pray**

   1. Yield—to the Holy Spirit. Ask him to lead you and to empower you.

   2. Humble—yourself before God. He will give you more grace (James 4:6).

   3. Confess—the anger, if you have sinned (Eph. 4:26; 1 John 1:9).

D. **Focus**—on Christ's imminent (any-moment-now) return (James 5:7-9). These people were mad at God because of their many trials. They were also impatient with him, thinking he had forgotten his promise to come back and get them out of their mess. James argues that God is like a farmer patiently waiting for the spring rain (the latter rain) to bring in a full harvest. He is patient with mankind, waiting for the last person to come to Christ. Can't we be patient with him? Nevertheless, realizing that the Judge stands before the door (he could come at any time) can also help us be more patient with people.

Back in the day of John D. Rockefeller, one of his senior executives made a decision that cost the company about forty million dollars in today's money. Most of the employees of Standard Oil Company steered clear of Mr. Rockefeller on that day, with a notable exception—Edward T. Bedford, a partner in the company.

When Bedford walked into Rockefeller's office, he was ready for him to explode. Instead, Rockefeller busied himself with a pencil and a pad of paper. After a few minutes he looked up at Bedford and said, "Oh, it's you, Bedford. I guess you've heard about our loss?" Bedford said he had.

"I've been thinking it over," Rockefeller said, "and before I ask the man in to discuss the matter, I've been making some notes." Bedford later told the story this way: "Across the top of the page was written, 'Points in favor of Mr. _____.' There followed a long list of the man's virtues, including a brief description of how he had helped the company make the right decision on three separate occasions that had earned many times the cost of his recent error.

"I've never forgotten that lesson," claimed Bedford. "In later years, whenever I was tempted to rip into anyone, I forced myself first to sit down and thoughtfully compile as long a list of good points as I possibly could. Invariably, by the time I finished my inventory, I would see the matter in its true perspective and keep my temper under control. There is no telling how many times this habit has prevented me from committing one of the costliest mistakes any executive can make—losing his temper. I commend it to anyone who must deal with people."[142]

Slow to anger—that's patience.

CONCLUSION

Through the Holy Spirit we find the **control** for anger, but through *forgiveness* we find the **cure** for anger (Eph. 4:31-32).

---

142 "Anger," Sermon Illustrations, accessed August 19, 2014, www.sermonillustrations.com/a-z/a/anger.htm.

There are many redeeming stories in Ernest Gordon's *Miracle on the River Kwai*,[143] which pop out like fireflies in the dark night of WWII. It dealt not with the problem of bitterness and hatred toward the prisoners' captors, the Japanese, but the prisoners' own lack of patience with each other. Arduous work, disease, not enough calories—all these things left tempers short.

But one afternoon something happened. A shovel was missing. The officer in charge became enraged. He demanded that the missing shovel be produced, or else. When nobody in the squadron budged, the officer got his gun and threatened to kill them all on the spot. It was obvious the officer meant what he said. So, finally, one man stepped forward. The officer put away his gun, picked up a shovel, and beat the man to death.

When it was over, the survivors picked up the bloody corpse and carried it with them to the second tool checkpoint. This time, no shovel was missing. Indeed, there had been a miscount at the first checkpoint. The word spread like wildfire through the whole camp— an innocent man had been willing to die to save the others!

The incident had a profound effect. The men began to treat each other like brothers. They began to have some patience with each other, forgiving each other for oversights and wrongs. And when the allies swept in, the survivors, human skeletons, lined up in front of their captors and instead of attacking them, they said, "No more hatred; no more killing. Now what we need is forgiveness."

Christ is the innocent one who died for us. Because he has forgiven us of so much, he urges us to forgive others. It is the cure for anger and the catalyst for patience.

---

143 Ernest Gordon, *Miracle on the River Kwai*, quoted in Ken Durham, "Miracle on the River Kwai," Sermon Central, accessed August 19, 2014, www.sermoncentral.com/sermons/miracle-on-the-river-kwai-ken-durham-sermon-on-forgiveness-for-others-81332.asp?Page=3.

ARE YOU A CHRESTIAN CHRISTIAN?
Galatians 5:22

Emma McCloud, a freelance writer, got on the Greyhound bus on a wintry night in Albuquerque, New Mexico, en route to Flagstaff, Arizona. It was a cold night, and she was glad to slide into her warm seat on the bus. Somewhere along the way a young American Native American boarded the bus. He looked very cold, disheveled, and tired, as though he had been walking some distance. Emma overheard him tell the bus driver that he needed to get off the bus in Holbrook, Arizona. "Would you please let me know when we get there?"

The Native American slipped into the seat in front of Emma and began to try to sleep. But he popped up in a few minutes, looked around at Emma, and asked her if she could alert him when they were getting near Holbrook. His sister's husband had recently died, and he was going to help her for a while. Unfortunately, both of them fell asleep, the bus passed through Holbrook, and the Native American snapped out of his sleep and wondered where they were. He woke Emma, and she didn't know either.

So the Native American went to the front of the bus and asked the bus driver, "Are we near Holbrook?" "We passed Holbrook an hour ago, buddy," said the bus driver coldly. "Oh no," exclaimed the young man, "I asked you to tell me when we got there." "I did," said the bus driver without sympathy. "You must have slept through it. You can get off at Winslow and get a bus back to Holbrook." "But I don't have any more money, and my sister is waiting for me." "Buddy," said the bus driver, "that's not my problem. You can ride on to Flagstaff and spend the night at the bus station." The Native American shuffled back to his seat, sat down, and put his head between his knees.

Suddenly, Emma found herself leaning forward and tapping him on the shoulder. She asked, "Young man, are you afraid?" With a proud but humbled look, he nodded and turned away in shame. "Young man, I have more money than I need. Here is some money for a phone call to your sister so she won't worry.... And here is some more money to buy some breakfast and a ticket back to Holbrook." With a stunned look on his face, the proud but forlorn young man took the money. Then he settled back in his seat to get some more rest.

After a couple of minutes, the Native American popped up, turned around, and said to Emma, "Can I ask you a question?" She nodded. "Are you a Christian?"

Are you? In Europe they like to distinguish between "nominal" Christians and "true" Christians. In America we make the same distinction with the terms "professing" Christians and "born-again" Christians. The distinction in both hemispheres is between those who call themselves Christians and those who have believed in Christ.

In Romans and Galatians, Paul makes two more distinctions among those who are "true," "born-again" Christians: (1) Christians who live according to the flesh versus according to the Spirit; and (2) Christians who live by the law principle versus the grace principle. Spirit-led Christians live by grace; carnal (flesh-led) Christians live by law (legalism). In order to enjoy the fruit of the Spirit, we need to be led by the Spirit. When we are, the fifth fruit listed in Galatians 5:22 ("kindness"—NKJV, NIV, NASB, ESV) is available to us.

"Kindness" is *chrēstotēs* in our Greek text. Can you see how close this word is to *Christos* (Christ)? This is the noun; the adjective is *chrēstos*—in fact, 1 Peter 2:3 (quoting Ps. 33:9 from the LXX) says, "The Lord is *chrēstos*," thus applying the adjective to the divine name of Jesus. Though the noun *chrēstotēs* is translated "kindness" in most versions and elsewhere as "goodness, friendliness, or easy" (Matt. 11:30), its most common usage in both the OT and the NT is to express the grace of God given to us in his covenant loyalty and his salvation.

Chrēstotēs is extended to those who confess their sins and repent in the Psalms of Solomon 9:7. This is forgiveness. Psalm 86:5 says, "For You, Lord, are good [*chrēstos* in the LXX], and ready to forgive, and abundant in mercy to all those who call upon You." Thus, it would appear that *chrēstotēs* comes very close to being a synonym for **grace** (*charis*). This was the conclusion of Konrad Weiss after his study of *chrēstotēs* in Romans 2:4; Ephesians 2:7; and Titus 3:4ff.: "In the apostolic age, then, the word expressed the comprehensive fullness of Christian salvation and was a full...equivalent of...***grace*** (*charis*)."[144]

In fact, the Gentiles began to call Christ *Chrēstos* and Christians *Chrēstoi*, since the words sounded so similar to them. This would be like our calling Christ "the gracious One" and calling Christians "the gracious ones." The point is that Christ and his followers were known and recognized by their grace orientation. We too can be recognized as ***chrestian Christians*** in these three ways:

I. OUR MESSAGE OF SAVING GRACE   Eph. 2:8-9

For by grace you have been saved by faith, and that not of yourselves; it is the gift of God, not of works, lest anyone should boast.

It would absolutely astound you to know how many professing Christians believe we ***must do*** something ***besides believe*** in order to

---

144 Konrad Weiss, *TDNT*, IX, 483-92.

be saved to have eternal life. Some churches think you ***must do*** seven things in order to ***merit*** grace (an oxymoron). To do something to merit grace is Neo-Galatianism pure and simple. By definition (grace is an ***undeserved*** favor) no one can merit (deserve) grace. Some of the Galatians wanted to add circumcision and keeping the Law of Moses to the simple requirement of faith. Paul says no man is justified by works of the law (Gal. 2:16).

Wendy Kaminer, a modern Jew trying to comprehend Christianity, confessed, "As an article of faith, this doctrine of salvation by grace and grace alone is remarkably unappealing to me. It takes, I think, remarkable disregard for justice to idealize a God who so values belief over action. I prefer the God who looks down upon us (in a very old joke) and says, 'I wish they'd stop worrying about whether or not I exist and start obeying my commandments.'"[145]

Or, as a professing Christian wrote to Charles Trumbull, "I have no hesitancy in saying I do not believe in your position. My entire experience refutes it…. I believe that salvation is brought about by the continuous desire and effort to gain it, and that it will not come without that desire and effort. I realize, of course, that no man can save himself, but I believe that God expects every man to do his part toward that salvation." That's Neo-Galatianism: faith + works.

II. OUR MANNER OF LIVING GRACE
Gal. 3:3; James 4:6a

Are you so foolish? Having begun in the Spirit, are you now being made perfect by the flesh? (Gal. 3:3)

But He gives more grace. (James 4:6a)

Once saved (justified) by grace, we can resort to trying to live the Christian life by the flesh (Gal. 3:3). Paul says that's foolish. It is a life

---

145 As quoted in Philip Yancey, *The Jesus I Never Knew* (Grand Rapids, MI: Zondervan, 1995), 152.

of legalism (trying to win God's favor through our own performance, energy, and abilities). The victorious Christian life, the Spirit-led Christian life (Rom. 8:14; Gal. 5:18), is by grace, not by law. We became Christians by grace. Now we need more grace to have victory over our sin nature (the flesh in Gal. 5). James 4:6 tells us that grace for victory over the lusts that war in our members will be given to the humble, but not the proud. Well, who are the humble if not those who cry out for God's power to live this supernatural life?

The *chrestian Christian* is grace oriented all the way around. He needs God's grace to get into the gates of heaven, and he needs God's grace to bring some measure of heaven to earth. C. I. Scofield wrote: "Most of us have been reared and now live under the influence of Galatianism. Protestant theology is for the most part thoroughly Galatianized, in that neither law nor grace is given its distinct and separate place as in the counsel of God, but they are mingled together in one incoherent system."[146]

Miles Stanford wrote:

> For most of us, it is time to stop asking God for help. He didn't help us to be saved, and He doesn't intend to help us live the Christian life. Immaturity considers the Lord Jesus a Helper. Maturity knows Him to be life itself. When we beg God for help in the Christian life, we are saying, "God, I'll do part and you do part. Together we'll get the job done."
>
> But, my friend, that portion of the Christian life we consider "our part" is that portion which hinders Christ in living out His life through us. And it is this very philosophy that we must do our part to help God perform the work of sanctification in our lives—it is this teaching, this demonic doctrine, which keeps so many Christians under the heavy yoke of bondage to the law principle which ultimately only stirs up a hornet's nest

---

146 C. I. Scofield, quoted by Miles Stanford, *Abide Above* (Hong Kong: Living Spring, 1970), 26.

of sin in their lives, which drives them into continued defeat and discouragement.[147]

Elmer Towns says it all in the title of his autobiography: *Walking with Giants*.[148] Although he has authored over fifty books and cofounded Liberty University with Jerry Falwell, Towns has always regarded himself as one of the little guys when standing next to a giant like Falwell. He tells the story of just an average guy from the country in South Carolina. His grades were average, his looks were average, and his height was below average. He wasn't a good speaker, and he wasn't a good writer. But God gave him at least two outstanding gifts: a fervent desire to be used by God and a tremendous amount of energy. When his sixth-grade teacher asked for a ten-page paper, he wrote fifty. He gave his life to serve Christ, and the Lord has used him like only a couple of dozen others in the last hundred years. As "just an average guy," Dr. Towns was never tempted to "do it on his own."

III. OUR MODEL OF GIVING GRACE
Eph. 4:32; Col. 3:12

And be kind to one another, tenderhearted, forgiving one another, even as God in Christ forgave you. (Eph. 4:32)

Therefore, as the elect of God, holy and beloved, put on tender mercies, kindness, humility, meekness, longsuffering. (Col. 3:12)

Here we are using *chrēstotēs* in its meaning of "kindness, friendliness, graciousness." The adjective is used in Ephesians 4:32 (*chrēstos*—"kind"), while the noun is used in Colossians 3:12

147 Miles Stanford, *The Complete Green Letters* (Grand Rapids, MI: Zondervan, 1983), 87.

148 Elmer Towns, *Walking with Giants* (Ventura, CA: Regal Books, 2012).

(*chrēstotēs*—"kindness"). Unfortunately, some Christians who will defend the message of saving grace are among the most ungracious of Christians. They are not **chrestian Christians**. We call it "in-your-face grace." Often they are the opposite of *chrēstos*; that is, they are harsh, judgmental, and dogmatic.

Such people may have the right message, but their negative, judgmental, self-righteous example causes both believers and unbelievers to run away faster than Deion Sanders could return a punt. A **chrestian Christian** is gracious in his dealings with people (see Luke 6:33; 1 Cor. 13:4; 2 Cor. 6:6; Eph. 4:32; Col. 3:12).

The Gospels record eight times when Jesus accepted an invitation to dinner. Three of these were friendlies—the wedding at Cana, Mary and Martha, and the men on the road to Emmaus. But the other five broke the social protocol: Simon the leper, Simon the Pharisee (where a prostitute showed up and wiped Jesus's feet), an unnamed Pharisee, and two tax collectors (Zacchaeus and Levi).

Why did the outcasts and social pariahs feel comfortable around Jesus, while the self-righteous but socially accepted did not? Philip Yancey suggested this principle from Jesus's life: Jesus brought to the surface repressed sin, yet forgave any freely acknowledged sin.[149] The woman caught in adultery went away forgiven, but her accusers walked away convicted of their own sin. Jesus treated her with kindness and forgiveness, while the accusers treated her with condemnation. C. S. Lewis wrote, "Prostitutes are in no danger of finding their present life so satisfactory that they cannot turn to God; the proud, the avaricious, the self-righteous, are in that danger."[150]

CONCLUSION   Luke 6:35-37

But love your enemies, do good, and lend, hoping for nothing
in return; and your reward will be great, and you will be sons

---

149   Philip Yancey, *The Jesus I Never Knew*, 152.

150   C. S. Lewis, quoted in Philip Yancey, *The Jesus I Never Knew*, 152.

of the Most High. For He is kind to the unthankful and evil. Therefore be merciful, just as your Father also is merciful. "Judge not, and you shall not be judged. Condemn not, and you shall not be condemned. Forgive, and you will be forgiven."

Here Luke calls for us to be merciful, as our Father in heaven is also merciful. He implores us not to judge one another, not to condemn one another, but to forgive. But can you see that the basis for this appeal to us to be merciful and forgiving is the *chrēstotēs* of God? It says he is **kind** to the unthankful and the evil—people who do not deserve kindness. Immediately following that observation of God and his character comes a "therefore." Therefore, based on what God is like, be like him. In so doing (the prior verse implies), we will "be sons" of the Most High. This isn't telling us we get into God's family by being kind to others. Note the word "reward." It is saying that by doing these things, we exhibit Christ-like, God-like character—we become mature sons of the Most High.

The parallel passage in the Sermon on the Mount makes this even clearer, because instead of saying you "will be" sons using the Greek word *esesthe* (the Greek verb for "to be"), Matthew uses the word *genēsthe*, which is translated "may be" from *ginomai* but has the idea of "becoming" (BDAG, *ginomai*, 4.a.). And the phrase "sons of your Father" does not speak of being in his family. No, it means "like your Father." James and John were the sons of Zebedee, but they were called "sons of thunder." Thunder was not the name of their father. Their personalities were characterized by thunder. And so, those who are able to love their enemies (those who have hurt them), become like God himself. After all, Jesus died for his enemies. Thus, the appeal in Luke to be merciful and forgiving and loving to our enemies because God is kind (*chrēstos*) promises not only great reward but Christ-likeness, the very goal of the Christian life. It's a call to kindness.

Pauline Kael was a film critic for the *New Yorker*. She was known for her caustic, critical reviews. It is said Pauline never met a movie she ever liked. *The Elephant Man* was an exception. She called it "a pleasurable surprise." Her one word description for the movie was "grace." She said:

> The grace in [David] Lynch's work comes from the care and thought: this is a film about the exhibition and exploitation of a freak, and he must be determined not to be an exploiter himself. The monster is covered or shadowed from us in the early sequences and we see only parts of him, a little at a time. Lynch builds up our interest in seeing more in a way that seems very natural. When we're ready to see him clearly, we do. By then, we have become so sympathetic that there's no disgust about seeing him full of deformity.[151]

At his death at age twenty-seven a mold was made of John Merrick's body and his skeleton preserved for science so the movie portrayed his appearance exactly as it was. He suffered from neurofibromatosis, a condition that caused tumors to grow all over his body, under his skin, around his nerves, even in his bones.

After a life of hellish suffering and abuse at the hands of others, Dr. Frederick Treves treated him, befriended him, and later wrote of him in a book titled *The Elephant Man and Other Reminiscences*.[152] Treves displays Christ-likeness in the movie, exhibiting a sensitivity and a graciousness (*chrēstotēs*) to Merrick that only could come from the heart of God.

At the end of his life Merrick has become something of a celebrity. His disease is incurable, and death is imminent. A friendship with a famous English actress, a Mrs. Kendal, has formed. She invites him to be her guest at the theater. After the play, she brings him on stage to a standing ovation of the well-bred Londoners. When Treves escorts him back to his room at the hospital, you can tell by

---

151 Pauline Kael, *Taking It All In* (New York: Holt, Reinhart and Winston, 1984), 82.

152 Frederick Treves, *The Elephant Man and Other Reminiscences* (London: Cassell and Company, Ltd., n.d.).

Merrick's childlike excitement that this night was the high point of his life.

After Merrick says good-bye to his friend, Dr. Treves, he pauses in front of his greatest work, a handcrafted cathedral, a replica of a cathedral outside his window. On the wall behind his cathedral is the sketch of a child kneeling beside his bed, praying. Then there is another picture where the same boy is now asleep in his bed, something Merrick couldn't do because of his difficulty in breathing. Now Merrick adds a final touch to his magnum opus by signing his name. It is finished. As Samuel Barber's "Adagio for Strings" begins to play, you have the feeling that Merrick is somehow finished too, that his life is now full and complete.

The camera pans slowly across the cathedral he has made, first horizontally, then vertically, almost as if it were making the sign of a cross. Merrick touches his head in response to what seems a sudden throb of pain. He looks at the picture on the wall of the child sleeping. Then slowly, methodically, he takes the pillows off his bed, one by one. He pulls down the covers, smoothens the sheet, and crawls into bed. He sits there a moment, then lies down. As "Adagio for Strings" plays on, the camera frames him, giving us a few last moments with this beautiful human being who has been imprisoned in that body for the past twenty-seven years. Slowly the camera moves from him to a picture of Mrs. Kendal, then on to a picture of his mother, on to the cathedral, then upward into the sky. The way the filmmaker shot the final scene underscored the sanctity of this man's life: the cathedral, the cross, the picture of the children sleeping, and the music.

Precious to the Lord is the death of his godly ones, the psalmist says, and as you watch the final moments before John Merrick's death, you sense not only the sacredness of his life but the preciousness of his death in the eyes of God. As we behold his hideous physical presence, one side of us wants to cry out, "God, you really messed up on this one." But as you watch that final scene, you realize John Merrick was not some cosmic accident or one of God's mistakes. Quite the opposite. In the closing moments of his life, the image of

God was stamped on him more clearly than the "normal" people who surrounded him with repulsion, with the exception of Dr. Treves.[153]

John Merrick was not a freak of nature. The movie made his faith in Christ quite clear. But the kindness, the graciousness, the *chrēstotēs* of one doctor redeemed his physical life. When I saw the film for the first time in a theater, no one left while the credits were being shown. We had seen someone who was sacred. In a sermon titled "The Weight of Glory," C. S. Lewis said, "Next to the Blessed Sacrament, your neighbor is the holiest thing present to your senses."[154] The question is, how will our neighbor perceive us? Are you a *chrestian* **Christian?**

153 Ken Gire, *Reflections on the Movies* (Colorado Springs: Victor, 2000), 156-57. Though not quoted verbatim, this analysis comes directly from the excellent mind of Ken Gire.

154 "C. S. Lewis Quotable Quote," Goodreads, accessed August 19, 2014, www.goodreads.com/quotes/28923-next-to-the-blessed-sacrament-itself-your-neighbor-is-the.

GOODNESS—HEAVEN'S CHARACTER
Galatians 5:22

When Obi-Wan Kenobi told young Luke Skywalker that the dark side of the force had seduced Luke's father, he was alluding in fiction to a real theory of the cosmos that is almost as old as man. The first to write about it was a Persian religious leader named Zoroaster. He taught that good and evil were eternal and had been in an eternal struggle for influence in the universe. He saw good and evil as two different forces, whereas George Lucas in his Star Wars series presents them as two different sides of the same force.

About five hundred years after Zoroaster (though scholars date him anywhere from 5500 BC to 600 BC), a Greek philosopher named Plato (400 BC) added a new twist. He believed good and evil were eternal, but he divided between the material and the spiritual. Everything material he labeled as evil, while everything spiritual was good. He also taught that souls were eternal but could not reach their highest level of existence without entering a human body for a period of suffering. The human body was evil and functioned like a prison for the soul. But through much struggle the soul could be released from its prison to go back to the spiritual side of the universe as a better soul because of its suffering.

Along came Jesus and his disciples. He was the God-man: undiminished deity combined with perfect humanity into one person forever and ever. But even in the first century AD the influence of Greek philosophy began worming its way into Christian theology. Plato's philosophy of material things as evil and spiritual things as good permeated the Mediterranean world, especially after Alexander the Great conquered that world and tried to spread Greek philosophy. When this philosophy merged with Christianity, a group called the Gnostics came along and said Jesus could not actually have been a man or his perfect spirit would have been tainted by his evil body. Thus, he must have just appeared to be a man. This philosophy grew in its influence almost up to the time of Augustine (d. AD 430).

Augustine, considered by some to be the greatest of the church fathers and certainly the man (outside the writers of Scripture) most responsible for what the majority of Christians believe in Western Christianity, plugged Plato's philosophy into Christianity. He knew the Bible did not teach that the human body was evil, but that old belief crops up now and then in his teachings. For example, he taught that physical relations between even a husband and wife to have children were evil.

Augustine performed the wedding ceremony between Athens and Jerusalem, and the offspring of this union is a far cry from biblical Christianity. The goal of Christianity, according to the early Augustine, is to get the soul out of the body and into heaven—just like Plato. Though the body is not evil, it is still a prison and should be denied any form of pleasure, since such gratification is either sinful or inferior to the pleasure of the spiritual world, the ideal world.

So, what does the Bible teach about good and evil? Can anyone really be good in this life? Must we postpone the experience of goodness until the next life? Not if goodness is a fruit of the Spirit and we have the Spirit now. So how do we reconcile these apparent contradictions? Let's look at goodness: its definition, our dilemma, and our deliverance.

I. GOODNESS—OUR DEFINITION

The Bible uses two words for "good": *agathos* and *kalos*. The latter word refers to an externally observable excellence. It would be used to describe a fine horse or an expensive car. The former word refers to an intrinsic, internal good—not necessarily something that can be observed with the naked eye or at first glance. This is the word used in Romans 8:28. God works all things together for **good** (*agathos*) to those who love God and are called according to his purpose. Many times things happen to Christians we would call tragedies. The world looks on and even other Christians look on and can see no good coming from one of these tragedies, but something **good** is happening. And the good is something only the Lord and the angels may see. It is something it may take the next world to unveil, although sometimes we see the good in this life (for example, Joni Eareckson Tada).

Certainly the supreme example of this *agathos* is the cross. Can you imagine being Mary or John looking at the suffering of Christ and saying, "This is a good thing"? But you and I, with the advantage of hindsight, can say, "Yes, that was a good thing." The good things coming out of that tragedy are too numerous to list, but it would not have been easy to see them when Jesus hung on the cross.

Agathos is the adjective we translate "good"; the noun is *agathōsunē*, which is the fruit of the Spirit listed here in Galatians 5:22 and translated "goodness." So we are talking about a **goodness** that is not necessarily observable to people on the outside. In fact, I would **define** this kind of goodness as "**any virtuous act or attitude, seen or unseen by men, which makes a positive contribution to the kingdom of God.**" We could call this "divine good" versus "human good." Our sin nature can produce human good that will not contribute to God's kingdom or open the gates of heaven. If this virtue of *agathōsunē* is a fruit of the Spirit, then it is divine good that will last forever.

It is important to realize, however, that the teachings about what is good from Zoroaster and Plato conflict dramatically with the Bible. In the first chapter of the Bible we see God at work in the material world. Seven times he calls his creative work "good" or even "very good" (Gen. 1:31). He clearly did not view the material world as evil.

Thus, all the teachings of the medieval church that we are to withdraw from the material world and that physical pleasures are sinful and inferior to spiritual pleasures are categorically wrong. That is Platonism introduced into the church by Neoplatonists such as Ambrose and Augustine. Augustine wanted to have a "beatific vision" of God like one of his favorite philosophers (Plotinus) claimed to have. The key to having this vision was to deny the flesh. He established an order for monks in northern Africa that taught celibacy and other forms of denial of the flesh. He actually helped depopularize the doctrine of the Millennium because of his revulsion over the anticipatory feasting in view of the return of Christ practiced by the Donatists (the majority of Christians) in northern Africa.

Some monks would not even take baths for fear of seeing themselves naked. The Gnostics didn't even think a person could go to heaven if he got married, calling such unions a "foul and polluted way of life." The man most responsible for translating the Bible into Latin was Jerome (Jerome's Vulgate), who wrote, "He who loves his own wife too ardently is an adulterer."[155] Augustine himself said the Patriarchs would have preferred to propagate the human race without connubial bliss (maybe a high five would do the trick), but since there was no other way, they performed reluctantly out of a sense of duty.

Fast-forward to the thirteenth century and things haven't changed much, if at all. Here is Thomas Aquinas's teaching: "Every carnal act [sexual] done in such a way that generation [pregnancy] cannot follow

---

155 Quoted in Roland B. Gittelsohn, *My Beloved Is Mine: Judaism and Marriage* (New York: Union of American Hebrew Congregations, 1969), 176.

is a vice against nature and a sin ranking in gravity to homicide."[156] Wow. Now pleasure with one's wife is the same as murder. No wonder John Calvin burned his stepdaughter at the stake when she was caught in adultery.[157] And Martin Luther (an Augustinian monk), who was one of the first monks to marry, said, "No matter what praise is given to marriage, I will not concede to nature that it [intercourse] is no sin."[158]

Do you get the sense here that there might be a bit of confusion over good and evil? The Bible does not teach the eternality of good and evil. Evil began with the sin of Lucifer. Good is eternal inasmuch as goodness is one of the attributes of God, and he is eternal. There certainly is a struggle between good and evil, but not a cosmic struggle between two impersonal forces or one force with a dark side and a light side. The main struggle between good and evil is in our hearts, which brings us to our dilemma.

II. GOODNESS—OUR DILEMMA

The fall of man changed everything about him dramatically. He was completely affected, body, soul, and spirit. The goodness within man departed. In fact, Jesus's response to the rich young ruler, when the ruler called Jesus a good teacher, was to say that only God is good. Why, Jesus wanted to know, was the ruler calling him good? He was asking this man if he believed Jesus was God.

Paul said, in his description of fallen man, "There is none who does good, no, not one" (Rom. 3:12). But Paul said even more about the human dilemma. Even after we become believers, he said, "For I know that in me (that is, in my flesh) nothing good dwells; for to will

---

156 Ibid., 177.

157 "Letter to Harold 'Hoot' and Annie Gibson," Reverend Know-It-All, accessed August 20, 2014, www.rev-know-it-all.com/2010/2010---12-19.html.

158 Ibid.

is present with me, but how to perform what is good I do not find. For the good that I will to do, I do not do; but the evil I will not to do, that I practice.... O wretched man that I am! Who will deliver me from this body of death?" (Rom. 7:18-19, 24).

This is the Christian dilemma—how to do that which is pleasing and good to God when we are humanly incapable.

III. GOODNESS—OUR DELIVERANCE

The Holy Spirit is our Deliverer from this wretched state of living. Through him we can experience divine goodness. It is one of his fruits. But we must distinguish between human good and divine good. Human good/goodness is sourced in our flesh (meaning our sinful nature); divine good/goodness is sourced in God himself through his Holy Spirit. Human good cannot gain right standing with God for the unbeliever (Isa. 64:6), and the human good of the believer will be burned up as wood, hay, and stubble at the Judgment Seat of Christ (1 Cor. 3:12-15; 13:1-3).

But when we allow the Holy Spirit to lead us, to empower us, and even to fill us, then divine goodness can be experienced and displayed in our lives. Divine Goodness came to earth to dwell in God's children through his Holy Spirit. The good that we would do **he can do** in us and through us. PTL!

Romans 8:2 discusses this deliverance through the law of the Spirit of Life in Christ Jesus. The moment we cease our struggle against sin and turn the problem over to Jesus, the deliverance process begins.[159] Some things fall away all by themselves. Other sinful habits may have a stronghold in our lives that require more time to break. But God did not save us from the eternal penalty of sin (justification) to leave us to serve the power of sin. The one who

---

159 C. E. B. Cranfield identifies the verb here as a use of the ingressive aorist. See "Paul's Teaching on Sanctification," *Reformed Review* 48 (Spring 1995): 220-21.

delivered us from the eternal penalty of sin also wants to deliver us from the present power of sin (sanctification). The Holy Spirit is the power source: if we walk by the Spirit, we will not fulfill the lusts of the flesh.

Jesus said we are supposed to be the salt and light of this world. How? According to him, we are to let our **good** works shine before men that they might be attracted to Christ and come to him for salvation (Matt. 5:14-16). Unlike Plato, the Bible does not relegate goodness to just the spiritual world. Goodness has invaded this world through the Holy Spirit and anyone who has the Holy Spirit living in him. It is through the Holy Spirit that the two universes (physical and spiritual) intersect. They are not parallel; they are intersecting.

In 2000, I traveled to Almaty, Kazakhstan, to teach a seminary course for students over there trying to earn master's degrees. I would teach from 8:30 a.m. until 3:30 p.m. Then four or five students would come for dinner and ask questions. One evening, after listening to their questions for a while, I asked them a question: "What do you think of democracy?" One student replied, "It's a good place for Adam." Of course, I had no idea what he was talking about. He went on:

> It is a good place for fallen man. The only reason democracy works in your country is because of the spiritual values on which it was founded. Take those values away, and it becomes a mess. On the first floor of this apartment is a brothel. Across the street is a restaurant owned by the Russian mafia. The president of our country was the former head of the KGB in our country. Soon after he became president he siphoned the oil money from the government into his personal account and quickly became a billionaire. It is easy for fallen man to exploit democracy.[160]

---

160 Interview with a student in Almaty, Kazakhstan, Summer 2000.

Human government does little to restrain evil. De Tocqueville observed this back in 1832.[161] Take spiritual values out of government, and it is just a matter of time until it runs amok. There is still a place for human government, but without Christians in human government, there is very little restraint. What will happen to America, or any nation, when spiritual values are completely set aside? Let me show you the steps in the "Decline of a Nation" from 2 Kings 21.

1. Forsake the Lord and his ways (v. 22).

Many think this began in earnest with the removal of prayer from our public schools in 1962. And it is interesting to look at the charts of immoral behavior shooting up after 1962 after remaining somewhat level for years. Nevertheless, the turning away from God began more around the beginning of the twentieth century. That's when most of our seminaries denied the Bible as the Word of God. That's when we began experimenting with eugenics as a direct result of Darwinism. The idea was that we could control our own evolution. The American program of eugenics was well established and well funded (the Rockefeller Foundation) by the 1920s and became the inspiration for the Nazi eugenics program. In fact, the Rockefeller Foundation helped fund the German program that trained Josef Mengele before he went to Auschwitz. In 1936, Harry H. Laughlin, a researcher in eugenics, was granted an honorary doctorate by Heidelberg University for his work on the "science of racial cleansing"[162] (see p. 25 in this book).

In 1933, John Dewey and others signed the Humanist Manifesto, which rejected creationism outright: "Religious humanists regard the universe as self-existing and not created.... Humanism asserts that the nature of the universe depicted by modern science makes

---

161 Alexis de Tocqueville, *Democracy in America*, trans. Gerald E. Bevan (New York: Penguin, 2003).

162 "Eugenics in the United States," Wikipedia, accessed August 20, 2014, http://en.wikipedia.org/wiki/Eugenics_in_the_United_States.

unacceptable any supernatural or cosmic guarantees of human values."[163] The second edition of the Humanist Manifesto published in 1973 reasserts their position:

> As in 1933, humanists still believe that traditional theism, especially faith in the prayer-hearing God, assumed to love and care for persons, to hear and understand their prayers and to be able to do something about them, is an unproven and outmoded faith. Salvationism, based on mere affirmation, still appears as harmful, diverting people with false hopes of heaven hereafter. Reasonable minds look to other means of survival.... Promises of immortal salvation or fear of eternal damnation are both illusory and harmful.[164]

2. Shed innocent blood (v. 16).

There were abortions in America before Roe v. Wade, but since that law (1973) over 56 million innocent children have been killed in this country alone. Since 1980, over a billion babies have been aborted worldwide.[165] I heard a speech by Bernard Nathanson (d. 2011) a few years ago. He and his father ran the largest abortion clinic in the world in New York. He told us how he, his dad, and some other physicians actually plotted to bring about the Roe v. Wade decision. After killing scores of thousands of children (sixty thousand), he was converted to Christ when making a movie of an abortion called *The Silent Scream*. He said America was asleep at the switch when he and his dad pulled off the legalization of abortion. But, he said, we are asleep at the switch again, only on a different issue: frozen embryos. He gave three examples of case law to illustrate how a generation is going to rise up that does not know its parents.

---

163 Humanist Manifesto, 1933.

164 Humanist Manifesto, 1973.

165 "LMTV Abortion Counter Background," *Life Matters*, accessed August 20, 2014, www.lifematterstv.org/abortioncounters.html.

3. Sex outside of marriage (v. 7).

This hardly needs much documentation, but Alfred Kinsey helped spark the sexual revolution. He was a homosexual whose favorite hunting grounds was in the Boy Scouts of America.[166] He also was an avowed Marxist. This was way back in the forties and fifties. Here is the Humanist Manifesto (1973) again:

> In the area of sexuality, we believe that intolerant attitudes, often cultivated by orthodox religions and puritanical cultures, unduly repress sexual conduct. The right to birth control, abortion, and divorce should be recognized. While we do not approve of exploitive, denigrating forms of sexual expression, neither do we wish to prohibit, by law or social sanction, sexual behavior between consenting adults. The many varieties of sexual exploration should not in themselves be considered "evil."[167]

Where is it now? One of my students is a high school football coach. He said the biggest problem they are having in his high school is lesbianism. I asked when that began, and he said around 2000. He said the girls see it as kind of cool. And what promoted all this? He named three TV programs that made it look chic.

4. Use of mediums and spiritists (v. 6).

We have a teaching site for our school in San Antonio, Texas. While visiting there recently, I was told of a gathering of witches and warlocks. This gathering took place at Randolph Air Force Base and was just for military personnel. There were 350 at the rally. Now that was really hard for me to believe until they told me what was behind it all—Harry Potter books. They became so popular with the kids that

---

166 Judith A. Reisman, *Kinsey: Crimes and Consequences* (Crestwood, KY: Institute for Media Education, 2000), 9.

167 Humanist Manifesto, 1973, tenet 6.

after they had grown up and were old enough to be in the military, they took their spiritism with them.

Ten years ago I rode up a lift in Switzerland with a couple who ran a Bible school in France. They told me there were more witches and warlocks in France than pastors. While teaching at Jordan Theological Seminary in Amman, one of my students was a Kurdish Iraqi refugee. He told me his sister had used a black market for passports and escaped to Germany to become a professional witch. She is a Zoroastrian who worships Shatan. So was her brother until he got ripped off by a fake passport that would not pass inspection. He was heading to join his sister in Germany as a warlock. Discovering his passport was a fake led him indirectly to Jesus.

5. Mocking of God's message and his messengers (2 Chron. 36:15-16).

I once had a disciple who was a committed believer and very intelligent. After some seminary classes at a conservative school and pastoring awhile, he decided to become a scholar. So he was accepted into a program for the development of NT scholars at the University of Chicago. They take only two students per year into this program. A couple of years into the program he no longer believed in the inerrancy of Scripture. I asked him to let me read whatever literature it was that had convinced him to no longer believe the Bible was without error in its original writing. He said it wasn't anything he read. It was the slow, steady drip of cynicism from his professors—mocking the message.

When I was finishing college, I took the only religious course on campus, a course in comparative religion. When my professor found out I was interested in seminary, he began trying to sell me on an Ivy League seminary or Oxford. He said he could get me a full ride. When I told him I was going to go to a conservative, Bible-believing school, he stood up behind his desk and fulminated for five minutes against fighting fundamentalists and ignorant Bible inerrantists.

Another friend recently applied and was accepted into a well-known European seminary, but he said if they found out he is an inerrantist, they will boot him out of the program.

I could go on and on, but you get the idea. When these five things coalesce, watch out below. It was General Douglas MacArthur who wrote:

> History fails to record a single precedent in which nations subject to moral decay have not passed into political and economic decline. There has been either a spiritual awakening to overcome the moral lapse, or a progressive deterioration leading to ultimate national disaster.[168]

What we are claiming in this study on the fruit of **goodness** is that through *chrestian* Christians the world has a chance to see the **goodness** of God in action. God is not the Holy Other who has isolated himself in a parallel universe while we self-destruct. Christ ascended and sent the Holy Spirit into this physical universe to show people a better way. When we walk by the Spirit, the fruit of the Spirit is on display for all to see the **goodness** of God.

---

168 "Douglas MacArthur, 1880-1964," Qotd.org, accessed August 20, 2014, www.qotd.org/quotes/Douglas.MacArthur.

FAITH—HEAVEN'S ASSURANCE
Galatians 5:22

It was Oswald Chambers who said, "Faith for my deliverance is not faith in God. Faith means, whether I am visibly delivered or not, I will stick to my belief that God is love. There are some things only learned in a fiery furnace."[169] With these words Chambers has struck a nerve in the body of Christ. Church pews or seats are filled with people who believe or have great faith as long as the blessings are flowing in their lives. But what happens when the divorce papers arrive, the layoff notice is given, the children don't turn out as dreamed and prayed for, ill health robs us of years of our life? Will the Son of Man find faith when he returns to earth?

In one sense, exercising faith is the easiest thing we do every day; in another sense, it is the hardest thing we will ever do. When we get in that car to drive to work or to go shopping, we exercise tremendous faith. We are confident that thousands of pounds of steel will operate properly to get us to our goal, and we trust in our driving skills and the skills of other drivers on the road to get us to our destination safely. In

---

169 Oswald Chambers, quoted in "Sermon Illustrations," Ministry127. com, accessed August 20, 2014, http://ministry127.com/resources/ illustration/faith-does-not-preclude-trials.

fact, we have so much faith in our cars and our abilities to drive them, we scarcely give it a second thought before we turn the ignition.

But give us a debilitating disease, a rebellious teenager, a layoff notice, and all of a sudden our fears and doubts can rob us of the confident life of faith we were leading. Or were we? Biblical faith is born in the cemetery of darkness; it flies best in the fog. It acts as an antidote to fear, and it counteracts foolishness. During the Age of Faith (before Immanuel Kant), people believed **so** they could understand; during the Age of Reason (after Immanuel Kant), people only believed **what** they could understand.

I'm calling us to become people of faith, because without faith it is impossible to please God (Heb. 11:6), and when Jesus returns to this little planet, faith is precisely what he will be looking for (Luke 18:8). So let's look at faith—its definition, its development, and its demonstration.

I. FAITH—ITS DEFINITION   Heb. 11:1

Faith is the substance of things hoped for, the evidence of things not seen.

The word for "faith" both in Hebrews 11:1 and the fruit of the Spirit listed in Galatians 5:22 is *pistis*. Almost every translation translates the word in Galatians 5:22 as "faithfulness." Normally, this word is translated as "faith," and I am sticking to that translation for these two reasons: (1) "faith" is the way *pistis* is translated 99 percent of the time; and (2) lots of non-Christians are "faithful"—to their wives, to their word, to their country, and so on. "Faithfulness" does not require supernatural ability. But the faith to continue to pour out one's life for the kingdom of God (Matt. 6:33) when the tide of public opinion has turned against you (Jesus) or there seem to be no resources for the task at hand (George Mueller) requires a supernatural faith in a God we cannot see.

Many see Hebrews 11:1 as the biblical definition of faith. Let's look more closely at a couple of words from the verse (see "Accusation of License" in chapter 5 for a shorter discussion):

1. **Substance.** This is the Greek word *hypostasis* and usually is translated "assurance."[170] About one generation after the Reformation began (1516), certain teachers in the

---

170 This understanding of *hypostasis* was popularized by Martin Luther, but really doesn't have much support in Hebrews or anywhere, for that matter. We are introduced to the word in Hebrews 1:3 where Jesus is said to be the *charaktēr tēs hypostaseōs autou*, the exact expression (*charaktēr*) of his _____. It doesn't make much sense to put "assurance" in the blank. "Essence" makes sense. That would be saying that Jesus and the Father have the same essence or makeup, a statement of ontology (the study of the nature of *being, becoming, existence,* or *reality*). BDAG (1040b, 1041a) says, "Among the meaning that can be authenticated, the one that seems to fit best here is *realization...in faith the things hoped for are realized or become reality....* Köster prefers *plan, project* [Vorhaben] for the passages in 2 Cor, and *reality* [Wirklichkeit] for all 3 occurrences in Hb, contrasting the reality of God with the transitory character of the visible world." The change made by Luther at the insistence of Melanchthon is discussed in TDNT (VIII, 586). He changed it from substance to "a personal, subjective conviction." TDNT rejects this out of hand because it doesn't fit the usage in Hebrews 1:3 and has no substantiation elsewhere. "In a formulation of incomparable boldness Hb. 11:1 identifies πίστις with this transcendent reality: Faith is the reality of what is hoped for in exactly the sense in which Jesus is called the χαρακτήρ [*charaktēr*] of the reality of the transcendent God in 1:3." Rather than the subjective, this meaning puts the emphasis on the objective reality of the spiritual world. Especially in Hebrews, the world that we can see and touch is passing away (Heb. 12). The real world is the spiritual world. "It is plain, then, that in Hb. ὑπόστασις [*hypostasis*] always denotes the reality of God which stands contrasted with the corruptible, shadowy, and merely prototypical character of the world but which is paradoxically present in Jesus and is the possession of the community as faith."

church began to separate "assurance" from the essence of "faith." That is, is assurance part of what makes up faith? We are talking about its essence. Assurance is essential to faith, or there is no faith. People wanted to know if they were elect or not. These teachers (Neo-Galatianists) told them they could find assurance they were elect by looking at the good fruit in their lives. Ironically, by separating assurance from being part of faith, assurance was destroyed in the lives of most of these people. They did not know if their fruit was sufficient or good enough to prove valid faith.

We would agree that assurance is part of faith. However, the assurance must be tied to the promise involved. If Jesus says, "I am going to heal you," and you believe his promise, then you have assurance before the fact that you are going to be healed. If you believe he will provide for your needs based on his promise in Matthew 6:33 that God will give everything you need to live this life if you seek first his kingdom and his righteousness, then you have assurance before the fact that your needs will be met. The assurance is tied to the promise.[171]

---

171 We belabor the assurance discussion for this reason. Some teach that one must believe in eternal security when he puts his faith in Christ for salvation or he is not saved. They also teach this is what Calvin and Luther taught. It is true that Calvin and Luther taught assurance is part of saving faith. But a recent dissertation has shown that the assurance they had was not in eternal security but rather that their sins were forgiven at the moment of faith. Luther never did believe in eternal security, which is one of the great contradictions in his soteriology. This is one reason the author says the theology of both Calvin and Luther was unstable. Furthermore, using Hebrews 11:1 to support this idea was brand-new and an idea from Melanchthon. It has the effect of destroying the assurance it

2. **Not seen.** Biblical faith is operative at its purest level when we cannot see our way. If we can see it, we don't need faith, by definition. Augustine himself said, "Faith is to believe what we do not see, and the reward of faith is to see what we believe."[172] Elijah was a great example of faith in that he kept his head bowed to the earth while he prayed and sent his servant to look out over the sea to see whether there were any storm clouds coming. Six times he sent his servant back to look. Elijah could not see, but his faith in God's promise of coming rain kept him praying (1 Kings 18:41-45).

The African impala can jump to a height of over ten feet and cover a distance of greater than thirty feet. Yet these magnificent creatures can be kept in an enclosure in any zoo with only a three-foot wall. Why? Because the animals will not jump if they cannot see where their feet will fall. Faith is the ability to trust what we cannot see. With faith we are freed from the flimsy enclosures of life in which we often allow fear to entrap us.

So much for our definition of faith. Now, how can we develop our faith?

is trying to promote. By making faith something subjective, now the person must examine his faith to see if he had the right kind of faith. Did you have assurance when you believed? If not, you did not have the right kind of faith. More self-doubt and introspection ensues.

172 Augustine, quoted in "Religion," ToInspire.com, accessed August 20, 2014, www.toinspire.com/quotes.asp?catid=28.

II. FAITH—ITS DEVELOPMENT

A. Through Miracles—Seed Faith

In our early Christian lives our faith grows by leaps and bounds when we witness the supernatural acts of God. This is like seeing a mountain moved into the sea as a result of faith as little as a mustard seed (Matt. 17:20). Philip Yancey says the new Christian needs this kind of faith to help buttress his faith that something supernatural really did happen in his life when he believed in Jesus.[173] But, Yancey suggests, these kinds of miracles seem to occur less and less as we grow in faith instead of more and more. You would think as our faith gets stronger, we would see more of the miraculous. After all, if faith as little as a mustard seed could move a mountain, what could we do with faith as big as a watermelon? But it seems to work just the opposite, and we shall see why shortly.

The sign miracles we read about in the gospel of John were selected by John specifically to engender faith (John 20:30-31)—"These [signs] are written *that you may believe.*"

B. Through Exercise—Repeated Faith

The widow who kept asking the judge over and over for justice (Luke 18:2-8) was an example of growing faith. Through many repetitions her faith was growing because each repetition was a little harder to do than the one before it. The parable ends with this question: "When the Son of Man comes, will He really find faith on the earth?" (Luke 8:8).

---

173 Philip Yancey, *Disappointment with God* (New York: Harper Paperbacks, 1988), 245-48.

C. **Through Testing—Fog Faith**

1. **Victory over Temptation**

   The victorious Christian life comes by faith (Gal. 2:20; 5:6).

2. **Victory over Trials**

   Our faith is purified by the fire of trials (1 Pet. 1:7) and made mature or complete (James 1:2-4).

Chippie the parakeet never saw it coming. One second he was peacefully perched in his cage; the next he was sucked in, washed up, and blown over. The problems began when Chippie's owner decided to clean Chippie's cage with a vacuum cleaner. She removed the attachment from the end of the hose and stuck it in the cage. The phone rang, and she turned to pick it up. She'd barely said hello when *sssssoppp*! Chippie got sucked in.

The bird owner gasped, put down the phone, turned off the vacuum, and opened the bag. There was Chippie—still alive, but stunned (you think?). Since the bird was covered with dust and soot, she grabbed him and raced to the bathroom, turned on the faucet, and held Chippie under the running water. Then, realizing that Chippie was soaked and shivering, she did what any compassionate bird owner would do: she reached for the hair dryer and blasted the pet with hot air.

Poor Chippie never knew what hit him. A few days after the trauma, the reporter who'd initially written about the event contacted Chippie's owner to see how the bird was recovering. "Well," she replied, "Chippie doesn't sing much anymore—he just sits and stares."[174] It's not hard to see why. Sucked in, washed up, and blown over...that would steal the song from any heart. And it does. That's why Jesus says in the parable of the sower (Matt. 13:21) that many Christians

---

174 Max Lucado, *In the Eye of the Storm* (Dallas: Word Publishing, 1991), 11.

grow, grow, and grow until the trials of life come along to blow them over. Then they just sit and stare. J. I. Packer put it this way:

> This is the ultimate reason from our standpoint, why God fills our lives with troubles and perplexities of one sort or another. It is to ensure that we shall learn to hold Him close. The reasons why the Bible spends so much of its time reiterating that God is a strong rock, a firm defense, and a sure refuge and help for the weak is that God spends so much of His time showing us that we are weak, both mentally and morally, and dare not trust ourselves to find or follow the right road. When we walk along a clear road feeling fine, and someone takes our arm to help us, likely we would impatiently shake him off; but where we are caught in a rough country in the dark, with a storm brewing and our strength spent, and someone takes our arm to help us, we would thankfully lean on him. And God wants us to feel that our way through life is rough and perplexing, so that we may learn to lean on Him thankfully. Therefore He takes steps to drive us out of self-confidence to trust in Himself, to—in the classic scriptural phrase for the secret of the godly man's life—"wait on the Lord."[175]

III. FAITH—ITS DEMONSTRATION   James 2:14-16

What does it profit, my brethren, if someone says he has faith but does not have works? Can faith save him? If a brother or sister is naked and destitute of daily food, and one of you says to them, "Depart in peace, be warmed and filled," but you do not give them the things which are needed for the body, what does it profit?

---

175 J. I. Packer, *Your Father Loves You* (Wheaton, IL: Harold Shaw, 1986), www.thinkpoint.wordpress.com/2012/05/12/does-god-want-us-to-feel-that-our-way-through-life-is-rough-and-perplexing/.

Faith without works is a dead faith. But "dead" does not mean "fake, false, spurious, or not genuine." We never use the word "dead" with such a meaning in the English language, and they didn't use it that way in Greek either.[176] Then what does "dead" mean? It means "lifeless, without vigor or excitement, without movement or action." A vibrant faith is a working faith. As Abraham Heschel put it, the biblical model of a vital, vibrant faith requires "a *leap of action* rather than a *leap of thought.*"[177]

During the terrible days of the Nazi Blitz, a father, holding his small son by the hand, ran from a building that had been struck by a bomb. In the front yard was a shell hole. Seeking shelter as quickly as possible, the father jumped into the hole and held up his arms for his son to follow. Terrified, yet hearing his father's voice telling him to jump, the boy replied, "I can't see you!" The father, looking up against the sky tinted red by the burning buildings, called to the silhouette of his son, "But I can see you. Jump!" The boy jumped because he trusted his father. The Christian faith enables us to face life or meet death, not because we can see, but with the certainty that we are seen; not that we know all the answers, but that we are known.

The following letter was found in a baking powder can wired to the handle of an old pump that offered the only hope of drinking water on a very long and seldom-used trail across Nevada's Amargosa Desert:

This pump is all right as of June 1932. I put a new sucker washer into it and it ought to last five years. But the washer dries out and the pump has got to be primed. Under the white rock I buried a bottle of water, out of the sun and cork end up. There is enough water in it to prime the pump, but not if you drink some first. Put about one-fourth in and let her soak to

---

176 Anderson, *Triumph Through Trials*, 85-113.

177 Abraham Joshua Heschel, *God in Search of Man* (New York: Farrar, Straus and Giroux, 1955), 283.

wet the leather. Then pour in the rest medium fast and pump like crazy. You'll git water. The well has never run dry. Have faith. When you git watered up, fill the bottle and put it back like you found it for the next feller. (signed) Desert Pete. P.S. Don't go drinking the water first. Prime the pump with it and you'll git all you can hold.[178]

Now if I were dying of thirst, it would take all the faith I had to take that bottle of clean, clear water and pour it down the hole to prime an old desert pump. That would be a clear demonstration of my faith in the promises of Desert Pete. Believing the promises of Desert Pete is one thing, especially if there is a skeleton or two near the pump. But believing God's promises is another. Nevertheless, what we believe (faith) will show up in what we do (actions).

CONCLUSION

It was George Mueller who said, "Faith does not operate in the realm of the possible. There is no glory for God in that which is possible. Faith begins where man's power ends."[179] Conversely, as Shakespeare wrote, "Our doubts are traitors and make us lose the good we oft might win by fearing to attempt."[180]

David, a two-year-old with leukemia, was taken by his mother, Deborah, to Massachusetts General Hospital in Boston to see Dr. John Truman, who specialized in treating children with cancer and various blood diseases. Dr. Truman's prognosis was devastating. "He has a 50/50 chance." The countless clinic visits, the blood tests, the

---

178 Paul Chappell, "Joseph's Understanding," Daily in the Word, accessed August 20, 2014, www.dailyintheword.org/content/josephs-understanding.

179 Quoted in "Quotes," GeorgeMuller.org, accessed August 20, 2014, www.georgemuller.org/quotes.html.

180 William Shakespeare, Measure for Measure, 1.4.77.

intravenous drugs, the fear and pain—the mother's ordeal can be almost as bad as the child's because she must stand by, unable to bear the pain herself.

David never cried in the waiting room, and although his friends in the clinic had to hurt him and stick needles in him, he hustled in ahead of his mother with a smile, sure of the welcome he always got. When he was three, David had to have a spinal tap—a painful procedure at any age. It was explained to him that, because he was sick, Dr. Truman had to do something to make him better. "If it hurts, remember it is because he loves you," Deborah said.

The procedure was horrendous. It took three nurses to hold David still, while he yelled and sobbed and struggled. When it was almost over, the tiny boy, soaked in sweat and tears, looked up at the doctor and gasped, "Thank you, Dr. Tooman, for my hurting."[181]

David had faith in Dr. Truman because he had some prior experience of the love and care of the doctor, his nurse, and his mother. It helped him face the pain. Have you experienced that the Lord is good, that his yoke is light and gentle? Then believe that he will only allow you to suffer pain for some ultimate good.

---

181 "Courage," Sermon Illustrations, accessed August 20, 2014, www.sermonillustrations.com/a-z/c/courage.htm.

MEEKNESS—HEAVEN'S COMPOSURE
Galatians 5:23

According to Bill Farmer's newspaper column, J. Upton Dickson was a fun-loving fellow who said he was writing a book entitled *Cower Power*.[182] He also founded a group of submissive people. It was called "Doormats." That stands for "Dependent Organization of Really Meek and Timid Souls—if there are no objections." Their motto was: "The meek shall inherit the earth—if that is okay with everybody." Their symbol was the yellow traffic light.

Sound like a club you would like to join? I doubt it. Sounds like a bunch of wimps. Is that what meekness is all about? If so, why would anyone want to be meek? After all, says the world, you only go around once in life, so you have to grab the brass ring. Assert yourself. Take a course in how to be self-assertive. Win by intimidation.

Besides, meekness = geekness. And geeks won't rule the world. Nerds rule the world, right? Just look at Bill Gates. Bill is a self-confessed nerd, but meek? No. Why would anyone want to be meek?

---

182 "Meekness," Sermon Illustrations, accessed August 20, 2014, www.sermonillustrations.com/a-z/m/meekness.htm.

Well, maybe because Jesus said the meek will inherit the earth. That is a pretty good reason to want to be meek. The Bible also says that Jesus was meek. If we want to be like Jesus, we need to learn meekness. But what is it exactly? Let's study meekness: the meaning of meekness, the mandates to meekness, the model for meekness, and the motivation for meekness.

I. MEANING OF MEEKNESS

A. Brokenness

"Meekness" is the word *prautēs*, which is a word used for a wild horse after it has been broken. A horse that has been broken is under the control of its master. The Christian who has been broken is living a Spirit-controlled life. He is not controlled by the lusts of the flesh (anger, jealousy, lust, ambition, and so on).

Some say, "Before God can use a man, he must break a man." Watchman Nee wrote that the alabaster box must be broken before others can smell the perfume.[183] Many believers come to God with their cleverness and their giftedness, but his use for them will always be limited until they are broken.

Jesus says until we learn meekness, we will not find rest for our souls: "Take My yoke upon you and learn from Me, for I am gentle and lowly in heart, and you will find rest for your souls" (Matt. 11:29). The word translated here as "gentle" is *praus* from the same root as *prautēs*. The first is the adjective; the second is the noun. So Jesus himself is meek and lowly in his heart. If we want to become like Jesus, we must learn these things from him. The bad news is that our hearts are puffed up and full of pride. The good news is that meekness is a fruit of the Holy Spirit and available to anyone who will release the Spirit to live the substitutionary life of Christ.

---

183 Watchman Nee, *The Release of the Spirit* (Cloverdale, IN: Sure Foundation, 1965), 12.

B. Complete Trust in God When Men or Life Seems Unfair

1. **No Anger**—Aristotle saw meekness as the midpoint between much anger and not anger. Whether he is right or not, Galatians 5:19-20 just told us that anger is produced by our sin nature, and James 1:20 tells us that the anger of man does not accomplish the righteousness of God. The meek man is not an angry man. James 3:13 speaks of the wise man living his life in "meekness of wisdom."

2. **No Revenge**—Jesus quotes Psalm 37:11 in Matthew 5:5— "The meek shall inherit the earth." It is a psalm of trust in God when the righteous suffer and the wicked prosper. Or in the words of R. G. Lee and his famous sermon, "Payday Someday." We don't need to seek revenge because vengeance belongs to the Lord. And someday he will settle up accounts. The wicked will not prosper forever.

3. **No Fighting for Rights**—the word is used next to *epieikes* in Titus 3:2 and 2 Corinthians 10:1. *Epieikes* is a word used to describe God in the OT when he had the legal right to wipe out Israel completely, but he chose not to press that right. The same word is used in reference to Euodia and Syntyche in Philippians 4:5 when they had a dispute. Part of reconciliation for them was to choose voluntarily not to press their rights. Another way to put it would be to adopt the attitude that the other person might be right.

C. Conclusion—meekness is a total trust in God that enables us to yield our personal rights and expectations to him.

J. I. Packer put it this way:

The meek are those who know themselves to be poor in spirit, who...in humility want only the will of God. "Moses was very meek, more than all men that were on the face of the earth" (Num 12:3). His meekness was shown in his acceptance of what God ordained, including endless battles with those recalcitrant and disappointing people whom he was trying to lead from Egypt to Canaan, including, even, the enormous disappointment of himself not getting into the Promised Land.[184]

D. Clarification

In 1 Peter 3:4, the wife is called to win her carnal husband to become a spiritual man with her meek and quiet spirit. But this is not an excuse for allowing abuse. Sickness allows abuse; meekness does not. The call to martyrdom is a very unusual call (Jesus and Stephen). Even Paul appealed to Caesar before ultimately dying for his faith. Meekness does not mean being a Christian Doormat. It deals more with our manner and demeanor. No, meekness is not geekness, and it is not weakness. Meekness actually requires strength.

II. MANDATES TO MEEKNESS

A. In the Church

1. To Preserve Unity

Ephesians 4:2-3 says, "…with all **lowliness** and **gentleness,** with longsuffering, bearing with one another in love, endeavoring to keep the unity of the Spirit in the bond of peace." Then Jesus was telling us to learn from him in Matthew 11:29; he put forms of these two words side by side when he said he was "meek and lowly." In Ephesians 4 above, the word for "meekness" is translated "gentleness." Obviously, peace and unity in a church are easier to maintain when people are not fighting for their rights or to prove they are right (see also Col. 3:12; James 3:13).

---

184 Quoted in "Meekness," Sermon Illustrations, accessed August 20, 2014, www.sermonillustrations.com/a-z/m/meekness.htm.

2. **To Preserve Doctrine**

Second Timothy 2:24-25a reads: "And a servant of the Lord must not quarrel but be gentle to all, able to teach, patient, in **humility** correcting those who are in opposition." This time the word *prautēs* is translated as "humility." Again, it is an appeal to peace in the church. Obviously, much of living out Christ-likeness is learning to get along with other people, and this fruit of the Spirit does much to help prevent church fights and splits.

3. **To Preserve a Brother**

In Galatians 6:1 we find: "Brethren, if a man is overtaken in any trespass, you who are spiritual restore such a one in a spirit of **gentleness**, considering yourself lest you also be tempted." Restoration of a brother does not work very well when the spiritual leaders of the church come to confront the offending brother swinging a big stick.

We can see from these passages that meekness is a real key to church relationships. It is the opposite of the proud, the pushy, the argumentative, the my-way-or-the-highway man. They say birds of a feather flock together. Well, the sidekicks of meekness are humility and *epieikes*, not pressing one's rights.

A truly humble man is hard to find, yet God delights to honor such selfless people. Booker T. Washington, the renowned black educator, was an outstanding example of this truth. Shortly after he took over the presidency of Tuskegee Institute in Alabama, he was walking in an exclusive section of town when a wealthy white woman stopped him. Not knowing the famous Mr. Washington by sight, she asked if he would like to earn a few dollars by chopping wood for her. Because he had no pressing business at the moment, Professor Washington smiled, rolled up his sleeves, and proceeded to do the humble chore she had requested. When he was finished, he carried the logs into the house and stacked them by the fireplace. A little girl recognized him and later revealed his identity to the lady.

The next morning the embarrassed woman went to see Dr. Washington in his office at the Institute and apologized profusely. "It is perfectly all right, madam," he replied. "Occasionally I enjoy a little manual labor. Besides, it is always a delight to do something for a friend." She shook his hand warmly and assured him that his meek and gracious attitude had endeared him and his work to her heart. Not long afterward she showed her admiration by persuading some wealthy acquaintances to join her in donating large sums of money to the Tuskegee Institute.[185]

B. In the World

1. To Attract with Our Lives

In Titus 3:2 we read, "Speak evil of no one, to be peaceable, **gentle**, showing all humility to all men." Many years ago, Christian professor Stuart Blackie of the University of Edinburgh was listening to his students as they presented oral readings. When one young man rose to begin his recitation, he held this book in the wrong hand. The professor thundered, "Take your book in your right hand, and be seated!" At his harsh rebuke, the student held up his right arm. He didn't have a right hand! The other students shifted uneasily in their chairs. For a moment the professor hesitated. Then he made his way to the student, put his arm around him, and with tears streaming from his eyes said, "I never knew about it. Please, will you forgive me?" His humble apology made a lasting impact on that young man. This story was told some time later in a large gathering of believers. At the close of the meeting a man came forward, turned to the crowd, and raised his right arm. It ended at the wrist. He said, "I was that

---

185 "Humility," Sermon Illustrations, accessed August 20, 2014, www.sermonillustrations.com/a-z/h/humility.htm.

student. Professor Blackie led me to Christ. But he never could have done it if he had not made the wrong right."

2. **To Attract with Our Lips**

Peter charges us with these words: "But sanctify the Lord God in your hearts, and always be ready to give a defense to everyone who asks you a reason for the hope that is in you, with **meekness** and fear" (1 Peter 3:15). Although George Whitefield disagreed with John Wesley on some theological matters, he was careful not to create problems in public that could be used to hinder the preaching of the gospel. When someone asked Whitefield if he thought he would see Wesley in heaven, Whitefield replied, "I fear not, for he will be so near the eternal throne and we at such a distance, we shall hardly get sight of him."[186]

III. MODEL FOR MEEKNESS

Clearly, Jesus was and is our model for meekness. As noted, Matthew 11:29 tells us he was meek, although the word *praus* is translated "gentle"—"Take My yoke upon you and learn from Me, for I am **gentle** and lowly in heart, and you will find rest for your souls." And in Matthew 21:5, when Jesus rode into Jerusalem for Palm Sunday, the day he officially proclaimed himself to be King of the Jews, we read, "Tell the daughter of Zion, 'Behold, your King is coming to you, **lowly**, and sitting on a donkey, a colt, the foal of a donkey.'" This time the same word (*praus*, LXX) is translated "lowly."

Jesus could have chosen a chariot or a white stallion fit for a king, but he was never showy. Someone has said: "The door of life is a door of mystery. It becomes slightly shorter than the one who wishes to enter it. And thus only he who bows in humility can cross its threshold."

---

186 Warren W. Wiersbe, *Wycliffe Handbook of Preaching and Preachers* (Chicago: Moody, 1984), 255.

The Handbook of Magazine Article Writing contains this illustration by Philip Barry Osborne.[187] "Alex Haley, the author of *Roots*, has a picture in his office showing a turtle sitting on top of a fence. The picture is there to remind him of a lesson he learned long ago. 'If you see a turtle on a fence post, you know he had some help.' Says Alex, 'Anytime I start thinking, "Wow, isn't this marvelous what I've done," I look at that picture and remember how this turtle—me—got up on that post.'"

IV. MOTIVATION FOR MEEKNESS

A. To Enjoy an Abundant Christian Life Today
Galatians 5:23—it's one of the fruits of the Spirit.
First Timothy 6:11—it's part of the abundant life.

B. To Enjoy an Abundant Christian Life Tomorrow
Matthew 5:5—the meek will inherit the earth...when Jesus returns.

CONCLUSION

The famous inventor Samuel Morse was once asked if he ever encountered situations where he did not know what to do. Morse responded, "More than once, and whenever I could not see my way clearly, I knelt down and prayed to God for light and understanding." Morse received many honors from his invention of the telegraph, but felt undeserving: "I have made a valuable application of electricity not because I was superior to other men, but solely because God, who meant it for mankind, must reveal it to someone and he was pleased to reveal it to me."[188] This is a meek man, one who does not vaunt himself or claim credit for something God did.

---

187 "Humility," Sermon Illustrations, accessed August 20, 2014, www.sermonillustrations.com/a-z/h/humility.htm.

188 Quoted in Tim Hansel, *Eating Problems for Breakfast* (Dallas: Word Publishing, 1988), 33-34.

Corrie ten Boom makes this comment about the Indian spiritual leader Sadhu Sundar Singh, whom she met in Europe after he had completed a tour around the world. According to her, people asked him, "Doesn't it do harm, your getting so much honor?" The Sadhu's answer was: "No. The donkey went into Jerusalem, and they put garments on the ground before him. He was not proud. He knew it was not done to honor him, but for Jesus who was sitting on his back. When people honor me, I know it is not me, but the Lord, who does the job."[189] Perhaps we sheep could learn something from donkeys.

---

189 "Humility," Sermon Illustrations, accessed August 20, 2014, www. sermonillustrations.com/a-z/h/humility.htm.

SELF-CONTROL—HEAVEN'S RESTRAINT

Galatians 5:23

In St. Petersburg, Russia stands the magnificent statue of Peter the Great, seated upon his horse, with his hand uplifted, pointing his nation onward and eastward. Peter was the maker of modern Russia. In many respects he well deserved the name "great." But he was also subject to maniacal outbursts of fury and anger. In one of these fits of rage he killed his own son. Toward the end of his reign, Peter the Great once remarked, "I have conquered an empire, but I was not able to conquer myself."

I wonder how many of us can echo those words. It was Solomon who wrote, "Like a city whose walls are broken down is a man who lacks self-control" (Prov. 25:28 NIV). Self-control is the last fruit listed in Galatians 5:22-23, but it may be the most elusive. Who among us has not regretted an impulsive response, an outburst of anger, an addiction to some desire of the flesh, an overwhelming lust, a consuming thought pattern of bitterness or greed, or an unhealthy love relationship, and on it goes? But truly, if we are ever going to claim to have lived, even for a short period of time, what we call the victorious Christian life, then we must conquer ourselves. Is that possible? Let's see as we look at the last fruit of the Spirit listed in Galatians 5:23.

I. EXPLAINING SELF-CONTROL

A. What It Isn't

1. Not Self-Abuse

This practice (usually called asceticism) arose out of the philosophy that the spiritual universe is good, but the material universe is evil. That meant our bodies are evil. Thus, in order to help drive evil out of our lives, we must punish our bodies through all sorts of self-imposed suffering.

One reason the word for "self-control" is not found in the OT is that the OT teaches the material world and our bodies are good, not evil. The Christian emphasis on material self-denial from AD 300 on betrays the influence of Greek philosophy on Western Christianity. Many of these monks were inspired by the teaching of Augustine who extolled asceticism. One such monk was Simeon Stylites.

Simeon Stylites was a Syrian monk who was disgusted by the worldliness he observed in his fellow monks. So he decided the best way to conquer worldliness was to live on top of a pillar.

It has been stated that, as he seemed to be unable to avoid escaping the world horizontally, he may have thought it an attempt to try to escape it vertically. For sustenance small boys from the village would climb up the pillar and pass him small parcels of flatbread and goats' milk.... Edward Gibbon in his *History of the Decline and Fall of the Roman Empire* describes Simeon's existence as follows:

In this last and lofty station (15 meters high and 1 meter square at the top), the Syrian Anachoret resisted the heat of thirty summers, and the cold of as many winters. Habit and exercise instructed him to maintain his dangerous situation without fear or giddiness, and successively to assume the different postures of devotion. He sometimes prayed in an erect attitude, with his outstretched arms in the figure of a cross, but his most familiar practice was that of bending his meager skeleton from the forehead to the feet; and a curious spectator, after numbering twelve hundred and forty-four repetitions, at length desisted from the endless account. The progress of an ulcer in his thigh might shorten, but it could not disturb, this *celestial* life; and the patient Hermit expired, without descending from his column. After spending 37 years on his pillar, Simeon died on 2 September 459. He inspired many imitators, and, for the next century, ascetics living on pillars, stylites, were a common sight throughout the Christian Levant.[190]

2. **Not Self-Help**

Self-control within the ethics of Greek philosophy meant to have enough power within yourself to control yourself. But another reason this word seems to be absent in the OT is that the Bible does not acknowledge the humanistic philosophy of the Greeks, who thought man could pull himself up by his own bootstraps and have mastery over himself.

When I was in college, my mother signed me up for a summer job that would take me away from a girlfriend she did not like. It was selling Bibles, and they sent me from my hometown in Nashville, Tennessee, to Shawnee, Oklahoma, to go door-to-door selling Bibles. Tough

---

190 Quoted in "Simeon Stylites," Wikipedia, accessed August 20, 2014, http://en.wikipedia.org/wiki/Simeon_Stylites.

work. But they introduced me to self-help books: *Think and Grow Rich* by Napoleon Hill, *The Power of Positive Thinking* by Norman Vincent Peale, *Psycho-Cybernetics* by Maxwell Maltz, and many others. One of these books suggested we begin every day standing in front of the mirror and repeating, "Every day in every way I am getting better and better." Now there is no doubt trying to replace negative, doubtful thinking with positive thinking can be a good thing. After all, positive thinking can be just another way of talking about faith.

The problem in positive thinking is the object of one's faith. In the self-help books the object of one's faith is one's self. The idea is that man is the highest power in the universe and has the power within himself to solve all his problems. The Bible begs to differ. You can stand in front of the mirror all day long telling yourself you are getting better and better, but you will wake up the next day with the same sin nature you had the day before. And your sin nature isn't getting any better—never will.

B. What It Is

1. **Power on the Inside**

   "Self-control" = *egkrateia* = *en* + *kratos* + *on* = in + power + having = having power within (yourself). So the word does speak of having power within.

2. **Power on the Outside**

   However, the power within is actually power from without, meaning the human being is powerless to have complete mastery over himself; that is, he cannot keep from sinning. We need an infusion of supernatural power in order to have victory over ourselves, namely, the power of the Holy Spirit. When we become Christians, God gives us the Holy Spirit to live inside of us. With his power within, we can exercise the fruit of self-control.

It is interesting that when Paul was witnessing to Felix in Acts 24:25, he chose three things to discuss: righteousness, *self-control*, and coming judgment. The fruit of self-control is appealing to an unbeliever because every person would like to be free from the control of his own lusts, urges, and passions. But only one with supernatural power within can enjoy this kind of freedom.

II. EXERCISING SELF-CONTROL

Because of our fallen condition, the battle between the flesh and the spirit is one we cannot win in our own strength (Rom. 7:14-24). In our own strength the good that we want to do, we do not do; the evil we do not want to do, that we do. Echoing the same idea Galatians 5:17 claims, "The flesh lusts against the Spirit, and the Spirit against the flesh; and these are contrary to one another, so that you do not do the things that you wish."

SPIRIT ⇐ (MIND ⇒ EMOTIONS ⇒ WILL) ⇒ FLESH

The battle here is for control of our soul (mind, emotions, and will—our inner self). If our sinful nature can control our mind, emotions, and will, it can control our body as well. In order, then, for me to enjoy victory over my sinful nature, I need to exercise self-control over my mind, my emotions, my will, and my body.

A. Control of the Mind—2 Corinthians 10:4-5

For the weapons of our warfare are not carnal but mighty in God for pulling down strongholds...bringing *every thought* into captivity to the obedience of Christ.

B. Control of the Emotions—1 Corinthians 9:25

Everyone who competes in the games *exercises self-control* in all things. They then do it to receive a perishable wreath, but we an imperishable. (NASB)

C. Control of the Body—1 Corinthians 7:8-9

Now to the unmarried and the widows I say…if they cannot *control themselves*, they should marry, for it is better to marry than to burn with passion. (NIV)

Steps to Immoral Slavery:[191]

1. **Natural Curiosity**—"I want you to be wise about what is good, and innocent about what is evil" (Rom. 16:19b NIV).

2. **Awakening of Conscience**—when we follow our curiosity into the arena of evil, our conscience warns us that this is not right (Rom. 2:15).

3. **Sensual Focus**—after we are drawn away by our own curiosity and lusts (James 1:13-14), Satan tempts us (Gen. 3:1-6).

4. **Questioning of Scripture**—Satan causes us to question God's Word and his love for us (Gen. 3:1).

5. **Violation of Conscience**—sin is born (James 1:15).

6. **Awakening of Guilt**—guilt forces a response; Adam and Eve hid and began to rationalize (Gen. 3).

7. **Response to Guilt**—we deny sin and enter darkness or confess it and walk in the light (1 John 1:7-9).

8. **Incomplete Repentance**—sorrow for consequences, but not for sin itself. The beginning of wisdom is to hate evil

---

191 Bill Gothard, *Institute in Basic Youth Conflicts* (Oak Brook, IL: Institute in Basic Youth Conflicts, 1975).

(Prov. 8:13). This gives rise to a secret world of fantasy where evil desires are met.

9. **Compensation**—incomplete repentance does not remove guilt; compensating activity begins.

10. **Frustration over the Lust Monster**—lust gets hungry and demands to be fed. This produces frustration and double-mindedness (James 1:8, 15).

11. **Redefining Morality**—there is continuous mental effort to justify personal immoral behaviors on the basis of the existing moral code. The code is usually reinterpreted to include as moral what was previously thought to be immoral.

12. **Argumentation over God and the Bible**—those who have "redefined" God or Scripture to fit in with their immorality will be quick to advance their ideas in order to "enlarge their world." In their world they have decided what is right and what is wrong. They are men of corrupt minds (Titus 3:10-11). They willingly believe a lie (2 Thess. 2:11).

A young college student set up an appointment. His family was in my church. He had been away from home going to college at a major university. As he came in my office, I could tell he had lost some weight, let his hair grow, and adopted a slovenly appearance—not too atypical for some college kids. But I really knew things had changed when he began praising Allah every third sentence. He had come to let me know about his conversion to Islam and why he rejected Christianity.

Well, about the tenth time he praised Allah in my office, I had had enough. So I said, "May I ask you a question?" Sure. "What moral compromise have you made that has caused you to give up your faith in Christ?" That made him furious. The decibels in his voice rose, and I had to invite him to leave. I wonder why he got so mad? A few months later he was kicked out of his university when it was discovered he was running a drug ring with some fellow students.

I rarely run into *intellectual* problems with Christianity among those who have turned from it after growing up in the church. Almost without exception a *moral* compromise precedes their defection. You see, Christianity speaks of accountability to God and the judgment that goes with it. For many people it is easier to get rid of the accountability and the God behind it than to overcome their immorality.

CONCLUSION

Only the Holy Spirit can give us mastery over our sinful thoughts, passions, and decisions—all of which control our bodies. But we praise God for his Holy Spirit, through whom we can enjoy true freedom from being controlled by the lust of our flesh (Gal. 5:16).

I would like to finish this exploration of the fruit of the Spirit by reminding us that our blessed Holy Spirit is more than just an enabler and a producer of fruit. He is also a Counselor, a Comforter, and a Connector.

In her book about writing and life called *Bird by Bird*, Anne Lamott wrote, "What people somehow (inadvertently, I'm sure) forgot to mention when we were children was that we need to make messes in order to find out who we are and why we are here."[192] By "messes" she is talking about more than the messes in a child's room. She is talking about relationship messes, conversational messes, and immoral messes. Messes we all make. Messes we all need to make while we are still at home where someone there can help us work through the mess. How else can we know mercy if we ourselves have not been in some kind of mess that required someone's mercy to get us out of or to find our way through it? How else can we know love

---

192 Quoted in Maria Popova, "Bird by Bird: Anne Lamott's Timeless Advice on Writing and Why Perfectionism Kills Creativity," Brain Pickings, accessed August 21, 2014, www.brainpickings.org/index.php/2013/11/22/bird-by-bird-anne-lamott/.

or grace or forgiveness while we are still young, if not through all the messes in all the rooms that make up our lives?

Judith Guest wrote a book about a family in trouble and bobbing up and down from the emotional wake of a tragic boating accident.[193] Two brothers are in the family boat when a sudden storm capsizes the boat, and the more athletic brother, Buck, drowns. The younger brother, Conrad, survives, but now he has to cope with the tragedy and the guilt of being alive. He doesn't cope well and attempts suicide.

Perhaps you recognize this story, which was made into a movie called *Ordinary People*. It's about a family in crisis, but what family goes through this world without a crisis? It is about all of us and our need to connect, especially in the midst of a mess or a crisis. Conrad can't connect with his mother because she's dealing with the whole messy crisis by organizing people right out of her life, including her son and husband. After all, they remind her of Buck, her dead son.

One night Conrad thinks he is about to connect with his grieving mother, but instead she just tells him to go clean up his messy room. His room is just a metaphor for his life—one big mess. He desperately needs to connect with someone, but his brother, Buck, is gone, and his mother is now chatting on the phone. He doesn't clean up his room.

Instead, Conrad goes to the restroom and splashes water on his face. The water triggers a flashback to his drowning brother. He runs out of the house crying, "Stay with me, Buck. Don't let go! Buck! Buck!" The only person he can run to is his therapist, Dr. Berger. Out of breath and trembling with fear, Conrad bursts into Dr. Berger's office. With genuine care and love Dr. Berger consoles and walks Conrad through his fears. Finally, the storm subsides in Conrad's life, as he collapses sobbing into Dr. Berger's arms and stays in his arms a long, long time.

Dr. Berger is a beautiful picture of the ministry of the Holy Spirit in our lives. The Holy Spirit is the Counselor, the one called alongside to help us and comfort us the way in which Dr. Berger came alongside

---

193 Judith Guest, *Ordinary People* (New York: Penguin, 1982).

Conrad. He listened. He asked questions. He made a few comments. But most of all he was there.

We were not forgotten back there when we were hurt so badly, wounded so deeply, crushed so completely. The Holy Spirit is mindful of our hurts and faithful in healing them. He is the Great Connector, especially when there is no significant other in our lives who will connect with us. That is why the flashbacks come. Because it is our time to be healed. The process is usually slow and most times painful. But the Holy Spirit is there for us. He will walk us through the messes, talk us through the messes, and most of all, love us right through the messes of life as well.[194]

---

194 Gire, *Reflections*, 99-108.

CPSIA information can be obtained
at www.ICGtesting.com
Printed in the USA
BVOW04s0959100317
478063BV00004B/124/P

9 780991 658855